Native State

Also by Tony Cohan

Broadway Books

New York

Native State

State

a memoir

Tony
Cohan

Author's note: Several names and identifying characteristics have been
changed to protect the identity of the individuals depicted. This book
makes occasional use of composite characters.

PRINTED IN THE UNITED STATES OF AMERICA

BROADWAY BOOKS and its logo, a letter B bisected on the diagonal, are
trademarks of Random House, Inc.

Photo of author on page 243 is courtesy of Ruthane Capers.
Used by permission.

Visit our website at www.broadwaybooks.com

First edition published 2003

Book design by Donna Sinisgalli

Library of Congress Cataloging-in-Publication Data
Cohan, Tony.
Native state : a memoir / Tony Cohan.—1st ed.
p.   cm.
1. Cohan, Tony—Homes and haunts—California. 2. Novelists,
American—20th century—Biography. 3. Hollywood (Los Angeles,
Calif.)—Biography. 4. Terminally ill parents—California. 5. Cohan,
Tony—Childhood and youth. 6. Fathers and sons—California 7. Cohan,
Tony—Family. I. Title.
PS3553.O416Z47 2003
813'.54—dc21
[B]
2002043904

ISBN 0-7679-1020-6

1 3 5 7 9 10 8 6 4 2

"What if man lingered on . . .

how things would then fail to move us.

The finest thing in life is its uncertainty."

KENKO,
JAPANESE PRIEST,
TWELFTH CENTURY

One

"I drew a deep dizzying breath
in which the perfume of star jasmine
was mixed with chlorine."

CHRISTOPHER ISHERWOOD,
THE WORLD IN THE EVENING

The memory has the luster of a dream.

In it, I stand holding my father's hand on a mountain at dusk. Beyond and below in every direction stretches the sparkling city where we've newly arrived: Los Angeles. Domed Griffith Park Observatory rises above us. My dad wears wing-tipped shoes, a handsome silk suit. The outline of his upturned magisterial jaw far above mine is backlit by the dying sky. Nearby sits a brand-new blue Buick Roadmaster, in which my mother, dressed in a tweed suit, is doing her lipstick in the car mirror.

Dad's arm, sweeping upward, seems to cradle the sunshot heavens as if they are a spray of flowers, embracing multitudes. Looking up into that oracular bowl of sky and clouds and emergent stars, which in memory is either the planetarium ceiling or the sky itself, clutching in my four-year-old fist a tiny crate of candy oranges to send to relatives back east, I sense heaven and earth to be conspirators, deeply in league about the excellent nature of things—as in the music-drenched climax of some feature-length cartoon.

Violet tints of dusk merging into dark. Spotlights scanning the foothills from below. Planes buzzing beyond. Smell of orange blossoms, sage. From some radio, "See the pyramids along the Nile . . ."

Then—a crack of lightning. Suddenly it begins to rain. People run for their cars.

"Mary Helen!"

"Mom!"

She isn't in the Buick. I notice an empty bottle of Gordon's gin on the seat. Drenched, we run around the parking lot, calling for her.

"*Señor.*" A man has found her, off the asphalt, a few feet down the mountain slope.

"Philip, my nylons," she calls up from the little ravine by the observatory where she'd fallen. Legs splayed, skirt up, garter belt showing, one black high heel pointed to the roiling sky. Fresh red lipstick smeared, confusion sketched across her eyes.

I look up and see my father's face, burning with rage.

This earthly paradise is infested.

2. Welcome Home, Stranger

The tan, featureless halls of LAX funnel passengers toward passport control. An orange-haired woman in a short-sleeved blue shirt inserts my passport into a machine and waits for the computer entry to pop up. She embosses a fresh stamp over the blue, red, and black collage of wanderings. "Welcome home," she says, smiling. "Next!"

I lug my shoulder satchel past suitcases tumbling onto aluminum carousels, feeling a little like a piece of luggage myself: tagged with overlapping destinations, waiting to be grabbed by its rightful owner. A customs officer takes my declaration form, searches my eyes. "Has anyone you don't know given you mail or packages to deliver? . . . What was the purpose of your visit to Mexico?"

I emerge from the terminal into tepid, sea-level air at dusk. In the taxi line I dredge my Mexico keys from my pocket and drop them into my shoulder bag, replacing them with the ones to the little cottage in Venice. In a parallel gesture I reach in my wallet and replace peso bills with greenbacks. The bicultural switcheroo: I can do it blindfolded.

From the back of the cab running north on Sepulveda Boulevard, I look up into the silver belly of a departing jet, close my eyes against the shattering roar, feel the wind shudder the cab.

Strange, how it's always the same. The closer I get to home, the more displaced I feel.

The call had come only hours after I'd arrived back in Mexico. Nell's weary voice: "Your father fell again."

Abruptly the fifteen-hundred-mile trip began to play itself in reverse. I hurried back up Calle Flor in the soft, mile-high evening air, along the darkening cobbled streets, past the parish church. At Viajes Vertíz, Malinda was just closing up but in deference to my *emergencia* turned the computer back on and snagged an Aeromexico cancellation the next afternoon out of León. I drifted back through the plaza among the roaming toy and balloon vendors, the milling teenagers making the Sunday-night *paseo* beneath the clangor of church bells, the Atotonilco marching band pumping out its sloppy, spirited Beatles medley in the pavilion.

Four days before, my family had gathered, as we did every April, at the suburban Los Angeles home where my father has lived since 1954. Dad had taken in the birthday proceedings from his wheelchair at the head of the table in a silly paper hat, mugged for the Polaroids. He'd managed to snuff out a couple of cake candles, even croaked the lead-in to an old joke whose punch line we all knew. Ninety-four years old. A festive day.

Now this. Is the true vigil beginning at last, the one we'd been dress-rehearsing all these years?

Arriving back at the house on Calle Flor, I considered its likelihood. Since my mother's death seventeen years earlier (from "smoking-related complications," in the Neptune Society death certificate's reductive phrase), Dad had been enacting one of history's longer fades. So many false alarms, few real crises, but affairs on chronic alert. All eyes on Dad: just the way he liked it. I'd urged him to move out of the big empty house and up to Santa Barbara, where my sister and her family lived, but he wouldn't budge. "You're going to have to drag me out of here feet first," he'd say.

The next morning, in Mexico, I repacked papers, books, laptop. I left a note for my wife, Masako, in Puebla shooting photographs for her new book on Mexican tiles. I locked the mesquite doors of the old *finca urbana* and climbed back into my friend Jorge's minivan. As we raced back across the Guanajuato plain toward the León airport, the radio spinning Mexican ballads and American rock oldies, even the weather seemed to run in reverse, unseasonable rain clouds gathering along the low peaks. Thoughts and feelings rose and dispelled on the air: anticipations, preoccupations, irritations. *This comes at a bad time. I have a new book to write. Is the old guy crying wolf again?*

But something in Nell's voice had said: This one may be it.

"He thought he was in Chicago," Nell says, greeting me at the front door.

As I step inside onto the beige carpet, the musty smell of arrested life hits me. The front door shuts softly behind. The rush to get here grinds to a tiptoed halt. In the silence, my head pounds with jet noise.

"Angela and I found him on the bathroom floor. He missed striking his head on the tub by maybe half an inch."

"How did he get to the bathroom?" Dad has been wheelchair-bound for months.

"We don't know," she says. Nell, an old family friend, has

been living at the house the last three years. "Somehow he got himself up in the middle of the night and hobbled in there. He must have forgotten he couldn't walk any more."

When he first began to lose sensation in his feet, I urged Dad to exercise, keep the circulation going. But he doesn't much like struggling against physical adversity, preferring to be taken care of by others. Angela the Filipina caregiver put it perfectly: "Your father is a worrier, not a warrior."

"When I found him," Nell says, "I asked him where he was. He said, 'In Chicago.' "

Chicago. It doesn't figure. Dad's from Connecticut. He did love to talk about taping a radio episode of the *Jimmy Durante Show* in Chicago during his radio days and meeting the Mafia figures the great comedian knew. With the years, as the realities of Dad's past became subsumed into myth—as he became a legend in his own mind, burnishing his bio, striking a line here, adding another there—it had assumed a brazen gloss: Famed Producer and Director of Radio's Golden Age. Had Dad been at some speakeasy in Chicago last night, quaffing bootleg with Durante and Capone, a memory (or invention) sufficient to stir him to walk when the doctors say he can't?

"We had to call in Bob from next door to lift him."

Dad isn't that big, but he's dead weight when he goes down. I've lifted him after many a fall. Neighbor Bob, a swing-music aficionado who covets Dad's collection of old Okeh 78's (Beiderbecke, Trumbauer, Dorsey, Satchmo), is no spring chicken himself. We're all getting old on Dad's watch.

In the shuttered bedroom, fragrance of medicaments. Angela is tucking in the corners of the bed. Dad has a cotton bandage above his left eye.

"Hi, Dad," I say softly.

Pale and reduced, afloat in his king-sized bed like a shrunken potentate, my father offers up a shiny, mottled hand.

"Welcome home, stranger," he whispers.

Dad has fallen back asleep. I've put in a call to Dr. Smith. Nell has retired to the room that used to be my mother's, Angela to the one forever known as "Tony's room" though I haven't slept there for thirty-five years. This beige California ranch-style monument to the American 1950s (Ozzie and Harriet *in situ*) that had once lodged a family of four is now a place of vigilance, a nursing home serving one client.

Welcome home, stranger. I saw him five days earlier, but he's forgotten, as he'll forget this visit. Even when he still had his marbles, though, Dad loved the comfort of repetition. In fact, his life here for the last forty-five years has always seemed to me little more than a series of endless reiterations, in suffocatingly minute detail.

Welcome home, stranger. I'm welcome here, because I'm needed now. But it has never felt like home. And I've always felt like a stranger here.

I get up from the bedside chair and slip out of the room. In the dim hallway I brush past the large painting of my mother: Mom the beauty, in blue robe and prewar bob, eyes chastely downcast—Madonna of the Lakes. At the request of a painter named Warshawsky she'd posed for the sumptuous, articulated oil now embalmed in the corridor's permanent dusk in its scalloped blond wood frame. According to Dad, the émigré artist had seen in Mom an idealized figure of the Virgin. Warshawsky's art studio on La Cienega was just a few doors up from the power pole cops found Mom wrapped around one night a few years later in Dad's Buick Roadmaster. They'd hauled her off to jail and booked her that time—a blessing in disguise, since it had effectively broken one of the worst of her terrifying benders.

How she hated California.

Crossing the open living room, I pass the Eames chair, the Exercycle, the Danish-modern coffee table, the tan-upholstered settee, the unplayed out-of-tune spinet, the unread Books-of-the-Month, the unregarded Matisse and Picasso prints. Living room merges into dining room, kitchen, den—the low-slung, open-plan house a prototype of a certain American postwar ideal. The upholstery is still infused with the unfiltered Chesterfield and Optima cigar smoke that once clouded these rooms, blending with the aromas of Nell's cocker spaniel—and loss's elusive effluvium.

My sister, Meg, who'd been ten years old when we moved here, says she always thought of this house as home. I never did. To me it was a place devoid of affect or nourishment, a museum to a life my parents had lived elsewhere in better days. Our family's bright beginnings in California, sunny new land of promise, had ground to a final halt in this muted dwelling, set in a barren subdivision at the time Dad bought it. After high school I'd been glad to be gone. If someone had told me then that I'd still be coming here this late in my own life, I think I'd have slit my wrists.

As the lights in his memory began to blink out one by one, then in clusters, Dad would sometimes say to me, "You know, I can't remember living here." It seemed like an odd thing to say until I thought about it. But Dad's real life had happened elsewhere: in Connecticut, in Manhattan, in Hollywood. Here he'd always seemed like an empty man, lost in a haze of passionless gestures and boring habitudes. As a young man I hadn't understood why, or felt the least compassion toward him about it. Cruelly, I'd thought of my father as the perfect exemplar of Eliot's hollow man, or the nowhere man John Lennon sang of.

No, I wasn't about to forgive him anything.

I sit down in the overstuffed den chair beneath the framed poster of the Steinberg *New Yorker* illustration in which America beyond Manhattan is rendered as insignificant. Dust motes explode. Family photo albums lie stacked on the table beside the chair. The grandkids when they visit love rummaging through Dad's carefully curated archives of kids and relatives, celebrities and stars, and show-biz memorabilia, the old black-and-whites bleeding into color as the family grows, disperses, ages.

Outside the plate-glass window, in the shadowy stand of eucalyptus trees bordering the trimmed lawn, birds warble. Angela's television plays softly in her room. Metal walking sticks Dad no longer uses lean against the bleached mahogany dining-room table. Nell's cocker spaniel, Raffles, snoozes next to the refrigerator.

Or was it Dad who had the photo albums out?

The top one is open to a black-and-white publicity still of me at fifteen, bent over a snazzy white pearlescent Ludwig drum kit, flailing away, a cool grin on my face, dressed in a hip one-button-roll suit and Chet Baker hair. A pianist, bass player, and tenor flank me. Inscribed on the television-stage scrim behind us is a treble clef with musical notes and the words *Spotlight on Youth.*

Drums: my first instrument of escape.

On the same table, next to the phone with the extra-large numbers to accommodate Dad's failing eyesight, sits a worn leather-bound address book. During visits home over the decades I'd marvel at the page after page of entries under my name, successively crossed out: Paris, Tangier, Barcelona, Berkeley, Kyoto, New York, San Francisco—spreading from "C" to "D," then commandeering "E" and "F." New pages were inserted to accommodate my tireless, unreadable wanderings, inscribed first in my mother's careful Parker penmanship, then, later, in Dad's flattened, angular scrawl.

The last entry is the house in Mexico. Inconceivable, that I'd been there only six hours ago.

The phone rings. It's Dr. Smith. I ask her about Dad's fall.

"Another infarction, most likely. Mini-stroke. Afraid there's not much we can do at this point."

"What inning are we in?" I ask Dr. Smith, a lifelong Dodger fan.

A pause. "The ninth," she says.

The street below my father's house winds through pines and eucalyptus to a tiny creek beneath a wooden bridge. Late-April air bears the scent of rosemary, honeysuckle, loam. Moonlight diffuses through the treetops. With the passage of years the little wild canyon has thickened with plants, trees, new homes. I stand at the oaken railing, watching shallow water flicker over stones on its silvery dance to the sea a half-mile away.

If it's really Dad's ninth inning, odds are he'll stretch it to the full count. He's always taken his time doing things. Why should he change now?

This means I'll be here for a while.

Work will slow, come to a halt even. I'd been planning trips deep into southern Mexico, Guatemala, Peru, Bolivia, Chile; then on to Indochina—Burma, Laos, Thailand, Vietnam. This spring a memoir of my life in Mexico had come out and I'd toured the country, reading from it. The "follow-up" is to be called *Turista,* a chronicle of the next round of the wanderings that have lately become my literary stock in trade. The publisher awaits first chapters and an outline.

Resentment floods me. Will I ever get clear of this vain, demanding character, my father? At moments like this it feels as if my entire life has been little more than a fitful struggle to wriggle free of his suffocating grip. Yet in another, necrophilic way—it doesn't even produce guilt any more—I welcome the grounding because of its occasion. How many times have I secretly wished for him to die?

Are there new blessings to be mined, revelations or reconciliations ahead for either of us in this protracted senescence? The feebler he's grown, the more I've come to doubt it. He's outlived his good days by so long. Forty-four years old when live radio ended, he's been hanging around for a half-century, swinging the clubs, reprising the old jokes and routines. Even mercy takes effort by this point—not just mine but all the family's. We're a worn, exhausted crew with an enduring old coot on our hands.

Frogs serenade each other across the stream bed. The odor of dank moss drifts up. In high school I used to slip out of the house and come down here to smoke a cigarette, drink a beer. Later, visiting home from college, or off the road from drumming or traveling, I'd stand by this creek pulling on a joint. Anything to get out of that house.

Headlights wobble, slicing the dark. A car crosses a speed bump. As it passes I see them, the lovers. How smoothly she fits into his shoulder! Unaware of me, they pull over at a turnout up ahead where kids still come to explore the mysteries. An old Marvin Gaye song twines into the air, lilting and aphrodisiac, an incense of the ear. Their heads, silhouettes in the rear window, bend to each other. It was in that same gravel turnout, in the backseat of a green Ford coupe, that Sandra finally let me have her. Her first time, and mine . . .

Proustian effects, nostalgic whiffs. Echoes and traces of a world I grew up in here along the home coast. In late summer, poison oak and diamondback rattlesnakes in the brush. I beheaded one once, I remember, with a hoe.

I glance over at the parked car. The boy's head lolls back, the girl's has disappeared. Some oldies station marks the pulse with *"You go back, Jack / Do it again. . . ."*

California had been my entry into desire and experience; yet I could never live happily here. Growing up along this coast—this "terminus at the end of a journey, on the rim of a void," in one writer's words—contained this firm instruction: Go. So I traveled, I moved, coming to understand stability as less a matter of a fixed abode than a good set of shocks. Returning here always occasioned claustrophobia, dread, and the longing to flee again. Still, I always knew that the flights and escapes, the long stretches away, the relentless testing of connection to landscape and origins, were inseparable from my youth here, and what happened to me and my family in California, and to the fading figure I've come back yet again to see on this late-April day of 1999.

Ocean mist fingers the trees. The frogs fall silent. I turn and glance through the rear window of the car ahead. The couple, deep in their raptures, has slid down out of sight. For a moment I think I see, in the misty space where their heads had been, the outlines of a secret self left behind, parked along these dry canyon roads, tangled in backseat investigations and bad habits, woven into the succession of characters I became, snagged in the underbrush of beginnings. A sudden hunger fills me to know who that self was, or had been, or had become, or not.

I suppose I've always imagined my life as taking passage from one shore to another—though what lies on that far shore remained shrouded, invisible. Soon now, the lifelong tug against the undertow of origins will be over, freeing me to leave this place forever. Gazing into the dark creek waters, a near-unutterable thought arises: What if *this* is the far shore I'd sought, *this* the one journey I've never made—the journey back?

The moon disappears in mist. I turn and trudge back up the canyon toward my father's house.

Morning sunlight seeps through the tall beige curtains of a Spanish colonial living room in a canyon north of Beverly Hills. A pair of ash drumsticks rests on a shiny black spinet piano. A boy in a bathrobe picks up the sticks, examines their chipped teardrop heads, rolls them in his palm. He listens to the resonant clicks they make against each other, reads the red letters stamped on the side of each stick: "Slingerland 5A."

In the hushed living room, I feel a shiver of transgression, invading adult precincts. My parents are still asleep. I am nine years old, no older, because before I turn ten Dad will lose his job and the family will move back to New York for a year while he looks for work.

The night before, crouched unseen at the top of the stairs, I'd watched my parents and their guests gathered around the piano. Songs, laughter, the clinking of iced drinks as Bing Crosby, Johnny Mercer, and Jimmy Durante regaled the assembled with song. My father played a bit of piano himself—Gershwin, Kern, Rogers—but he'd deferred to his betters last night. Dad was at the top of his game, producing and directing the *Jimmy Durante Show* on CBS Radio, shaping comics, stars, gag writers, and musicians into a live nationwide program each week.

He'd bought the rambling two-story house in Coldwater Canyon from the actress Dorothy Lamour. Ever keen to impress upon me his involvement with celebrity, Dad referred to her as "Dotty," just as he always wanted me to call the bandleader

Paul Whiteman "Uncle Paul," and Jimmy Durante "Uncle Jimmy." Sometimes he took me along to script meetings at Uncle Jimmy's house on Beverly Drive, where I swam in the pool, observing through a water-spotted diving mask the great comic and his cohorts conjuring gags in canvas pool chairs. Some weeks, Dad took me to the studio, sat me in a swivel chair in the glass-enclosed control booth during live shows, and let me hold his stopwatch as the radio actors and entertainment icons of the day—Jack Benny, Rita Hayworth, Orson Welles—stood before fat mikes, fingers to ears, shaping air into syllables that gripped a nation. This grown-up world, confident and smart and celebrity-rich, seemed to move on its own wide current, leaving me alone in its wake, jerked from coast to coast, school to school, in a blur of train trips and maids and lonely bedrooms. I experienced myself as a tiny shadow, or cipher, in the elaborated drama of my parents' lives.

Later, when it was all over—when Dad's entry into the Brown Derby on Vine Street no longer caused a stir, and showbiz luminaries didn't recognize him or pay him much notice—Dad would seem permanently diminished by this loss of success and easy access to fame, coming truly alive only when recounting his intimacy with the entertainment greats. (Once, decades later, he asked me to meet him at the Brown Derby for lunch, and I arrived to find him staring quizzically at a façade of graffiti-splashed plywood: the fabled stars' watering hole had closed its doors.) But that morning in Coldwater Canyon, fondling the pair of smooth drumsticks in the morning light, I must have understood them as tokens of energy, action, participation—access to that glittering grown-up world I observed from childhood's shadows.

Uncle Jimmy Durante had an entourage of pals from his

vaudeville days of working the joints, Lower East Side Italians and Jews of rough origin. They clustered on Uncle Jimmy's patio, fetched drinks, roared at the comic's malapropisms, made book on the races at Hollywood Park, Santa Anita, Del Mar. They were always friendly to me—Eddie Jackson, a chubby, grinning ex-hoofer; Jack Clayton, a small-time singer who looked more like a slick croupier in cream golf slacks and expensive wing-tip shoes; a short, bespectacled one-armed man named Louie whose function was unclear but seemed to have something to do with "accounting." My father, by contrast, presented a certain element of class among these Damon Runyon types—a dapper New England Jewish college graduate married to a beautiful WASP former stage actress.

Among Uncle Jimmy's cronies was a natty, silver-haired man in a blue suit who always had a pair of drumsticks protruding from his jacket pocket. No drum kit, just sticks. To this day I don't know what Jack Ross did other than rap piano-top accompaniment to Uncle Jimmy's "Inka Dinka Doo."

In that early-sunlit living room, I turned Jack Ross's sticks, left behind after the party the night before, in my hands. White wood yellowed by varnish; narrow and tapered, with elongated knobby heads. They'd left a tracery of marks, like tiny hooves, on the black-lacquered piano top that didn't dust off when I ran my fingers over them.

Casting about for instruments of desire, we can only choose from things at hand. These sleek, paired incitements to gaiety and laughter were artifacts from a world my parents found far more interesting than me. Slingerland: where was that? I wanted to go there.

That night before, my mother had spotted me peering down at the party from the top of the stairs in pajamas and come up to pack me off to bed. Leaning over me in the darkened room, enveloping me in the powerful penumbra of odors that always meant they were either going out or entertaining—a smell almost as strong as the dank, nutty one my parents' sheets exuded when I crawled in with them in the mornings—she'd delivered the comfort of a good-night kiss, then receded to the door. In silhouette from the light of the hallway, she'd paused and said, "Good night, sweetie." I see her there, petite and elegant, dressed smartly for the party. Then the closing door, leaving me in darkness with the lingering smell of lipstick, perfume, cigarettes—and the liquor that I will later learn she desperately wanted to hide. By faint light bleeding through the doorjamb I inscribed my signature, over and over, on the support slats of the empty bunk bed above my head, listening through a rich gauze of loneliness and abandonment to the clamor downstairs: Johnny Mercer crooning "Atchison Topeka and the Santa Fe" at the spinet, Jack Ross tattooing the piano top.

How could any of us have known this was to be the last party?

In the living room the next morning, absorbed in Jack Ross's drumsticks, I heard my father coming down the stairs. Guiltily I set the sticks down on the piano top and stepped away. The Slingerland 5A's clicked and resonated—impossible for those sticks to be silent, they were so alive—then rolled off the piano and dropped into the carpet's dense, deadening plush.

I never saw Jack Ross again, that natty wizard who coaxed rhythm from available surfaces with such minimal, portable means. With the years, as I'd move from tabletop to practice pad to snare to full ensemble, entering the greater world of promise embedded in those ash drumsticks, I'd glimpse shadow visions of Jack Ross, chomping gum, summoning a clickety web of beats on piano top or tabletop, riding rhythm's magical surge.

That fall, the Jimmy Durante radio show was canceled. Live radio, glamorous theater of the mind, was sliding silently into the dark. Tiny white faces flickered in silvery ovals in living rooms now. Dad was out of a job, and Mom was packing the family's bags for the move back to New York. Through the control-booth window I watched my father, stopwatch in hand, cue his last show, as a chesty announcer quoted doctors on the medicinal value of cigarettes, made a final call for Phillip Morris.

Out the window of the Santa Fe Super Chief: rising steam, receding palms, red desert, iron cities. I played canasta with my sister in the club car, met Casey Stengel, the manager of the New York Yankees, and at my father's urging—he seemed more excited than I—got his autograph.

In Manhattan we settled into an apartment in the East Fifties. After I suffered a schoolyard beating at public school, Mom enrolled me in a private academy with a headmaster and uniforms, where we played soccer instead of stickball and called the teachers "sir." Through the closed doors of the apartment I heard my parents' muted quarrels. I took buses around the city alone, tasting my first independence.

A year and some months later, the family had resettled in a reduced, less sunny California. Uncle Jimmy, Uncle Paul, and Uncle Bing were gone. The piano lay silent. Mom wandered about the Coldwater Canyon house in a bathrobe nipping gin, under the lash of some anguish I could feel but not see. Dad worked the phone, trying to land something in television, and took long trips back to New York.

The good times were over, for good.

I retain from that period a scrapbook bulging with autographed glossies of the stars, inscribed to my father's son: "To Tony. Keep your dukes up. Rocky Marciano." "To Tony. Happy Trails. Roy Rogers and Silver." "To Tony, I Got a Million of 'em. Uncle Jimmy Durante." "To Tony. Musically yours, Nat King Cole." These signed photos would arrive at an ever-lessening pace throughout the 1950s, until finally they stopped altogether. (A few years ago, I woke up one night in a sweat in a hotel room in Japan, racked with a desolating thought: did my father forge those autographs?)

As Christmas approached that year, my parents asked me what I wanted for a present.

"Drums," I said.

Blinks, blank stares, polite coughs.

My announcement fell into a void for a while. Then, at dinner one night, my father said, "That's fine, son. But before we invest in drums for you we need to find out if you have any talent."

"Talent" was a big word around our house. Dad adulated talent, identified with it. After all, hadn't he worked with the great talents of the day? Talent was a mysterious, God-given absolute that few people possessed, like a high IQ. Some people were musical, others not; some funny, most not. Talent showed up early. If you had it, you were granted special dispensation to pursue it; but if you didn't, there was no way you were going to get it, so you shouldn't waste your time or anyone else's. My mother felt similarly, from a more severe, Calvinist angle: Do not be self-indulgent, vain, put yourself above others. Do not imagine you are great or smart or handsome, for probably you are not; and if you are, you shouldn't gloat about it. Unless you're a Picasso—and he is a horrible man, you know—you have no business presuming to make art. Eschew personal glory. Make yourself useful. Help the starving, the poor, the less fortunate.

So my simple expression of desire was immediately pitted against my father's self-perception as an arbiter of great talent and my mother's stern disapproval of art's self-indulgence.

This drumming business arose at a time of great shifts within the family, things I couldn't possibly understand but could only experience, like changing weather, alterations in pressure and light, the arrival of clouds or sudden gusts of wind. That summer, my mother's drinking had reached frightening proportions. My sister and I first noticed this when my father returned to New York to work on a television show with the comedian Garry Moore, an old radio crony. Possibly Mom and Dad had "separated," though the word was never used, then or later. Suddenly Mom was different somehow, slurring and staggering around the house, lipstick cockeyed, smelling funny, dropping things. We'd run to the kitchen clamoring for dinner to find Mom lurching about in oven mitts, colliding with the appliances, sloshing scalding water over the countertop, burning the food. We'd withdraw to our places at the table in the breakfast nook to await the arrival of small hamburger patties the shape of tennis balls rolling about in the middle of the plate, seared charcoal-black on the outside, cold and red inside. We'd nudge each other under the table, roll our eyes, scheme on how to slip the food to the dog, then raid the kitchen later for graham crackers, Mallomars, Oreos.

As Mom's binge flared out of control, neighbors discreetly looked in or took us to their houses to feed us. I was given whispered instructions and phone numbers "just in case." Friends quietly removed the car keys from the house to prevent Mom from driving. My sister was farmed out to family friends. A doctor came to visit.

The drama spread like a stain through our days, Mom alone and utterly helpless, Dad back in New York trying to hack it in television. I'd come home from school to a silent house, the door to her room closed. Then she'd suddenly appear, looped out of her mind, purse on her arm, lipstick plastered in the vicinity of her mouth, having decided to drive down Coldwater Canyon into Beverly Hills and go shopping and insisting I accompany her. Even now thinking about those car trips raises the hairs on the back of my neck.

Surely I began to turn against my father then. As I read it, he'd abandoned us, leaving me in charge of my mother and sister, Mom adrift on some tossing sea far beyond a ten-year-old's powers to becalm, and my sister, four years younger, innocent and helpless. Where was Dad when Mom was falling apart? Wasn't he supposed to be in charge? My father's seemingly benign emotional and physical distance had turned lethal. I couldn't count on him, then. With the passage of years I'd easily forgive my mother's drinking but not his neglect of us.

Late that fall of 1950, things came to a head. Mom, drunkenly trying to steer the station wagon down the steep driveway, veered into the hedge of oleander bushes bordering the asphalt, nearly pitching the car into the neighbors' driveway, fifteen feet below ours. Hearing the crunch, I ran outside to see the car's front end hanging precariously in space, the rear end up in the air, wheels spinning. Mom sat frozen at the wheel, a rivulet of blood running down her forehead, staring intently at the dashboard, trying to light a Chesterfield. Neighbors came running and removed her just before the car toppled into the neighbors' driveway.

This incident brought my father back from New York in a hurry. Mom disappeared into a sanitarium for a while, and Dad began looking for work in Hollywood.

It was in the face of these developments, and with Christmas approaching, that I'd flung out my simple wish to take up drumming.

After more days of demurring, Dad called a drummer he'd known at CBS during radio days and set up an appointment for me to take a "talent test" at a drum shop in Hollywood. I suppose he thought this might place a small obstacle in my way, a hedge against a kid's passing fancy. With the family fortunes precarious and no new work in the offing, the idea of buying percussion paraphernalia and lessons to go with it must have unsettled Dad, ever prudent about money. Then there was the racket the drums would unleash in the house while Mom was "recovering." Added to this was the heavy business of talent: who has it, who doesn't.

On the Saturday before Christmas, Dad drove me to Hollywood in the big blue Buick. We parked on Vine Street and walked down an alley. The sound of clattering percussion from behind a high metal door flooded me with that gut-clenching admixture of excitement and panic that would stay with me for as long as I drummed.

The drum studio was also a shop selling equipment, with towering mountains of bass drums stacked against the wall, gleaming rows of metal kick pedals laid out like shoes on display, piles of whispery coiled snares, and cubbyholes crammed with paired sticks of varying sizes and weights. Facile drumming exploded from behind closed doors: rolls and bangs, cymbals and booms. At length a small, thin, gum-chewing man with slicked hair emerged from one of the rooms.

"Phil." He reached out a hand to my father.

"Dick, this is my son, Tony. Maybe you could try him out on a few things, see if you think he has any talent."

While the two men talked, I gazed about Dick Monahan's drum shop. The cork walls were covered with glossy inscribed photos of drummers: "To Dick. Keep Swingin'. Yours, Buddy." Or Shelley or Max or Art or Cozy or Sid. In most pictures, grinning drummers flailed at glistening arrays of equipment, hands raised in paroxysms of rhythm. In a few, they sat imperiously behind their sets, arms crossed, sticks gripped in their fists. About half of the drummers were black, a fact I registered without having anything to relate it to. Large bass drums tended to have the drummer's initials painted on in ornate gothic script beside a brand name: Gretsch, Slingerland, Ludwig, Rogers. A Turkish cymbal called Zildjian seemed to merit almost every drummer's endorsement.

"Come on in here, Tony," Dick Monahan said.

He led me into a tiny soundproofed room with, to my surprise, no drums. He seated me on a stool in front of a mounted square of wood with a round black rubber pad at its center. Sticks were introduced into my hands: Slingerland 5A's, just like

Jack Ross's. Dick Monahan arranged them, the right one held like a hammer, the left cradled like a telephone receiver. (Over the years, as my hands and arms became strong, I'd develop thick veins along the top of my right forearm and beneath on my left.)

Dick Monahan guided me through a stroke or two, his hands cupped over mine. I doubt he'd ever given a talent test before, because surely no such thing exists. How can you tell in a few minutes if a ten-year-old has "talent" on an instrument he's never touched? My father had concocted this freighted ceremony in part—I sensed even then—to assert his eroding sense of self-importance.

Dick Monahan was like a lot of drummers I'd meet over the years—gaunt, wiry, intense, with a hummingbird metabolism, seeming to be on coke or amphetamines whether they were or not. I could smell the Fan Tan gum he chomped, and whatever greasy concoction he wore on his hair.

"Okay, let's play the left." He held my wrist, correcting my grip. (I can still feel the light pressure of teachers' hands as traces in my flesh on forearm, wrist, palm.) "Good. Now the right. Now left, right. Left, right."

I simply did what he told me, though my strokes had no force or evenness. Left, right. Left, right.

"Good. That's called a 'single stroke,' " Dick Monahan said. "Okay, now left left, right right."

Left left, right right.

"When you do it fast, that's a press roll."

Then: Right left right right. Left right left left. I played the asymmetrical pattern a few times awkwardly.

"That's a paradiddle," Dick Monahan said.

I looked at him.

"Paradiddle. *Left* right *left left. Right* left *right right.* A paradiddle is one of the twenty-six rudiments every drummer's gotta learn." He pointed at the wall behind me.

I turned and looked up at a chart that said "Table of Rudiments." There was a ladder with numbered rungs. Each rung had a cluster of vertical stick lines with little "x"s beneath them—drumming's form of musical notation—and enticingly playful names: flam, ruff, ratamacue. Midway down the ladder I found the paradiddle: *Right* left *right right. Left* right *left left.*

"Look," Dick Monahan said, taking my sticks. He played evenly on the pad: *Left right left left. Right left right right.* Slowly at first, then faster and faster, until his hands were a blinding Mixmaster blur—*leftrightleftleftrightleftrightright*—weaving a pattern whose individual strokes were no longer discernible, but making an effect clearly different from the single stroke (left right left right) or the roll (left left right right).

"Okay," Dick Monahan said. "That's it." He patted me on the shoulder. "You're okay, kid."

He led me back outside and said to my father, "Yeah, Phil, I think he's got some talent."

Dad nodded soberly, rubbing his chin. "Well, Dick, maybe we could start him out slowly with a few lessons. See how it goes. Don't want to get him in over his head."

While Dick Monahan and my father made arrangements for a drum teacher to come to our house once a week, I listened to the drummers crashing and clashing in the other rooms. They all sounded like virtuosi to me. Never in a million years would I be able to play like them. Surely they, not I, were blessed with that mysterious elixir, "talent."

Once, years later, having drummed by then with some of the same artists as those flailing masters in the glossy photos on

Dick Monahan's wall, I sat in the central square of Marrakech for several days running, listening to a troupe of black African drummers, the Gnaoua. A boy who must have been ten or eleven sat to the side, making tea for the players, intently watching them, absorbing it all. Near the end of the second day, they let him play for a few minutes. The boy's eyes shone with excitement as he rose to join the troupe. It seemed so natural, the learning and apprenticeship, the ripening of the boy's desire. How different from my introduction to the drums—the family's caution and reserve, the talent test, the mechanical "rudiments" and prescriptions—artificially framing the experience from the outset, my desire first held up to skeptical scrutiny, then quickly routed into a world of measurement and potential, of tests and exams.

This was how white folks got rhythm—or lost it. All around the country there must have been thousands of kids like me, drawn to rhythm's mysteries. I'd see them in years to come, marching on the floors of football stadiums at halftime or in parades: uniformed rows and columns of them, whamming bass drums, smashing great cymbals together, rolling and flamming "street beats" on tubby drums suspended from epaulette-drenched shoulders, high-stepping behind arm-waving band-meisters and scantily clad baton girls, making the thunderous noise of a mighty nation on the march. Later I'd see them—join them—behind kits in combos at dances and weddings, and in dark dives where another drumming lived: the alter-world of "swing" and "bop" and "rock," the thrilling, libidinous flow of syncopation that black funeral-band drummers in New Orleans had released into America's bloodstream: John Philip Sousa subverted by way of West Africa and Baby Dodds, unleashing drumming's call to passion.

I'd drum in the junior-high-school orchestra, the marching band. I'd flail publicly on the floors of coliseums and school-auditorium stages. With time I'd pile my traps into the back of cars and drive to Elks and Rotary clubs, Shriners' conventions, weddings, fraternity parties. I'd keep a whispery brush beat for cheek-to-cheek couples at dances, slam rock-and-roll backbeats for kids doing the "bop." I'd drum for cool-voiced thrushes and rockabilly shouters, suave crooners and blues honkers, in little demo studios off Vine Street with egg-crate walls and four-track consoles. I'd enact lightning ceremonies of bebop virtuosity in smoky dives. I'd come to understand drumming's secret, oracular contract with the body: that drums—whether used to goad troops into battle, pulsate a listening experience, incite dancers to abandon, or induce ritual trance—are Eros, encoded desire.

"Well, son," my father said in the car on the way home that day. "Dick says maybe you've got some talent."

I tried to imagine Dick Monahan having dared to say to my father, "Sorry, Phil, your kid doesn't have any talent." On the basis of what? He'd simply suffered my father's posturing enough to log another student on the rolls.

It was okay, though. I'd gotten through it. With Dad, I was learning, nothing would ever be simple.

That Christmas morning, beside the tree, I found a silver snare drum on a tripod stand, a swivel stool, a hi-hat cymbal rig with a foot pedal, and a pair of Slingerland 5A's.

In the snapshot in Dad's photo album, I'm sitting in a bathrobe before the snare drum, flashing the sticks aloft, an elated grin on my face. Why not? Here was a road out, a way to effect distance from that murky undifferentiation of self and family, breathe my own air at last. Maybe by picking up those sticks I'd revive the family's happy days, rekindle Dad's fading fortunes, restore Mom's beauty and joy, which were fast being sapped by drink and despair. At the least, I'd get to hit something—punishingly, violently, stick to hide, stick to hide—bang my way out of the family's narrowing walls.

In my parents' end would be my beginning.

4. Golden Land

From the 10 Freeway heading east, the L.A. basin, swept clear by a dawn offshore breeze, looks crystalline and sharp. The flatlands to the south are visible all the way past the airport to Signal Hill. North along the run-up to the Santa Monica Mountains, the silvery palm branches shimmer like streamers and the low stucco buildings look fresh-scrubbed in the morning light. Ahead, Mount Baldy's distant snowy peak appears as close as a hood ornament.

This light, diffusing through what William Faulkner once called "the vague high soft almost nebulous California haze," aroused in him, and most writers who came here, a sense of menace. The painters, though—Hockney, Diebenkorn, Ruscha—reveled in it.

I roll the window down. East of the 405 interchange, the air abruptly loses its saltiness, warming by five or six degrees. Some days a gentle wind lofts the sea air farther inland; I've smelled it as far east as Chinatown, seen seagulls in Pasadena. People pay extra for view homes perched on the granite slopes of the Hollywood foothills, though many days the picture windows offer little more than a pall of particulate waste.

Odd, to be back again so suddenly. I've begun reoutfitting the little craftsman cottage in Venice, laying in provisions. Masako will remain in Mexico for now as planned, working on her book. This is, after all, my death watch: hers will come later, in San Francisco, her parents younger than mine by a decade.

This morning I'm making a run to the storage bin in Glendale, where our remaining household goods await—imagined essentials from a climactic garage sale when we left L.A. fifteen years ago. I haven't a clue what's in there. Storage, in a city of low-slung dwellings with few basements or attics, has become a growth industry, the rented unit an extension of the home. Even owners of sprawling, two-story spreads with large garages maintain storage bins for the spillover. Some use them as daily offices; others, I suspect, sleep in their concrete cubicles. These monuments to the conditional, the temporary, the transient, typify a town everyone expects to be leaving at any minute. When I was growing up, my parents and their cronies—gag writers, crooners, ingenues, exiled Weimar composers—used to parade the stock joke that they only bought Coke by the bottle, never a six-pack, because at any minute they might be returning to New York, London, Rome, or Berlin. In fact, nearly all the ones I can think of stayed on and died here.

Yesterday afternoon, Nell called from Dad's house in a panic. Angela the caretaker had gone to see a lawyer about her immigration papers and hadn't returned or called. Dad was lying unattended, and Nell was too old to lift him into his wheelchair or turn him over. She was afraid Angela had had a freeway accident or been picked up by immigration officers and deported. I rushed over. I could smell Dad the minute I opened the door. I found him in his bedroom, lying in his own waste. Gaily he waved and called, "Hiya, Tony boy."

Over the years, my father had become ever more lonely, wobbly, and imperiled. His driving had turned near-homicidal, but he wouldn't hang up his spurs. L.A. is a terrible city to grow old in: its elders, stripped of drivers' licenses, are broken-winged birds trapped in their nests. First Nell moved in, then Angela.

By now Nell has become deeply invested in taking care of him, finding great meaning in the work—and a salary, and a place to stay. Angela depends upon the job for money and immigration papers. Relieved at first that help had arrived, I now find that, instead of one person to worry about and keep afloat, I have three. We're burning through Dad's savings. Hunkered down, immovable, he's straining all our capacities.

I was about to wade into the mess and try at least to turn Dad over and swab him off when Angela arrived. She'd had to stay late to see the immigration lawyer and couldn't get to a phone. Angela has a life too, with its needs. Together she and I cleaned Dad up, then sprayed the room with air freshener.

Accelerating, I feel the buffeting breeze rush through the open window. I think of Joan Didion's Maria Wyeth in *Play It as It Lays*, daily driving these interchanges "as a riverman runs a river." L.A. as sensory text, a kind of Braille for the sighted: a city in code, bearing letters in place of a name. But then freeways subvert the very idea of a city, which says: Slow down, enter the density, relate. Speed provides a substitute for experience—a quick release from history, especially one's own. The on-ramp ascent, with its sudden velocity burst, is irresistible. The moment I got behind the wheel of a car at sixteen, I was lost to my parents forever. Every southern-California kid has the contours of this hurtling topography inscribed in his blood. Some lost it all driving ("Tell Laura I Love Her," "Dead Man's Curve"), the romance of road death conferring twisted, bloody immortality (James Dean, Carole Lombard). Surf rockers Jan and Dean were in my high-school class; Jan never did recover from his crack-up.

Robertson, La Cienega, Fairfax. The off-ramps fly by, each sign laminated with memory. We moved from house to house so many times—and I moved so often later on my own—I can probably claim fifteen neighborhoods as mine. Just past the Fairfax turnoff and before the La Brea, I catch a glimpse of the hillside of one of our first L.A. houses—a two-story Spanish right above the Sunset Strip, behind Preston Sturges' Player's Restaurant, a block west of the Château Marmont. My parents forbade me at six years old to walk the three blocks along Sunset to Schwab's Drugstore to buy comics, their fears of my molestation or abduction unvoiced but keenly felt, the air thick with show-biz scandal. Even playground conversation revolved around troubled kid actors, dads arrested for marijuana use, starlet moms' headline divorce settlements. My best friend Bobby's dad was an alcoholic screenwriter from Yale, his mom a tall Texas model. They lived right behind the Château Marmont, and Bobby and I would sneak into the hotel pool and swim among the legends, minnows among the famous whales, or fetch ice for Montgomery Clift at the Liquor Locker on Sunset. Across the street, at the Garden of Allah, oasis to the stars, I talked baseball with the bartenders and busboys while Dad smoked cigars with Uncle Jimmy and Bob Hope in poolside chairs. When Bobby told me the singer Johnny Ray had been arrested for giving some guy a blow job in a public lavatory, effectively ending his career, I nodded gravely, as if I had the slightest idea what a blow job was. (Later, when I did learn, I still didn't get it: why "blow," which seems like the antonym of the act; and "job," when pleasure, not work, is usually involved, at least in voluntary circumstances?) At the house, Dad held scatological telephone conferences with Uncle Jimmy, all-night script meetings with the CBS gag writers around the kitchen table. It was almost all I saw or heard of him in those furious, high-riding days. Radio had four years to go.

Past the Hoover exit, I bank left across the downtown interchange, the office towers ebony monoliths backlit by morning sun. In my years away, entire neighborhoods have been reconfigured by earthquake, riot, fire, erosion, ethnic shift, decay. (L.A.'s routine destruction in disaster movies is always considered a victory *for* civilization.) The smog has lessened, though today's toxins already gather at the base of the San Gabriels. When, in 1934, Faulkner wrote his short story "Golden Land," the term "smog" didn't exist, though it was probably a chemical component of his "California haze." Still, there was that baleful, noxious undertone in his description: too damn much sun.

Mom hated the sun. Maybe Faulkner was describing a hangover, the kind she knew too well. One morning in that house off the Sunset Strip, I found her frantically stuffing clothes in a drawer, in her bathrobe, weeping, the venetian blinds and organdy curtains drawn against the punishing brightness. I didn't know what was wrong; but that must have been the first time I realized there was distress, and sensed my father was the cause. Mom would have been thirty-three then, whip-smart and high-strung, needing intellectual company she wasn't going to get from Dad. In later years, after she stopped drinking, she still abhorred California life to her bones. To an asthmatic with emphysema (a pack a day of Chesterfield Kings almost to the end), the smog was lethal: you could say that, in a quite literal sense, L.A. killed her.

Downtown recedes, traffic clears ahead. Crossing three lanes at seventy miles an hour, I veer onto the Golden State Freeway. *The sun, strained by the vague high soft almost nebulous California haze, fell... with a kind of treacherous unbrightness....* Ominous, Faulkner's description, partaking of a stylization he and Chandler and West didn't quite invent but brought to a high gloss: California as suspect, ersatz Eden, needful of un-masking. It was L.A.'s good luck to have had these alcoholic ge-niuses to deconstruct its Arcadian face, erecting a countervision to the empty claims of developers, boosters, and hawkers: a lit-erature of scorn. But nobody can scorn L.A. better than those of us who grew up here.

Edging onto the Griffith Park turnoff, I catch a glimpse of the observatory, inscribed in memory of first arrival—and later, indelibly, in *Rebel Without a Cause*. Nick Ray, the director, got it way off, we all thought: James Dean's hair was wrong, his walk bogus—and *nobody* in L.A. wore a *red* windbreaker. Mineo: strictly East Coast. Same with *The Graduate*. Nobody was get-ting California right.

A block from the storage facility, I idle at a stoplight in the heat of high noon, inhaling the aroma of eucalyptus, exhaust, mowed wet grass. Across a railroad yard, in a vacant parking lot, a school marching band is rehearsing: "California here I come / Right back where I started from." I watch a tumbleweed blow across the road until the light turns green. At the security gate I enter a code and drive slowly down identical, numbered corridors. I slip a key into a rusted lock, lift a corrugated metal door, and gaze helplessly at a tangle of driftwood washed up from a former life.

I am standing beside a bass drum as tall as I am, dressed in a
military-looking uniform with braid and epaulettes, at the back
of our junior high school concert band. We are posed in a semicircle on ascending risers. The photographer must have been
mounted on a very tall ladder among the school auditorium
seats to shoot us like this. The panorama, printed on a thick
matte paper, unrolls like a Japanese scroll.

"That me?" my father mumbles from his wheelchair beside
me in his living room.

"No, Dad," I say. "That's me."

We were highly rated among local school bands, I remember, our concert programs of military marches, light fantasias,
and reworkings of Gershwin favorites sure to fill school auditoriums. When we marched at halftime in football stadiums to
snappy street beats and updated arrangements of "Stars and
Stripes Forever" and "Colonel Bogey's March," I experienced a
kind of release: the trombones' blurry bleats, the saxophones
honking on the wind, the trumpets smearing the air, the swaying tubas' shiny wide bells mirroring the whole scene in minia-
ture as rows and files turned in tight formation. Passing before
the parade-reviewing stand, we exuded the proud, beefy aroma
of 1950s American moral uplift, proof against the twin enemies
of lust and disorder.

This concert-band picture, in its staged symmetry, repre-
sents that very American center that would not hold. Already

the skinny thirteen-year-old at the back of the school-band photo, bass-drum beater in hand, was in the grips of shadowy, nameless desires destined to subvert the dictated order.

At thirteen, I was trying to read some kind of pattern into the larger elements arrayed around me. Family, school, society: each seemed to have something in mind for me, but I couldn't connect with any of it. I felt like a Martian or a spy set down among a world of strangers. Viewing the noisy, self-important dramas around me through a watchful filigree of detachment, I couldn't fathom what made my family or schoolmates laugh or weep, what moved them. If I could slip through a day unnoticed, without being jostled onto the stage of events, I was content.

There was nobody—had I even been able to speak of it—to whom I could confide any of this. My parents' problems preoccupied them utterly, leaving me on my own much of the time. Junior high school, outside the band room, was a bright, shadowless panorama of anxious sexuality and physical confrontation where boys tested each other with verbal taunts inciting after-school fights, and girls in tight skirts and fresh breasts pushing out of pink angora sweaters wriggled across the schoolyard, making it impossible to concentrate in class. I lived in a seething erotic stew, wildly shy, fearful of sudden violence or sexual confrontation.

Early one morning, I woke up flooded with feeling, the lingering traces of a dream of girls' bodies passing off my mind. My heart pounded and my penis throbbed. The bedsheets were wet with a strange salty substance. From then on, it seemed I woke up with erections, got them in class or sitting at dinner or in cars. I coveted images of women, saw through their clothes, ravished them in my mind. Some mornings, as we approached school on the bus, I felt myself getting hard. Panicked, I'd try to "think" it down, pressing my schoolbooks into my lap as if to squeeze it off somehow, desperately rearranging my Levi's as I stood to enter the schoolyard.

At night, in a private theater all mine, I reviewed the girls at school, mentally undressed them, envisioned doing things they'd never consent to in reality. My prick was a summoning wand, a goad to imagination. This new rhythmic summoning (a "single stroke," on the Table of Rudiments) fused somehow with drumming: things to do with my hands that bore me away from the dismaying realities of family, school, community.

While my sexuality burgeoned and my parents' world shook, a drum teacher from Dick Monahan's school dutifully arrived at the house once a week. I'd long since learned to play a roll, that blur of alternating taps which can sound like thunder, or water, or the churning of time itself. I'd mastered the flam, the ratamacue, the paradiddle, the rest of the Western percussion catechism. I'd made a great racket in the living room playing to my father's 78 rpm record of Benny Goodman's "Sing Sing Sing," on which the gum-chewing Gene Krupa (famously arrested on marijuana charges) took a peerless drum solo.

My sound grew louder, my playing faster and more certain. I began to explore the dance-band vocabulary; for surely my drumming future, if there was to be one, didn't lie in school marching bands. I learned how to play "time," to keep the beat, to "swing." Setting a pulse with my right hand on the big ride cymbal, clicking my hi-hats with my left foot on the off pulse, I added embellishing thumps with my right foot on the bass drum and snappy comments on the snare with my left hand. I learned how to play "Latin" and waltzes and "rock" to records, becoming a well-oiled, four-limbed percussionist, edging ever closer to going public with my skills.

This meant adding paraphernalia; and so in my thirteenth-birthday picture there is a pearl-white bass drum and a big ride cymbal atop it to go along with the snare and hi-hat. I'm wearing a suit with wide lapels, a square knit tie with a stickpin. My hair is greased in a Presley waterfall. Smiling through braces, I lean over the kit, looking just a little bit more like those hotshot drummers I'd first seen in the photos on the wall of Dick Monahan's drum shop.

Later I'd add a small tom-tom above and behind the snare, then a big freestanding floor tom-tom to my right. I'd add to that a wood block and a cowbell mounted upon the bass drum, a sizzle cymbal, a third tom-tom, ever elaborating my kit. For a drummer, like a bicyclist or a drug addict, is nothing without his paraphernalia, whether it's simply hide stretched over wood or clay, or the tooled gimcrackery of late-twentieth-century percussion. (Years later, on the day when I'd get rid of my last set of traps, I'd lose not only the act but the relationship to the tools: the carefully personalized equipment, the iconography, the brand names, the burnishings and cleanings, the rituals of setting up and tearing down.)

A well-known film-music conductor at MGM lived next door to us. His wife, Betty, was always home alone. She, like my mother, had a drinking problem, though Betty's was more languid, chronic, less theatrical. Some afternoons I'd take the path between our houses and knock on Betty's back door. She'd greet me in her low-cut housedress, a glass of Scotch in hand, and invite me in for cookies. As Betty bent into the fridge to take milk out, or wiped a stain off the table, I'd crane to catch a glimpse of the nipples crowning her large, swaying breasts, but never quite caught more than their suggestion.

All the neighbors knew our family was having troubles. They saw my sister and me as abandoned kids, to an extent. So there was nothing peculiar about my visits to Betty, who one day invited me deeper into the house, past the two Steinway concert-grand pianos in the great silent living room, to the darkened den far in back, where she watched television alone and drank in the inert afternoon. As I sat beside Betty on the couch, it seemed she deliberately found reasons to bend over and change the channels so I could ogle those soft, swaying tits I coveted. A hard-on filled my jeans, and I didn't try to disguise it. Betty couldn't fail to notice the thirteen-year-old with the short white tee shirt, bare midriff showing a beach tan, his swollen member stretching his tight Levi's. On successive afternoons, Betty and I sat like this, gazing at the dim, near-soundless black-and-white television, me with my hard-on, Betty in her loose housedress. I suppose I hoped she'd move toward me, though I didn't dare do anything myself. I desperately wanted to touch myself in front of her, lunge for her breasts, then have her touch me somewhere; but the moments passed and nothing happened. Later, at home in bed, I'd envision, in precise detail and in endless variation, the longed-for upshot of those afternoons with Betty.

Did she think of me too, alone in that shaded den, hand beneath her dress?

A saxophone player at school told me that a local dance band's drummer had just enlisted in the army and they were auditioning replacements. A few days later, a large, lumbering man of thirty or so dropped by school and tried me out on a few tunes in the band room during lunch. Afterward he handed me a green business card that said "The John Melli Orchestra. Dances Weddings Parties." He told me to show up at the Beverly Hills YMCA Saturday night at seven. I'd get paid seven dollars.

That Saturday, packing my drums for my first job, I was less worried about playing than about the ignominy of having my father drive me there. Surely I'd be the only musician under driving age. Pondering this problem, I unscrewed the aluminum foot pedal from the wooden rim of the bass drum and fit the big drum into its black reinforced-cardboard case, the ride cymbal into its cloth pouch—initiating that drummer's ritual of dressing and undressing I'd enact night after night, down through the years, in clubs and bars and lounges, in theaters and auditoriums and recording studios in a dozen different countries, always taking longer than the other musicians. I fit the smaller cymbals and the snare drum into a cardboard case on wheels where an inset shelf, like a mechanic's toolbox, held drumsticks and brushes, the hi-hat stand and foot pedal, and the metal keys used to tune the drums.

As I finished packing, my father called me into his den, which smelled of cigars and pipes, the walls festooned with pictures of Uncle Jimmy, Uncle Paul, Peggy Lee, John Wayne, Jack Benny, Al Jolson—anyone important who'd ever appeared on a radio show of his. I found Dad perusing an old book he'd pulled down from a shelf. It was about jazz in the thirties. There was a brief mention of Dad and a show he'd produced, carefully underlined in red. After pointing this out to me, as he'd done a number of times before, he put down the book and lit his pipe. I wanted to leave but knew I shouldn't.

"You know, son, your dad was a pretty good musician himself."

Dad began to hold forth about his own early years as an amateur saxophone player in college. My first outing as a drummer seemed to have raised in him a compulsion to regale me with his past glories, real or imagined. (This terrible need would worsen over the years, any sign of attainment on my part setting Dad to bragging about his own past. Still, there was nothing to be done. My father had begun the great unconscious project that would last him the rest of his life: emblazoning himself in his own and others' minds as a show-business legend.)

That night, dressed in suit and tie, I loaded the drums in Dad's Buick. I'd told him the job started a half-hour earlier than it did, hoping the other musicians wouldn't see the fourteen-year-old novice drummer being delivered to the gig by his father.

Driving down the canyon into Beverly Hills, Dad continued reminiscing about his early days in music. I could barely hear him, swept by my own fears. I'd never played with a live trio, let alone a ten-piece dance band of experienced men. When we arrived at the YMCA, I asked Dad to let me off in the deserted side parking lot.

"No, I'll help you come in and set up, son."

"That's okay, Dad. Really. I'll see you afterward."

I entered the empty, crepe-paper-draped YMCA gym and crossed the polished wood floor. To my relief, none of the other musicians had arrived. I propped open the breaker doors to the parking lot and dragged my drums inside. While I was setting up on the auditorium stage, the other players began to arrive. They all looked to be in their twenties or older. They nodded to me brusquely or else ignored me, unhousing their instruments, sucking on reeds, spitting into mouthpieces, chatting among themselves about new Stan Kenton and Modern Jazz Quartet records.

The John Melli Orchestra used part-time musicians from L.A.'s West Side, the repertoire drawn from stock arrangements of standards or from "fake books"—illegally circulated compendia of pop tunes. The leader, a tall, shaggy man with simian arms and a cheap suit too short at the ankles and wrists, handed sheet music around.

Young dancers drifted into the gym and hovered expectantly along the edges of the floor: shy boys in charcoal-gray suits, girls in strapless pink-and-white gowns. The lights dimmed. I settled behind my drums, stomach knotting, hands trembling. John Melli, a Selmer tenor hung from his neck by a strap, raised his arm and gave the downbeat on "Moonglow." Three saxophones, three trumpets, trombone, bass, and piano burst into sound. Music bled out into the gym, borne on my ragged pulse. The strokes and routines I'd practiced at home for three years suddenly conjoined with nine other instruments: a total shock, like being suddenly dunked underwater for the first time. I heard the various instruments, all facing away from me, as backdrafts of sounds that didn't quite blend together. From my perch above and behind the band, I felt alone, confused, powerful.

The first dancers took the floor, merged and swayed. I tried to keep time to "Moonglow," but the music felt disjointed, gluey, out of order. There was no problem with technique or repertoire; I'd already looked through the "charts," the sheet music, and knew all the tunes. But playing along with drummers on record was nothing like *being* the drummer, making time for others; it was the difference between being driven in a bus and driving one. I'd greatly underestimated the concentration involved.

A tenor saxophonist turned and glared at me in consternation. Fearfully I fixed on John Melli, his palms pressed frantically downward, signaling me to slow down. My cheeks burning, I slavishly matched his arms as they hacked the air, trying to settle onto the pulse.

By the second chorus I seemed to have found a sort of sync with the band, both carrying and being carried by the rhythm. For a while I did nothing but focus on John Melli's semaphoric limbs, trying to maintain the beat. Then, gradually, my attention began to drift to the dance floor. Balloons bobbed on the ceiling, stirred by the orchestra's breath and the dancers' motion. Girls' skirts swayed and boys drew closer. As "Moonglow" wound to a close with its little stop-time coda, the dancers slowed, arced in time, clung to each other. Silence fell over the auditorium; then scant applause trickled forth.

I looked down, expecting to meet the horn players' angry eyes, but they were leaning forward in their chairs, shuffling sheet music for the next tune. John Melli kicked off "In the Mood," its bounciness inciting some dancers into a kind of jitterbug, others into the more liberated "bop." I whapped backbeats on two and four, dropped bass-drum accents, more confident up-tempo; but then the band seemed to gallop away from me, and there was John Melli's arm chopping the air, urging me to speed up.

Gradually I settled to the beat again. The dancers whirled, the horns congealed. As we blew the last choruses, a couple broke into some virtuoso dance activity on the floor, a circle forming around them, and for a minute the gymnasium was locked in a single act, band and dancers hitting a groove. Then it was over. I heard applause, saw the dancers' heads raised to the bandstand.

Alternating between my Slingerland 5A's and brushes for ballads, I drummed on. John Melli's glowers abated and his arms fell back to his sides. During the fifteen-minute break at the end of the first hour, while the other musicians smoked and talked in the parking lot, I sat alone backstage on a metal chair, clutching my sticks and staring at my shoes, waiting to be chewed out by somebody. But I was simply paid no attention.

During the second set, I concentrated on keeping steady time; for a drummer, if he does nothing else, must keep time. The band began to fuse. Now I dared to look out again upon the scene of teen romance unfolding below: kids swaying in each other's arms or flirting along the wall, the censorious chaperones rigid before the currents of edgy, innocent sexuality surging through the room. I wanted to make a tender, dreamy space for the lovers with the swish of my brushes, caress them with my cymbals. Alone behind my drums, having nobody to hold myself, I'd fuel their dreams with my own. A girl was looking over her boyfriend's shoulder at me, and I began playing to her. "Dream when you're feeling blue. . . . Dream it's the thing to do. . . ." As we ended, another couple lingered deliciously in a kiss.

We played "Happy Birthday" for somebody. Then kids started snake-dancing around the floor to my crisp triple rim shots at the end of each phrase of "The Bunny Hop." There was a request for "The Mexican Hat Dance," which the band knew from memory. Musicians and dancers alike seemed to share some inherited common repertory of music, American but then not quite: more a crazy quilt of folk songs, pop tunes from radio and old records, and songs from the countries people's parents came from.

When we launched into "Rock Around the Clock" (evidence that The John Melli Orchestra was hip, cool, in on the rock-and-roll thing), boys' jackets came off and girls shook their crinoline dresses, beehives bouncing. The chaperones eyed one another gravely. Finally, when the dancers had cooled off, we wrapped up the evening with a slow rendition of the Everly Brothers' "All I Have to Do Is Dream," the lovers pressed into each other, wishing away the garments that separated them. As we held on the final note, I single-stroked my mallets on the cymbal in a shimmering, sustained shudder of release.

The lights came up, the dance was over. The musicians began packing their instruments, lighting up cigarettes or pipes, and chatting. A trumpet player nodded to me, betraying neither censure nor praise. John Melli passed out envelopes. I peeked in at the five and two ones, then shoved the envelope in my jacket pocket.

I disassembled my drums slowly so I'd finish after the other musicians had driven off in their cars. Finally, when it seemed I was alone in the auditorium but for the janitor sweeping crepe paper into a corner, I noticed a pretty girl lingering at the edge of the stage, sparkle in her hair, a balloon tied to her wrist. Dreamily she watched me pack up the last of my kit. I looked down at her and smiled; she smiled back. Then her escort emerged from the rest room, a lanky blond jock with a pomaded crew cut. As they walked off across the empty gym floor, hand in hand, the girl cast a quick glance back at me. I felt a flush of attainment, sensing another of drumming's possibilities.

Dad was waiting in the parking lot by the Buick, smoking

his pipe in the warm night air. I loaded my drum cases into the car.

"How did it go, son?"

"Okay," I said as we drove off, quietly elated but reluctant to share the experience, either the good or bad parts.

"Get paid?"

I pulled a five and two ones from the envelope and held them up, but Dad didn't seem to notice.

"You know, on my first job—well, I don't remember how much I got paid, but it was probably a little more than that. Must have been around 1924. I was good, you know, in demand. I couldn't read, but I could improvise on C melody, so the band-leaders would let me take the 'hot' solo. Of course, later on, when I produced my own shows with all the greats—Dorsey, Trumbauer, Teagarden, Satchmo—naturally I had an edge, be-cause, hell, I was one of the guys myself. . . ."

We drove through Beverly Hills, Dad laughing at the plea-sure of his own recollection, the names and cadences taking him back to a luminous yesteryear, a landscape already as tiresomely familiar to me as my own breath.

We wound through Coldwater Canyon to our little street. Drawing up the long driveway, I saw that the two-car garage door was open. Mom's station wagon was gone.

Dad braked and ran inside. Slowly I began unloading my drums, hauling them up the long stairs to the house. All the lights were on inside, but Mom was nowhere to be found. Upstairs, my little sister, Meg, was asleep in her bed.

The call came in the middle of the night. Mom had plowed the station wagon through a bakery window on La Brea Boulevard and was in jail at the Hollywood station. Dad left me in charge of my sister and went down to bail Mom out and get her admitted to a clinic somewhere to dry out.

I sat up the rest of the night, filled with the thrill of the drumming and the dance—replaying the good moments, the humiliating miscues, the lingering image of the rapt girl at the fringe of the stage afterward—while my parents' lives tumbled through space.

6. The Duffer

Dad sits in a bathrobe in his wheelchair before the silent television, an old family-photo album perched on his blanketed lap. Demoted from walker to wheelchair, he no longer leaves the house. He can't hear well, remember, follow conversations. His short-term memory shot, he riffles the old celebrity picture albums, coming alive, it seems, only in these representations of a vanished time.

Over the last decade, decrepitude has gradually chipped away Dad's patina of decency and politesse. I've hauled him to clinics where he regales strangers about his bowel movements, grabs nurses' asses. He whispers obscenities in his granddaughters' ears. ("Poppa! Shame on you!" the girls will say, brushing his hand off a skirt hem.) I've steadied him on his walker, winced at the old jokes, picked him up when he fell. He talks to me as if my life hasn't happened and I still live here. Our old quarrels, absurd relics, seem no longer worth the candle when I only see helplessness in his eyes. A grudging intimacy has settled between us. After you've pulled your father's pants down in a public lavatory and helped him get properly pointed at the potty, this happens.

As his mind unspools, our conversations become weirdly comic, Beckett-like. The stock platitudes and polite locutions that always formed much of his patter now fire off at random, *non sequitur*, detached from any dialectical logic:

"It's warm today, Dad."

"Fine, thank you."

"You sleepy, Dad?"

"Good for you."

And: "Please give my regards to . . . uh, uh [fishing for a name]." "Thank you very much. And you?" "Don't think anything of it." "Glad to hear it."

At his ninety-fourth-birthday party, observing his new rubberized wheelchair, I'd said, "Nice wheelchair, Dad."

"One day, son," he muttered, accomplishing what will surely stand as his last joke, "this will be yours."

In the den I sign a few checks for Nell at the mahogany desk shipped out from Manhattan over half a century ago, now festooned with photos and mementos of family and erstwhile career. The shelf behind me groans with vintage books and swing records, transcriptions of wartime shows for the troops (his live transatlantic broadcast of Django Reinhart and the Hot Club of France; the special with Paul Robeson to protest Germany's invasion of Czechoslovakia). This time-warped booty is earmarked for me, and I don't want any of it. I'd trade it all for closure, deliverance, and a ticket out of here.

More celebrity and family photos line the walls, an aerial survey of an avocado ranch he'd bought in Santa Barbara when radio died, a snapshot of the old duffer in checkered slacks and golf hat, brandishing a wedgie. Among a rack of shiny pipes—unsmoked for years, though their aroma still pervades the den—I see the yellow, white-rimmed calabash pipe, a key icon in my father's personal mythology.

He always took credit for having coined Jimmy Durante's signature closing line, "Good night, Mrs. Calabash, wherever you are," during a late-night script meeting when Dad had been smoking the gourd pipe that now holds pride of place among his collection. But a close friend of his who wrote a definitive book on the radio era credited someone else with the line.

So there was the gilding, the bluffing. It was so long ago, who remembers or cares? Who among us doesn't limn his ré-sumé, effect a little spin, augment the size of the fish caught? With Dad it was always so embarrassingly transparent. But self-perception is a narcissist's Achilles' heel.

Seventeen years ago, not long after my mother died, my father and I were walking along the beach in Santa Monica. Extra family attentions were proffered during that period, which we assumed would come to a natural end when he'd regained his balance, established a new life as a widower, perhaps taken up with somebody else.

"Son," he said suddenly, fixing me in his gaze, "I'm count-ing on you to take care of me."

I looked back over my shoulder, figuratively, to see whom he might be addressing. He was seventy-six at the time, in perfect health. Never a headache, a hack, a hospitalization. Financially he looked set for the duration. For years we hadn't had much to say to each other; he seemed closer to my sister and her family. Much of my adult life had been lived at a distance from him. Conflicts that had erupted between us in my teens and smol-dered for decades had never been resolved; since then a wary ci-vility ruled our relations. We'd never agreed about much of anything—work, art, politics, religion. In truth, I didn't take to him all that much, and I assumed—no, I knew—he felt the same about me.

No, this is putting it too mildly. My father had been my nemesis, the guy blocking the light. I had many grievances against him. His unquenchable egotism and insecurity obliged him, however unconsciously, to undercut his son at every turn.

If to others he was simply a "nice guy," to me he was repressive and controlling, a toxic entity who sucked up all the air in the room. The main thing he seemed to want from me was unconditional, conspiratorial support in shoring up his self-esteem, which meant ascribing to his version of the world. This I stoutly refused to do, partly to withhold from him the satisfaction but, more important, to achieve my own. I suppose I laid my mother's sorrows at his feet too. Where had he been when Mom was falling apart, leaving me at ten years old the family caretaker? My idea of hell would be being trapped for eternity in a room with my vain, self-serving father. In turn, I shudder to think what his opinion was of me: wastrel, reprobate, wanderer, bohemian dabbler, ingrate—implicit judgments I'd seen in his eyes if not heard from his lips.

But it had long ago ceased to matter. It turned out a decent notion of me was less stingily withheld by the greater world, and over the years my accomplishments had matched if not superseded his. Fortunately, a good love had abided between my mother and me in spite of her difficulties. My needs for my father—and his for me, I'd always assumed—had been over by the time I left home at seventeen. Whatever I'd looked to him for, I'd either gotten by then or wasn't going to. We'd arrived, so I'd thought, at an unambitious, semipolite *modus vivendi,* our business with each other long ago, however unsatisfactorily, finished.

So, that afternoon on the beach, my father's call for some new, undefined interdependency this late in both our lives completely blindsided me. I couldn't imagine delivering whatever he might be asking for with any loving spontaneity. He expected to construct his widowerhood around *me,* the distant, peripatetic son? It flew in the face of all that lay between us.

Was I expected to replace Mom (who I considered to have died early from the strain of having serviced this egomaniac)? For years he'd barely given me the time of day; now, suddenly, he seemed to be calling for unalloyed devotion. When Dad delivered his pronouncement, I don't remember what I said in return. Nonplussed, I probably just nodded grimly.

In the days following, I began to wonder: What is he setting me up for? A chance to fail him yet again? With Dad, I'd learned, you always had to slip behind the words to get the message. And there was *always* a message.

Before long, the amazing, unwelcome reappearance of my father in my life began to take concrete shape. He called constantly with requests for visits and attentions, demands to run errands. "Call me tomorrow around ten, would you," or "Hope I'm not interrupting your writing. Know you're on a deadline, but I need a little help around the house." When I asked him exactly what he needed, he'd vaguely allude to a lightbulb, a noise in the garbage disposal, a family document. By the time I got to his place, he couldn't remember why he'd asked me to come— because of course it wasn't about that.

I began to interpret his pronouncement that day at the beach to mean something like: The entirety of what you imagine to have been your adult life until now—your silly rites of separation, your dubious achievements, your frivolous travels, your inept moral decisions, your sketchy family life (divorced and remarried, with daughter)—has been nothing but a puppet's dance at the end of a rubber band stretching away from the fact of servicing me, your father, the true reality.

I kept waiting for Dad to right himself, snap out of this. Surely the old charmer would soon take up with a new woman and that would do it. At the same time, I found it difficult to say no to him. I had my own standards to meet in this situation, regardless of how I felt; I bore regrets about my rude and wayward youth and the strains it had inflicted on him and my mother. In another, dawning sense, I was beginning to feel I owed my mother certain attentions to him—as tribute to what she'd borne, now that I saw what it was. So I often obliged, miserably. Dad loved the attention; I felt trapped.

One afternoon, he was telling me one of his repetitive, self-glorifying Hollywood anecdotes, dropping names of long-forgotten celebrities. Noticing my attention waver, he said, "Hey, listen up. You might want to use this in a book someday."

Never, I thought. You're the last person I'll ever write about.

Dad's escalating entreaties began to interfere with my movement, my independence, my work. I hunted for any excuse to slip out of town, spend time away. Even if it was only overnight, Dad would insist I call him before leaving and again the minute I got back. At the age of forty-five, I was on curfew, recalled back to childhood.

I lost sleep; Masako and I quarreled over trifles. Finally I couldn't stand it any more. Masako and I sublet a friend's apartment in Paris for the summer. Dad got wind of it and invited himself along. We canceled the trip. Soon after, we moved to Mexico for a stretch of months, thinking our long absence might drive Dad up to Santa Barbara, near my sister's sizable and loving family. But he dug in, adjusted to where he was, made do. He found a few new golf buddies at the local links and an occasional lady for a date at the movies. I could hear the lonely plaint in the phone calls I made home every Sunday from Mexico, but he seemed intent upon staying put.

Years passed. Dad never remarried, and lived alone. He outlived his ladies, his friends, his brothers and sisters. Kindly neighbors kept tabs on him when I was gone. He slowed by small degrees, gradually becoming grizzled, incontinent, shaky, but unbowed. I returned to California ever more frequently to deal with his doctors, his car, his finances. Finally I arranged for the place in Venice, anticipating longer stretches here.

My attentions were modest but steady. I dragged Dad to medical clinics, sat with him while he gummed his food, picked him up when he fell. I presented myself unfailingly at every birthday and holiday celebration, then left town again. When he began to fail seriously, the visits necessarily increased. Meanwhile, the subtext of our early battles, never resolved but simply outlasted, lurked behind our eyes.

Gradually, as Dad lived on—and on, and on—I began to decode the real messages behind his request that day at the beach: fear, remorse, terror of death; desolation, dread of abandonment—and a father's plea for a son's forgiveness.

"Tony boy? You there?" I hear the querulous call from the living room.

In his den, I close the checkbook and slip it back inside the desk drawer.

Dad beckons me to the chair beside him. A photo album lies open on his lap. He fumbles for my hand and holds it in his crabby, cold one. Instinctively I draw back. He grips harder. I brush the crumbs that had fallen from his lips off the open page of the photo album and onto the plaid blanket around his knees.

Dad frowns, then lights up in recognition. His querulous finger stabs the picture. "That Uncle Frank?"

"No, Dad. That's Nancy Sinatra, his daughter."

Only the tinny music of yesteryear seems to bring my father out of torpor.

This is what's odd, though. Sitting imprisoned among the memorabilia and lacunae in conversation, the oldies and the goodies, the detritus of long ago and far away, wending our way down Memory Lane, my addled dad and I, we each have business to conduct.

As I lead him back, he leads me back.

Drew was a trumpet player in my high school. He didn't gig around town weekends with dance combos, like me and my bass-player friend Chaz. He studied with a classical teacher somewhere in my neighborhood. Drew was in the concert band for a while but dropped out, too delicate for our robust repertory of street marches, swing medleys, and show tunes. A small, pale boy with an odd interior grin and a vague, nodding walk, Drew was into something very private. I hadn't an inkling of what it was until one afternoon he invited me over to his house.

Drew, it turned out, had vaulted ahead of the rest of us in musical consciousness. While Chaz and I were into Shorty Rogers and Gerry Mulligan and Chet Baker and Shelley Manne—facile, crew-cut West Coast white jazz guys with limpid styles—Drew was drinking deep of the serious contemporary black innovators: Thelonious Monk, Miles Davis, John Coltrane, Ornette Coleman. I sat on the edge of Drew's bed as he mouthed solos and licks along with the records in a wild scat, his new, advanced modalities of expression obliterating my old sensibilities in a stroke. Drew's bedside table was littered with alluring unfamiliar paperbacks—Kerouac, Lawrence, Henry Miller, Sade—his shelves stacked with Lenny Bruce and Lord Buckley records, a book of erotic prints by Egon Schiele. But Drew seemed to be testing me for something else besides musical hipness and vision. When he invited me to come along and visit "somebody cool" the next day, I agreed.

The following afternoon, we drove to a large, run-down ho-tel off the Santa Monica boardwalk. We crossed a deserted lobby, took an elevator to the fourth floor, and walked to the end of a dank, malodorous hallway. A black man with red-rimmed eyes unbolted a door and let us in. Hard bop pulsed from a cheap hi-fi. When Drew introduced us, I recognized his name: a bass player on a legendary series of early-fifties jazz records with the trumpet genius Clifford Brown and the drummer Max Roach. It was a shock to see him here like this. A half-dozen people, black and white, sat around on mattresses, emitting wisps of fractured words, nods serving as rejoinders. A sickly looking girl drifted out of the bathroom in a bathrobe, a man's tie cinched around her sore-infested forearm, a syringe in her hand. Somebody rolled up what looked to be dusky green tobacco cut-tings in a cigarette paper, lit it, sucked on it, and passed it around. Giggling, Drew followed suit, then handed it to me. I tried to do what he did and choked. Watery-eyed, I passed it along.

Coming out of the waterfront hotel into the glare of late af-ternoon, I knew something had changed, though I wasn't yet sure what.

I arrived home at dinnertime, still blurry from the conse-quences of the strange visit to the hotel. I slipped into my room and changed into a jacket and tie for a gig that night, then joined Mom, Dad, and Meg at the table.

Our family's life had changed radically since the glamour days in Coldwater Canyon. Migrating westward across Los Angeles, we'd landed first in a small rented house in Brentwood, where Mom had embarked on a climactic, harrowing, months-long drinking tear that nearly killed her and traumatized the rest of us. Since coming out of the sanitarium that time, she'd managed, with the aid of some syncretic mix of AA, Indian metaphysics, and psychiatry, to stay off drink. She adhered to a severe personal daily routine, rising with us in the morning to send us off to school, then looking after my father and the house. Dad often let it be known that my mother's sobriety was something to admire, as of course it was; though the possible reasons for her mysterious fall were never alluded to.

Now, settled into this one-story house in a new suburb a mile from the ocean, a temple to Mom's sobriety and Dad's enforced career quiescence, my parents had drawn a half-curtain over their lives, it seemed, linked to the outside ever less by experience and more by television. Dad, a part-time "show-business" specialist at an ad agency now, devoted an increasing number of his hours to cultivating his garden and his radio memories. At seventeen, I was preoccupied with music, girls, and basketball, and checked in at home only to eat and sleep.

Mom was in the kitchen in an apron, ladling out chicken à la king onto plates. She couldn't cook to save her life when she got married, and during Dad's big radio years there'd always been maids and cooks. By now she'd managed to master a half-dozen "balanced meals"—a meat, a starch, a vegetable—to feed the family each night. Dad, blessed with good health and a kind of dogged, Reagan-like innocence that he somehow managed to enlist those around him in helping him preserve, didn't seem to understand my mother's problems—or anyone else's—particularly well; but by not entirely abandoning Mom when she was drunk, he'd incurred her eternal indebtedness in some uneasy way, binding them in a noble, if dull, peace.

My father still liked to take me into his den to regale me with past glories. I, sulky and unresponsive, counted the days until college in the fall. By this point we disagreed about nearly everything. When Dad offered to ask a friend at the ad agency to help me get into Stanford, I refused, accusing him of moral hypocrisy and influence-peddling.

Now, as I tore into dinner, my father said, "So where are you playing tonight, son?"

"The Hollywood Palladium. With Nancy Sinatra."

Even as the word "Sinatra" left my lips, I knew what was coming. Our L.A. high school was packed with show-business celebrities' kids—Mitchums, Sinatras—and teen hotshot singers and actors like Jan and Dean and "Gidget." Nancy Sinatra, skinny-legged and thin-lipped, had recently decided she wanted to be a singer like her dad. We'd rehearsed a couple of times at her mother's house in Beverly Hills—some pop standards, a little bleached rock and roll, a couple of her dad's hits. Chaz and I had kept a straight face through rehearsals with the future purveyor of "These Boots Are Made for Walkin' " (her younger brother had yet to begin his dubious crooning career). Tonight Nancy was making her public debut at a senior graduation dance at the Palladium.

At the mention of Sinatra, Dad unleashed a wearying recollection of a radio show he'd produced in the 1940s with Frankie as guest star. Mom, with surprising fervor of her own, admitted to having had a consuming girlhood crush on Sinatra. Dad, undeterred, continued with his anecdote.

"Gotta go," I said, getting up from the table.

Driving off in Mom's Studebaker, I thought about the visit with Drew to the hotel room that afternoon, my first glimpse of a subterranean hipster world. Those images of smiling drummers I'd first seen in the glossy photos on the walls of Dick Monahan's drum shop when I was ten now merged into the disturbing reality of a brilliant bass player holed up in a seedy hotel room shooting dope. Maybe real art had a component of dissolution and alienation, frightening but necessary. I thought of a phrase of Henry Miller's I'd read at Drew's: "All the room is at the bottom." Give up everything, gain the comfort of oblivion, seek revelation in the shadows. Here was a counterlogic that had a certain allure. My family life, a pleasant façade to outsiders, was a barely disguised wrecked vessel, foundering on the shoals of my mother's alcoholism and Dad's career collapse. High school was checkered with hostility, as the pop, pep, and pap of the Eisenhower years curdled into delinquency and violence. McCarthyism hung like a shroud over the American culture I was being groomed to enter. The dance-band vocabulary I'd labored to learn—standards, waltzes, mambos, ballads, rock backbeat, Latin interludes, cool jazz stylings—I could play in my sleep now. There had to be something more. Panels of dissonant realities slid by as I drove the darkened, vacant L.A. streets.

I picked up Chaz and his bass on a street corner a block from his house in a poor neighborhood off Sepulveda Boulevard. A month before, I'd gone to fetch him for a gig and walked in to find his father, a car mechanic, raging drunkenly at Chaz for showing him up by making his own money in music. As I'd watched, he'd picked up Chaz's bass and smashed it against the wall. We'd fled the house, and Chaz had broken down crying in my car, adding to his shame. Music was all he had, his only road out. The concert bandmaster at school had arranged for him to borrow a school bass so he could keep working while his instrument got fixed. He'd stored it at a friend's house down the street for safety, which is where I picked him up.

Chaz slid his bass across the back seat of the Studebaker atop my drum cases, its neck sticking out of the rolled-down window. We drove off in uneasy silence. Chaz and I had discovered music together, working our way from marches to orchestral music, then on through Kenton, Brubeck, Bartok, and Mahler. Earnest and musically astute, Chaz had always led the way. We worked around town together, forming one of the better local rhythm sections. Chaz idealized my parents, so polite and well heeled compared with his, their difficulties invisible to him.

Driving down Sunset to Hollywood, I brought up the subject of Drew the trumpet player and the musical culture of Monk, Miles, and Coltrane he'd revealed to me.

"Those guys don't play clean," Chaz said. "Miles splits his notes."

"Maybe clean isn't the same thing as art," I ventured, opening up an aesthetic breach that would soon drive us apart.

A hired photographer snapped press pictures that night at the Hollywood Palladium. Corsages, tuxedos, prom dresses—pink, of course, though the photos are monochrome. Everyone is smiling but me. I sit behind my drums, arms folded, looking less sullen than blank, gazing into the camera as if challenging the photo's very reason for being. Chaz, standing beside his borrowed bass, is looking at me quizzically, as if to ask: What's happening with you?

A second photo shows the band with girlfriends. Standing beside me is mine, Sandra, fifteen and blonde and pretty in a strapless party dress, her intelligent eyes sweetly sad. She'd gotten a ride to the dance with Chaz's girlfriend so I could take her home afterward. (She'd sit patiently waiting, as musicians' girlfriends do night after night, on a folding chair backstage or down front, dressed for the dance but with no partner until the dance was over.) My arm is around her waist. In my expression I see, or think I do, the first hard-eyed, deadpan slash of alienation, cleaving me from realities I still inhabited but no longer believed.

"You seem funny tonight," Sandra said after the dance, as I drove us to a lonely spot in the hills above her house, our sexual stomping ground.

"Do I?" I shrugged. We'd been going steady close to a year, each other's first serious love. Sandra, quiet and bright and studious, was a year behind me in school. Desire, fear, adoration, jealousy: we'd felt their power for the first time together. Neither of us had had sexual experience. Her parents were churchgoing Lutherans, and the rules were clear: nothing was permitted. If every kiss was a stolen kiss, we'd become deft thieves. Advancing inch by inch, we'd pursued a slow, creeping erotic path, each step a sweet agony. Months had passed before I gently forced a tongue past the barrier of her damp, quavering lips. Many weeks later, embracing in the backseat of a car, I pressed my hard-on against her and knew she felt it. A month after that, entangled with her on a couch, I came in my clothes. In weeks to follow, my hands brushed about the hillocks of her breasts like moths before finally alighting upon the tender leaf of her blouse. Then, one breathless evening, my cramped hand scuttled inside her tight bra, cupping the soft, strange flesh, the springy nipple. At home in my mother's chest of drawers I practiced unhooking a bra, though it turned out to be Sandra's bathing-suit halter top I untied in a single swift pull two weekends later, in a poolhouse, her sweet breasts mine at last to fondle and kiss. Weeks preceded each new, inevitable step, charging us with bittersweet anticipation and private arousals of imagination. If our schoolmates were already (as the guys claimed) fucking like bunnies, Sandra and I were sexual retards, engaged in a tender, ruminative exploration, ascending sex's Everest in slow, demarcated steps: mapping, surveying, conquering. We never spoke of any of this, having no language for it. The early hours of our evenings together—movies, dances, studying— were but shadowy, tremulous preludes to the intent, absorbed submersion in flesh to follow: alone in a car, on her parents' couch, on some friend's bed. Our slow-motion waltz of delicate permissions: rape's precise opposite.

Sandra's father was a professor, her mother heavily involved with church charities. They'd begun pressing for Sandra to bring me to church, so, obligingly, I'd gone the Sunday before and stood singing "Onward Christian Soldiers" with the congregation, my eyes scanning the unfamiliar hymnal. I knew Sandra's parents were testing my uncertain religious status to see if I might be steered along the righteous path to matrimony.

For weeks Sandra and I had been brushing hips and thighs with hungry hands, edging ever closer to those last untouched redoubts. Finally, one night, I grabbed her hand, held it firmly against me through my clothes, and whispered the cheap line I'd rehearsed: "I want you to know me." She gasped, tried feebly to withdraw, then let her hand lie inertly there. The next time we reached this point—we never backed up—she touched it, took its measure, began to play with it. By now the time between each step had shortened to a week or days even, as new urgencies drove us. I'd be off to college in the fall; a new social tone of promiscuity among other kids pressured our delicate sexual hothouse; and lust itself forced each new step hot upon the heels of the last. The week before the Palladium gig, while

Sandra had stroked me, I'd clutched at her through her underpants, my finger dowsing along the elastic edge of her soaked panties.

Tonight, parked at the end of our little hillside cul-de-sac, we kissed hard and deep. Maybe it was my stormy confusions, or simply that we were losing control, tumbling down desire's rapids in a vessel we could no longer steer. Bypassing our usual careful procedures, my hands swarmed Sandra's thighs, then scooted her skirt up; her legs spread wide in welcome. While she unfastened me and fished hungrily inside, I gingerly slid a finger past the elastic into that hot mystery I'd coveted for so long. It was slippery, and I couldn't find my way around. Sandra flinched, murmured something into our locked mouths, redirected my hand forward. I'd fished past the mark to her anus.

Recovering, my finger must have found its way to the right spot: for Sandra gasped, breathed deeply, grabbed me as she'd never done, and held my hand to her. In a crescendo of whimpers and sobs, we climaxed. Overcome, we wept into each other's shoulders, my pants and the back of her hand gunked with semen, my fingers clotted with her scent.

We struggled into our clothes, blank and frightened, raw with exposed emotion. Amid crickets and jasmine aroma, I fished for the keys and started up the engine. I drove through the silent suburban streets, Sandra nestled into my shoulder, my arm around her, the pink dice she'd knitted for me swaying from the rearview mirror, wrapped together in peace or satiety or closeness, and an aching sadness for all we'd lost, and losses to come.

Drew called the next week to tell me he'd landed a weekend gig at a new jazz club in Hollywood. He'd lined up a hot young black tenor and bass player from South L.A. and a good pianist from the Valley. I canceled my dates with Chaz and our regular band. I spent that week immersing myself in the albums Drew had loaned me, absorbing the fluid, slashing bop drumming language of Philly Joe Jones, Roy Haynes, and Elvin Jones.

The night of the gig, I hauled my kit up the back stairs of a cement building into a smoky, underlit room of black-clad, unsmiling customers of different races. Before the first set, I shared a joint with the others in the band in the alley. Taking the stand, we carved savage, energized improvisations, angular and probing, out of some invisible block of ebony, daring disorder and risk, peeling away the surface of life around us, searching for a new, ugly beauty—like the cries of sweet pain Sandra and I had made on the dark hillside.

Nell is the only living person outside the family who knew my mother well. Their friendship went back to New York days, when they were single working women. Nell had been a studio singer, her husband, Roy, a composer and singer, Mom an aspiring stage actress. Roy and Dad, golf buddies, had been friends since live radio's heyday. They'd all migrated to California, the friendships held, and the kids knew each other.

As an adult, I never really knew Nell, but her sudden arrival at my father's house three years earlier when she was eighty-five years old had brought an unexpected boon. A quiet, insightful person with Eastern spiritual perspectives, she has things to tell me about my family. Over coffee one afternoon, while my decrepit father sleeps, revelations surface.

During Mom's darkest drinking years, when she'd hole up for days in her bedroom with a cache of gin, it was Nell who'd come to the big house in Coldwater Canyon, listen to her woes, and try to dig her out. When there was no food in the house, when the neighbors became so frightened about what was going on in Dorothy Lamour's big place on the hill that they put out distress signals, Nell would come and take me and my sister in.

Now it is Nell who, on a sunny May afternoon, in the deep twilight of my father's life, divulges what had triggered Mom's operatic binge when I was ten. Dad had run off to New York with another woman.

Nell came from the same part of the country as my mother,

the Ohio—West Virginia area. Mary Helen Foster, my mother, came from Steubenville, Nell from Akron; both had spent their teen years in Cleveland. Mom's family—English, German, Irish—had lived in Steubenville since the early nineteenth century; my grandmother's grandfather, "Squire" Robert Love, had presided as mayor there until his death in 1906. His wife, the former Mary Ann Dougherty, was born there too, as her mother had been. Pittsburgh was the big city for shopping trips and baseball games, ending with a train ride home on the Pennsy. Mom's paternal great-granddad, Colonel William Freudenberger (pronounced *"Frood*enberger"), headed up the local Spanish-American War Veterans' Association, striding the streets of Steubenville in his starched uniform and handlebar mustache, as seen in a surviving daguerreotype. An oil operator and real-estate investor, he was purportedly tricked out of an oil fortune by John D. Rockefeller and remained bitter about it to the end of his days.

"Your mother's Irish temper," my dad would often say, as if to explain away her sudden eruptions. Her vulnerability to drink he attributed to the Irish pedigree as well, whereas I recall more tenderly the "Tura Lura Lura" lullabies at bedtime. Bob Foster, my mother's father, was a charming rogue who made and lost several fortunes; he even did time in jail for embezzlement, according to my father. In the spirit of American self-invention, he'd changed his last name from Freudenberger to Foster when World War I broke out. (My dad's immigrant father, from another, more put-upon culture, had had his name changed for him at Ellis Island.) Bob Foster married Mary Wilhelmina Fisher of Wheeling, an auburn-haired beauty who died of pneumonia when her daughter, my mother, was twelve. The Loves, Freudenbergers, Fishers, and Doughertys all attended the First Methodist Church in Steubenville and today co-occupy a sizable family plot nearby, I'm told.

I gaze at a snapshot of a great-great-aunt and -uncle taken in their yard in Steubenville on their fifty-seventh wedding anniversary. Back in those days, the Heinz Co. was famous for having fifty-seven tomato products, including their flagship ketchup, and any couple celebrating a fifty-seventh anniversary would receive a box containing each of their items. Bald Uncle Elmer in bow tie and ill-fitting white suit, Aunt Lillian gray and bespectacled and stuffed into a summer dress: proud elders, paragons of church and Rotary and Kiwanas and Elks Club civic uplift, standing proudly in front of their Heinz booty in the backyard of a frame house.

To me, growing up in California, such sketchy gleanings of Ohio and West Virginia origins seemed as remote as the far Caucasus. That some unimaginable conjoining of blanched Steubenville loins wended westward to my family's Hollywood existence of comics and drunks, spiritualists and starlets, surfers and swamis, was probably my first inkling that California wasn't quite like the rest of America, and that our cross-country trip on the Santa Fe Super Chief had about it something epic and irreversible.

How to figure the cost to my mother, the passage from stultifying provincial America to Manhattan and Hollywood? After my grandmother's early death, Bob Foster remarried a stern woman who made Mom go to a Presbyterian church and thank God for taking her mother away to heaven, refused to let her talk to boys, and made her bind her breasts with strips of cloth to flatten them. By then Mom despised everything about small-town Midwestern life. She escaped to the Laurel School for Girls in Cleveland, where Granddad Bob, flush then and widowed a second time, installed them in a big house with chauffeur and maid. Mary Helen Foster, already beautiful, drew the attentions of the local star athlete, who later ended up in the Football Hall of Fame; but her best girlfriend was from a cultured, intellectual Cleveland Jewish family who took her off to Paris with them for a year. It was the Roaring Twenties, she had French boyfriends, she awakened culturally, and surely she drank. Her new surrogate family must have nurtured an ease with Jews which would have helped when she met my father: mixing, let alone marrying, was still uncommon in those days.

She returned from Europe in 1929 to find her father had lost his fortune. With no money for college, she moved to New York, sold encyclopedias door to door, then ended up onstage under the name of "Merrill Foster" in Pearl Buck's *The Good Earth*. Her father followed her there and married his third wife, my step-grandmother Edwina, a flamboyant Southern woman who worked at the haute-couture house of Mainbocher on Fifth Avenue. They lived in a grand apartment on Sutton Place South, overlooking the East River, for thirty-odd years, until one day Edwina kicked my grandfather out. Granddad Bob Foster showed up on our doorstep in California at the age of eighty-two without a dime, and my parents took him in.

My father told me after my mother died that her drinking long preceded the episodes in Coldwater Canyon. He described parties in New York when they were still dating and Mom would get so drunk she'd pass out and he'd have to carry her bodily up her apartment stairs to her bed. Later, when she stopped, he tended to idealize her recovery to us, perhaps even to himself. I don't think he understood alcoholism or indeed any form of intemperance, being such a steady Joe himself. But this reverence toward Mom's abstinence created an odd space in the home, Mom never occupying a middle ground but appearing either as sinner (the abject, fallen drinker) or saint (the disciplined, recovered renunciant): a perfect California mom, in a way, embodying both Eden and the Fall, the utopic and the dystopic. (Bertolt Brecht, who lived in nearby Santa Monica during his exiled war years, probably got it right in seeing L.A. as both heaven *and* hell—site of bright, sunny possibilities and arroyo dead-ends.)

I always loved my mother, evenly, no less when she was drunk and no more when she wasn't. I never held the binges against her or considered that I'd been damaged by her drinking. Kids are clear-eyed and figure things out quickly; they forgive mightily, and they love long and hard. Actually, Mom was more interesting—certainly more dramatic and funny, if frightening—as an active drunk than as a recovering one, her abstinence leading her, ironically, into a life of renunciation and discipline not unlike her Puritan forebears, at times mimicking the severity of that stern stepmother she'd so feared and despised.

So Nell knew some secret family history. She admired my mother's sobriety but even more her intellectual and metaphysical heft. If it was AA that first helped Mom pull out, it was her studies in Hindu Vedanta philosophy with that quirky, brilliant klatch of southern-California British neo-mystics—Isherwood, Huxley, the philosopher Gerald Heard—and her classes with Jungian psychiatrists, Egyptologists, and Mayanists, that proofed her against relapse. Mom, who always regretted having lost the chance at a higher education during the Depression, read assiduously and took classes at UCLA in history, archaeology, mythology, filling scores of little notebooks in her tight Parker penmanship. A scholar manqué and proto-feminist, she'd likely have been a professor in today's world. Instead, she poured her ideals and love of language into me.

The thing that disturbed my mother most—what frightened her, shook her to her bones—was when her tendencies toward excess began to appear in her son.

"So who was she?" I ask Nell, who pours more coffee. "The one my dad ran off with?"

Simple curiosity drives me to ask, though I'm not so sure I want to know. I fear her answer will disgust me. I don't need more ammunition against Dad, such a helpless figure now. News of his infidelity isn't a surprise somehow. What does it matter whom Pop was boffing in a berth on the eastbound Santa Fe Super Chief, tangled in some pedestrian midlife affair that brought such misery down upon the family? I doubt it could change how I feel about him at this late date. In my eyes, he doesn't have much of a pedestal left to fall off.

There are other things I'd rather not know about him, such as his stance toward the House Un-American Activities Committee when he was given a list of allegedly "pink" writers by the vigilante group Red Channels and a strong-armed invitation to fire any "commies" from his CBS shows. Dad—politically cautious, assimilated, mainstream across the board—was a get-along, go-along guy who cared desperately what other people thought of him, not one to rock boats. With the passage of years, I'd heard him reshade his stance on the blacklist issue. But I'd come to cut him more slack on this than I had in youth. How could I possibly understand the insecurities of growing up in his situation in his time?

A singer, Nell says.

Wouldn't you know it. A vocalist, a thrush, a siren, a canary. Dad was always a sucker for a good song. He loved music; and just as it would rescue his son from the oppressions of home and family, so had it earlier rescued him from his. In times when I'd found little in my heart to thank him for, I'd always exempted the gift of his love for music.

Dad's instrument had been the C-melody sax, and a little piano he learned from his sister. There was always music around the immigrant house in Meriden, Connecticut, led by the scholarly Polish-immigrant granddad I never knew (he died when I was four), a fiddler back in Łódź, I was told, and Dad's two older brothers and sisters played too. But it was the new swing and jazz that caught the teenage saxophonist's ear—Beiderbecke, Joe Venuti, Satchmo, and Paul Whiteman, whose coast-to-coast radio show Dad would later produce and direct—an enthusiasm that crossed ethnic lines in Meriden, helping my father break out into the brimming new egalitarian world of American popular art. After college he got a music-production job at the old Paramount Studios, married a pretty *shikse* in a ceremony performed by a reformed radio rabbi, settled three thousand miles away from his clan, and never looked back. (Until later, of course, when that's practically all he did.)

In some ways my father was as distant to me as a grandfather. He remained in the grips of alien cultural and religious ambivalences I couldn't fathom. Though he'd forsaken practicing Judaism in college, he observed private silences on the holy days, and a few times a year a salami and a loaf of corn rye from Canter's Deli would show up on the breadboard, pungent exotica among the canned tuna, mayonnaise, Wonder Bread, peanut butter and jelly. He golfed at an interdenominational country club rather than Hillcrest, the Jewish show-business one. At Christmas we always had a tree but no star on top, a compromise he and Mom had negotiated, it was explained to me. But what was wrong with a star? A matter of five points or six, I was counseled. Later in life, Dad seemed to have come partway back to Judaism for consolation if not faith. As for Mom, she had little good to say of her Midwestern Protestant upbringing. So neither religion was much present in the house, my parents defining themselves loosely as freethinking agnostics—a heritage I'd be grateful for later, actually, because it left me with few shibboleths to cast off.

But once when I was around thirteen, they must have decided I should have some sort of exposure to religion. One Friday night, Dad took me to a temple on Wilshire Boulevard and we stood in back for a while listening to a cantor until Dad became so discomfited that we quickly slipped away. The following Sunday, Mom took me to a Presbyterian church in Beverly Hills, where we encountered instead of a service the wedding of the son of a well-known television-show host. We milled outside among throngs throwing rice, then drove home, Dad excited at news of the celebrity wedding, since he claimed to be friends with the groom's father. So much for religious education.

Still, ethnicity remained important to Dad. He always wanted to know my friends' last names—"Conner. Irish kid, eh? Ortiz. That Mexican or Spanish?"—whereas on California's eclectic schoolyards it never occurred to us to parse our racial stocks or religious pedigrees so finely. "Miller. German boy? English? Jewish?" How could I explain to Dad that the new teen culture of Elvis and surfing and hot rods obviated most of that stuff, that California dreaming was less about origins than release from them?

I see now that my father had made a journey at least as distant as mine, from an immigrant home across the far fields of music and show business to the trimmed lawns and golf balls of the California suburbs. He so loved the great early popular tunes and their composers—Berlin, Gershwin, Rogers and Hart— whom he'd known, or claimed to have known, that when I went off to college I was amazed to learn that my schoolmates didn't know who Harold Arlen, "Yip" Harburg, Johnny Mercer, and Jerome Kern were, or which tunes they wrote and in what musicals they'd first appeared. When Dad sat at the spinet and played "Someone to Watch Over Me" (in C or G, the two keys he commanded), a soft smile played across his face and his burdens lifted.

Of course it would have been a warbler who stole Dad's heart.

"Is that you, Tony boy?"

I hear Dad's faint, reedy voice from his bedroom. Raffles the cocker spaniel barks. Angela scurries off to Dad's room. Nell gets up from the table and rinses our coffee cups in the kitchen sink, our séance over. A few minutes later, Dad emerges in his wheelchair, his sparse silvery hairs combed across his head, another photo album on his lap.

9. *Honey*

I'd always drummed summers—at a jazz club if I could, or else a hotel, a cocktail lounge, a restaurant. With my junior year of college drawing to a close and no gig in sight, the prospect of having to find a straight day job loomed uncomfortably.

The previous fall, I'd transferred from Stanford to the University of California's Santa Barbara campus. Stanford, an attempt to please my father's ambitions by proving I could do well at "the Harvard of the West," had been stultifying, conformist, better suited to engineers and Young Republicans. If Berkeley and San Francisco stirred with alternative culture and political protest, Palo Alto could have been a thousand miles away. Only trips to San Francisco to hear Miles, Cannonball Adderly, and Charles Mingus live at the Blackhawk and the Jazz Workshop had gotten me through. Stung by literature, I'd come south to Santa Barbara to join a hungry interdisciplinary wolfpack feasting, in tiny seminars on campus or at the teachers' houses, upon a stunning colloquium of literary minds: Aldous Huxley, Christopher Isherwood, the brilliant Pound and Yeats scholar Hugh Kenner.

The week before finals, a jazz pianist I'd been working with around Santa Barbara called me for an audition. Just bring sticks, Art said; there's a drum kit there. The next afternoon, I drove to a sleepy stretch of one-story establishments on the south end of town and pulled up in front of a long, narrow one-story stucco building. A sign on the roof, etched in neon letters entwined with a martini glass, said: DUKE'S SUPPER CLUB. Beside a green Naugahyde-padded entry door, a poster invoking the draconian authority of the Alcoholic Beverage Control sternly warned anyone under twenty-one (I was nineteen) against entering. I opened the door and passed into the rancid, melancholic dim of every nightclub on earth by day.

As my eyes adjusted, I spotted Art on a raised bandstand in a corner behind a runway jutting out into the room. A bald, tubby man in a Hawaiian shirt was running sloppy scales on a bruised trumpet. Art introduced me to Remo Bono, who ran the house band at Duke's. Remo needed a drummer and a pianist for the summer. There'd be no bass player, which meant Art would have to play a lot of left hand and me a lot of bass drum. We'd each get $125 a week, I'd have to lie about my age, and we'd have to join the local musicians' union—if we passed the audition.

I sat down behind a worn drum kit. Remo ran us through a few standards—"When You're Smilin' " (shuffle beat), "Just a Gigolo" (same). Then a tall young woman in shorts, halter top, and black beehive hair stepped out of the shadows and clumped up to the stand in high-heeled pumps. She passed sheet music around. Remo introduced her as Crazy Legs, a stripper from New Jersey.

"Exahtic dansah," she corrected Remo.

Crazy Legs began to walk us through her routine. I just tried to hit something hard every time her hips moved.

"Theah. Hit it *theah*," she kvetched. "No, da bump comes *heah*. Can't you read music or what?"

Remo turned to us and rolled his eyes, made the gesture of masturbation.

Later, when Art called and told me we'd gotten the gig, I

drove to the local union building, wrote out a dues check, swore allegiance to James Petrillo, the national union boss, and agreed to attend two general meetings a year. At the Salvation Army I bought a used white tuxedo, a ruffled shirt, a snap-on black bow tie, and black pants—the outfit I'd wear every night for the next three months.

During finals week, I shuttled between Duke's and classrooms, composing severe critical papers on Chaucer, Donne, and Wallace Stevens; etching dense commentaries on Benjamin Whorf's studies of Hopi linguistics; writing pithy exegeses of Beckett, Ionesco, Sartre, and Pirandello plays—then banging the kit for Crazy Legs and a Lenny Bruce–like scatological comic until after midnight. When school was over, I moved to a small cottage closer to town. Afternoons I spent with Art, intently decoding the new Blue Note LPs pouring into the record bins weekly, and getting in some practice on my drum set at the club, always empty by day. At nightfall, Duke's neon sign lit up again.

In the summer of 1959, a visiting foreigner, horny salesman, or furtive cleric could scour nearly any California town from one end to the other and encounter no allusions to sex in any form. College students and businessmen privately circulated phone numbers of a few local prostitutes, abortionists, drug contacts. Aficionados were known to hoard little stashes of grainy 16mm black-and-white stag films that cost a fortune to buy. Homosexual life was near-invisible by necessity, and harrowing to those who lived it. Laws against any manner of perceived deviance were tough and unforgiving, curfews strictly enforced. State and local agencies closely monitored liquor sales and licenses; and possession of a joint, let alone paraphernalia, could mean years in prison. Those in search of something illicit usually headed for a bar or a club, someplace where there was live entertainment and liquor was served. These were the provinces of the lonely, the restless, the perverse.

Duke's Supper Club was Santa Barbara's lone outlet for such soft sin. Dinner was served until the show started, though few came just for the steak and seafood with breadsticks and a side of Louise's special pasta, served on red tablecloths with fat candles glimmering in frosted glasses. The nightly floor show consisted of a "legit" act—a singer, a ventriloquist, an off-color comedian—and a stripper or two. This mix of naughty and nice kept Louise the proprietor from incurring the wrath of the city fathers, who visited Duke's on occasion themselves. (Jack the bartender took nasty delight in pointing out a city councilman, a church deacon, a police captain. Once, Louise told us to be at a well-known restaurant off State Street the next afternoon with our instruments; there, in a private back room, we put on a floor show with a stripper who took it *all* off for a klatch of red-faced, whooping Rotary Club stalwarts.)

Louise was a chunky, florid Italian with a businesswoman's brusque manner. She always dressed in the same tight black dress and high heels. It was rumored that some lesser Mob figures had set her up with a little spot "out on the Coast" for unnamed favors, and twice during the summer, groups of Italians appeared unannounced from "back east" to be ostentatiously wined and dined by Louise, then set up for discreet dates after the show with the "talent."

The "talent"—excepting those who had enough money or contacts to lodge elsewhere—stayed in a two-story clapboard structure behind Duke's, a warren of tiny rooms accessed by way of a rickety exterior stairway. Louise lived there too, functioning as den mother and chaperone. This might sound peculiar, considering what the girls were doing for a living; but they often needed protection from customers who developed rather frightening, obsessive interests in them, and from the local vice squad as well. Turning tricks after hours was strictly forbidden (some girls did, some didn't).

I pulled into the parking lot next to Duke's on a balmy midsummer Saturday night. A full moon hung over the sputtering neon sign—"*UKE'S *UPPER *LUB" in red, the martini glass in green. Entering the noisy, lit cavern reeking of smoke and alcohol and lust, I felt my stomach tighten, my loins tingle, a kindling anticipation fill me.

I slipped through the dressing room, mounted the bandstand, and settled behind the kit. Below me, the wooden runway snaked out into the darkened room. Rough-handed cowpunchers from the Ventura ranches, in for a Saturday-night whoop-up, clustered along the runway's apron, which was also a bar. Shadowy figures gathered at tables in the room's dingy recesses. Cigarette smoke billowed up through tiki mesh hung from the ceiling and green, red, and blue cellophane spotlight gels.

The lights dimmed. I gave a drum roll, a cymbal crash. Suddenly, from behind the black curtain, shaking to "One Mint Julep" like some divinity-blinded dervish, Honey Bare, the Texas Bombshell, hit the boards. The runway barflies, their lust-dulled eyes running up her glistening thighs, fumbled for their wallets.

The Remo Bono Trio downshifted into a slow, sinuous "Harlem Nocturne." The lights went blue. Honey, in Daisy Mae pigtails and cutoff jeans, her gaze cast out into the lights, was all legs and pelvis now, a good girl gone bad. Off came the check-ered blouse, down came the pigtails. Her shiny plump breasts spun aloft the pasties, little helicopters revving up. I let out backbeats, bass-drum thumps, and cymbal shimmers like an angler feeding line.

Settling on her haunches, Honey ground the customers one by one, working her way clockwise around the runway's fringe, getting those bucks up on the bar—just the way Louise liked it. Remo Bono's embouchure dripped, his toupee jiggled as he pumped his bent trumpet into the air. My rim shots were pistol cracks. We segued into "Tequila," Art grinning at me from be-hind the piano. Honey, streaming sweat, painted lips puckered with sex's seriousness, shoved her G-stringed moneymaker at the gaping, slack-jawed marks.

Seen from a nightclub bandstand, the world is a strange place. The shape of human need reveals itself in the flow of the action below: the customers entering and leaving, the acts mov-ing on- and offstage. Here comes old white-haired Hetty and her young escort Eugene, in from Montecito, taking their regu-lar table, trolling for a little naughty party play after hours. And here is the mysterious dark-haired girl with violet lips and bangs who comes in alone every night and sits at the bar, sip-ping Singapore Slings through a straw, peering up at me through long false lashes, lost in some crush.

From my vantage point above the action, I watch Jack the bartender run a short-change routine on a customer. The mark orders a whiskey sour, lays a hundred down. Jack says, "Your change, sir," and while the man's eyes tunnel into Honey's squirming fundament, Jack counts out against the edge of the bar ten, twenty, forty—a twenty floats down to the floor behind the bar—sixty, seventy—another floater—eighty, and a hundred. "And I thank you, sir!" The bleary customer leaves Jack a fat tip to boot. Each night after closing time, Jack and his partner, Eddie, lift the floor slats and scoop up the extra take—often running into the hundreds—and split it. But one of a dozen observable scams being run out on the floor.

"Night Train" was Honey's finale, the bumps built into the melody, sharp and pelvic. I jockeyed her home with bass-drum bombs, cymbals, flams. She caught my eye, flung me a thrust. As the Remo Bono Trio held sustenato, Honey pulled the black velvet scrim at the back of the runway around her butt, shook it, then disappeared to drum roll, cymbal crash, applause.

Slowly the customers came to, stirring as if from a dream. In the vacuum left by the dying shimmer of the music and the dance, the bartenders' glasses clinked, the cash register rang. Waitresses in fishnet stockings and teased hair began their drift through the room to settle tabs, take fresh orders. Cigarettes flared, men stumbled off to the rest rooms or the exits.

In a second-rate joint like Duke's, everything was an imitation of someplace else. The décor was modeled after some nameless sleaze parlor in Reno or Atlantic City. Our band mimicked Louis Prima's fabled Vegas lounge unit. Honey's routine was an unabashed knockoff of a bigtime Texas stripper known as Jenny Lee, the Bazoom Girl. Lissa, a blonde local singer who sometimes worked with us weeknights, aped June Christy's sultry crooning style on "Something Cool" and "Midnight Sun," and even bobbed her hair the same. Smokey Whitfield, an off-color black comic, was our cut-rate Redd Foxx. Miss Scarlett O'Hara, 300 Pounds of Joy, chalk-white with dyed orange hair, was a pint-sized Sophie Tucker, feet planted wide on the stage, belting "Bill Bailey" and "After You've Gone" and "Nobody Loves You When You're Down and Out." Lord knows where

Louise found these people. Strippers, dirty comedians, ventrilo-quists, crooners, bird acts, contortionists—second-line acts, mostly, between gigs in L.A., San Francisco, Vegas, Reno. Young hopefuls on their way up, or old headliners on their way down, booking in for a week or two for some extra money, or a little stay by the sea, or perhaps because they owed Louise or her Italian pals a favor.

I didn't know whom I was supposed to be imitating, but I'd become a pretty good strip drummer at Duke's. I'd learned to lock snare and cymbal, tom-tom and bass drum into the female anatomy, guide the dance. It's all a matter of emphasis: You get to know the girl, blend with her music, her cues. You become her telepathic lover across a dozen feet of space, help her ascend a ladder of fake orgasm. Just as with the real thing, you incite her irritation with a missed stroke, or raise her another notch with a well-placed bass kick. Glances across the space during performance between dancer and drummer set up resonances that sometimes play out offstage later.

The night's first floor show was over, and the stage went dark. Remo, Art, and I slipped offstage. Parting the black cur-tain, we descended the three rickety stairs into the cramped dressing room behind the runway. Honey Bare sat slumped, out of breath, on a metal soda-fountain chair before a cracked oval makeup mirror, half its bulbs dead. The table was strewn with used lipsticks, communal cold cream, crusted nail-polish jars, wads of tissues and cotton balls, stale drinks with puckered lemon rinds floating in them. Glitter glistened in Honey's teased, damp hair, spilled down her shoulders and sweating breasts. Pulling the tassels off your nipples, the girls said, gives you a rash.

Honey looked sullenly at us in the mirror. Remo made an

obscene sucking sound and mugged at her. "Fuck you," Honey said. She couldn't stand Remo's lechery; none of the girls could. Then, as Art and Remo passed on through the door into the club, Honey's eyes snagged mine in the mirror. She reached back and tugged at my tuxedo sleeve.

The night before, after work, Jack the bartender—a gaunt ex-sailor with a tattoo on his forearm that said "Yokohama Mama"—had told me Honey was hot for me. "Don't miss the chance, kid," he'd said, polishing his bar glasses, white shirt-sleeves rolled up, black bow tie hanging unfastened. "You think she sizzles onstage. I hear she's dynamite in the sack." I'd thought about her later that night in my own bed, and not for the first time.

At Duke's that summer I'd lived in erotic overdrive, regularly invited to engage in acts I've barely dreamed of. Women—and on occasion men—approached me backstage or out on the club floor and expressed their desires in the most unabashed ways, rubbing their bodies up against me, or grabbing my crotch and importuning: "Hey, whaddya got in there?" or "How about a little action tonight?" I found this crude, overt sexual communication disconcerting, scary, exciting. The confidence of the women, the clarity of the transaction: nothing could have been further from the delicate minefields of high-school erotics Sandra and I had tiptoed through, or the tits-and-ass obsessions and braggadocio of teenage boys. Even in college, "nice girls" still didn't, preferring to barter bits of sexual anatomy as if they were stock futures or gold bars. I'd had more sexual encounters in my first six weeks at Duke's than in my entire life up to that point. One night Lissa the singer told me to "stop by after work, I'm having a few friends in," and when I got there she greeted me at the door in a sheer negligee, whereupon she promptly fell to her knees and began fellating me. Sex simply because you want it: what an idea! Another night I was invited to a party at Eugene and Hetty's, where an amateur stripper danced to full nudity for a small circle gathered about her (as if she were a campfire), then took the men one by one into the adjacent bedroom to deliver the implied culmination of every strip act. There was seldom a night at Duke's that didn't involve an invitation to an erotic transaction, large or small.

Honey Bare was a vision of lust incarnate, clearly a voracious sexual acrobat, far beyond me in experience. I, suave purveyor of innuendo, urgings, and accents behind the safety of my drums, remained shy and callow offstage, easily intimidated. How could I possibly take her on?

In the cramped dressing room behind the runway, Honey's hand dropped from my sleeve and drifted across my butt. Her red fingernails traced my thigh through the tuxedo pants. She turned from the mirror and looked directly up at me, parting her ruby lips.

"Ah fancy you, drummer boy," she said.

I mumbled an awkward, unheard retort and lurched through the door into the crowded club, the trace of the Texas Bombshell's hand on my ass.

Hard-core devotees of the lascivious stayed away from Duke's on Saturday nights, deferring to the raucous rubes who crowded in from the outlying areas. Louise always made the talent work the floor between sets on Saturdays, because it raised the take, the customers buying the girls expensive drinks poured from separate, illegally watered-down bottles. So, when, minutes later, I saw Honey emerge from the dressing room and head for the bar to circulate, I pushed through the crowd and stepped outside.

I stared up at the full moon, inhaling a Kent. If I didn't make it with Honey, Jack the bartender would spread it around. If I did and it went badly, the same thing would happen. Either way, I was on the spot. Desire and terror, counterpoised: youth's leitmotif. I had no real lover's skills. My sexual immersion at Duke's had consisted so far of feel-ups, blow jobs, quick throw-downs on mattresses or beds, and gropes in the club washroom, but had yet to include a serious session with a woman who expected a man to know what he was doing.

I heard Remo's racetrack trumpet flourish from inside, summoning us back to work. I flicked my Kent onto the dark asphalt and stepped back inside the club, still irresolute. Uneasily I mounted the bandstand.

After the last set, flush with the confidence performance brings, I waited until Remo and Art had passed through the dressing room, then whispered in Honey's ear that I was having a little party after work the next night at my place. Would she come?

"Wah, ah'd love tew," she said into the mirror.

Having some people over to my place, I figured, would socialize my "date" with Honey, take a little pressure off. So after work I invited the club regulars over the next night, as well as some of my artist and writer friends from college (word quickly circulated that I was "dating a stripper").

That next morning, a Sunday, I was awakened early by my

mother, calling from L.A. to remind me she and Dad were coming up for a visit that day. Deep in the throes of my obsession with Honey, I'd completely forgotten. They planned to stay on and hear me play at my summer job.

"We're so looking forward to the show," Mom effused over Louise's special pasta at Duke's that evening. Earlier I'd tried to intimate that "supper club" encompassed a little more territory than the term might suggest, but sensed I wasn't getting through.

Mom and Dad considered themselves worldly types, having spent their twenties in rough-and-tumble Prohibition New York; and of course Dad's big show-biz years in Manhattan and Hollywood qualified him as a sophisticated character, certainly in his own eyes. But they'd spent the last decade in the sequestered calm of southern California's suburbs, ministering to my mother's separation from drink, and it was impossible for me to measure what their response would be to the scene at Duke's. Then there was Honey, and the "party" afterward. Thank God Mom and Dad were returning home that night.

My father had ordered another Scotch and was holding forth about a summer job playing saxophone at a resort in the Poconos when he was in college—an oft-repeated account illustrating his "wild" youth—when the lights dimmed, my cue to report backstage.

The opening act was Smokey Whitfield, a black comedian who stood at the mike in a cloud of smoke telling sex and dope jokes. I remained onstage during Smokey's performance, punctuating his punch lines with drum rolls and cymbal crashes. Smokey was genuinely funny, and even after a week of hearing his repertoire I still liked to watch him shade his delivery to the room he was playing to. I laughed when he hit his lines, and not just to play the shill. The jokes tended to involve sexual mixups: a man gets on a train but climbs into the wrong berth, mistaking a man's toupee for his wife's pussy. Smokey's pot jokes featured a couple of stoned, paranoid characters driving around in cars avoiding the police. (An entire subgenre of this material existed on the chitlin circuit years before Cheech and Chong refigured it as hippie humor. In one, a dopehead hears a police siren behind him and says frantically to his buddy, "Turn left, man! Turn left!" His buddy looks at him: "Turn left? Man, I thought *you* were driving!")

I glanced down at my parents, sitting stiffly at a corner table, Dad gripping a fresh Scotch, Mom working a Chesterfield and a Coca-Cola. I thought how hard it must be for her to be in a liquor-steeped room, a main tenet of her sobriety being to avoid temptation.

Honey's routine that night was a whoop-dee-doo cowboy number that began in Stetson, boots, a lariat, and a little wooden horsie she made good erotic use of as the routine wore on. Remo and Art blew "I'm an Old Cowhand" while I tapped something laconic and equine on the woodblock, gradually steaming it up on snare and tom-toms as the Western gear began littering the stage and the tassels went into orbit. Near the dance's frenzied end, Honey began shooting me hot gazes and doing things with her tongue, premonitory allusions to our night ahead. I glanced down into the darkness, searching for my parents, wondering if they'd noticed.

Afterward I joined Mom and Dad at their table. "Well," Dad said, flush-faced and woozy, "that girl sure is, has a, uh . . ."

Mom fiddled nervously with her hands. "You've become quite good at this," she said, the ambiguity of her comment thickening the air.

As Honey passed by on her way to work the floor, I watched my father's eyes hang on her sequined, swiveling ass all the way to the barstool.

"I'm afraid your father has had a little too much to drink," my mother said. "I think it's better we don't drive home tonight."

"No, no. I'm fine," Dad protested slurrily.

Panicked, I flagged down a waitress and ordered him coffee. I led him by the elbow to the men's room and tried to freshen him up.

When we arrived back at the table, Mom reiterated determinedly that he shouldn't drive back to Los Angeles in his condition.

I had an extra room at my place and they knew it. If they insisted on staying over, I'd have to call off the "party." At the same time, here was an easy out if I wanted it, a chance to bail on my assignation with Honey. But I'd already invited the club folk and my friends over; and our heated flirtation during the floor show had left me aching for her.

I told Mom I'd be happy to put them up but a friend was staying over in my other room. Then I went to the club phone in back and booked them a room at a nice motel a few blocks away, by the beach.

By the time I came back, Smokey Whitfield was heading backstage for the second show. I walked my parents to the parking lot, propping Dad up by the elbow.

"Good night, Mom, Dad. Thanks for coming."

"So long, son."

During the second show, Honey mimed rabid sex under the spotlight in my direction. The wooden horsie she rode was me.

Each whack of my stick was a pelvic thrust. The rest of the band and the audience had disappeared, and I was one bucking buckaroo back there behind the drums.

Afterward I waited in the parking lot for her to come out. We didn't dare hook up inside the club, where nothing escaped Louise's radar gaze. She emerged at last into the warm night in a light, clinging summer dress, her hair teased up, some sparkle still on her face, and kissed my cheek. She smelled like magnolia, and musk. We climbed in my car, and the gang from the club—Smokey, Lissa the singer, Art, Remo, Scarlett O'Hara, the waitresses, Jack and Eddie the bartenders—followed me home.

Entering the small hillside cottage with bags full of ice and liquor, I found my scruffy boho poet and painter friends already there, half drunk and curious to see whom I'd taken up with. As the sounds of Muddy Waters and Ray Charles spun out into the jasmine-tinged night, my college friends and the show folk mixed. Talk flowed in the kitchen; couples danced on the porch overlooking the field in back. Mick, a sculptor and amateur wit, traded drunken routines with Smokey Whitfield, while Remo Bono danced with Moira, a zaftig poet, his face buried in her bosom. Scarlett O'Hara sang a filthy sailor song *a capella*, rotating her girth and pulling her skirt up to flash her chalky, dimpled thighs, sending everyone into howls. Honey and I hovered along the wall, talking, whispering, holding hands.

At last people cleared out, leaving us alone. We fell hotly to each other against the bedroom wall. My hungry hands swarmed over this body I'd drummed into motion night after pounding night—the taut Texas flanks, the tassel-twirling breasts that seemed already mine somehow. Our kisses grew deep and sloppy, clothes fell away. We stumbled toward my bed.

So far I was in familiar territory—petting's slow, curvy foothills. Working my way south with kisses and licks, I arrived at my first surprise. Strippers shave so the G-string won't expose hair, and to avoid rashes from the sweaty gyrations. Some leave a narrow tuft around the labia, others razor it all off. Honey's was bald as a baby, and a little spiky against the grain—not unlike a shaved face.

She began calling out instructions—where, when, how much, and with what: tongue, lips, fingers. Girls from school passively took whatever I dished out or didn't, lying there as if receiving an inoculation. "Yes! Now suck on it, hard!" she cried exuberantly. Her exhortations grew more precise, technical. Slavishly I followed her commands until I heard her call out, "Oh, give it to me! Now!"

I struggled to my knees, dazed, mouth dripping like that of some swamp creature, fumbling to meet her request. As I scooted into position, Honey reached down hungrily and, before I could get my bearings, fed me quickly, expertly into her. Grabbing my ass with both hands, she began rotating at the eggbeater speed she deployed in her "Night Train" finale at Duke's. My cock was a pencil being fed into an electric sharpener. Taken hopelessly off guard, I bucked a couple of times, then went abruptly off.

If a woman can pretend she came, there's no way a man can pretend he didn't. My panicky attempts to disguise my sudden bang, with its attendant whimper, were to no avail. Helplessly I shrank away. I lay atop Honey, a beached seal, panting and humiliated, the silence in the room a shriek.

"Oh, sweetie," Honey said, coming to. "We was just gettin' started."

Vainly summoning language's dissimulations to my aid, I whispered, "I haven't been with anybody in weeks."

"It's all right, drummer boy," she whispered, stroking my head like some abject child's.

Honey didn't mope for long but, intent upon getting her own pleasure, found other things to do with me until I was up again—a brief interlude, because I was crazy with desire. I did things she told me to do, she found things I liked and did them, and this time I lasted awhile.

Our investigations lasted through the night—focused, technical, athletic. We coiled and uncoiled like wrestling snakes. At sunrise we were still awake, mining sensation. When Honey grew dry, I found some Vicks Vapo-Rub in the medicine cabinet, mentholating us and the bedding as well. At some point we must have slept for a few hours, for I remember waking to midday light, and she was awake too. We did it again, raw and sore, running the edge where pain and pleasure meet.

At last we arose, shaky-legged. Heading for the kitchen, I thought I smelled smoke. I stumbled upon Mick, passed out on the bed in the next room. I'd thought everyone had left the night before. In the kitchen I found coffee already made. A lipstick-rimmed Chesterfield was burning down to its nub in an ashtray with a note beneath it.

"Didn't want to wake you, dear," the note said in neat penmanship. "Just stopped by to say goodbye and drop off a few fresh clothes for you. I noticed you could use some."

Had Mom peeked in and seen us? A discreet woman, she'd never tell. My mother's son, I knew I'd never ask.

I found Honey out on the porch in her summery sundress with nothing on underneath, looking out across the field. She looked almost plain without the makeup and fake eyelashes. In the sunlight I could see little flaws in her body and her skin, signs of wear, which made me like her more somehow.

I embraced her from behind, kissed her shoulders and neck. She threw her head back and purred.

"You sure have a lot of books around your place," she said.

"College."

"You read them all?"

"Most."

We sipped coffee in between silences.

"I grew up in a place that looks sort of like this field," she said. "Outside of Port Arthur."

"Is that where you started dancing?"

"Yeah, in a little local bar. I was fifteen."

"How did you end up there?"

"You don't want to know." She sighed. "I had a kid."

"At fifteen?"

"Fourteen."

"Were you married?"

"Actually, I was."

"Where's the child?"

"Jimmy's with my mom. I send her most of my salary to raise him."

"What about the dad?"

"Oh, he's long gone."

"How old are you?"

"Eighteen."

I was stunned. I'd figured Honey for twenty-five at least. She seemed so assured, so experienced. Impossible that she was younger than I was.

"What's your real name?"

"No matter. Honey's fine." She shrugged, then turned around and took my hand and looked at me. "You have a girlfriend?"

"Not really. Not since high school."

"You do it with her?"

I blushed. "Not the same as with you."

She giggled, then reached over and patted my ass. "I like you, drummer boy. You keep up a good beat."

I told her I liked her too, and I meant it.

She nestled her head on my shoulder. "You made me shy, you know that? Back in the club. I couldn't get up my nerve to tell you I was sweet on you."

"Why?"

"You're so damned good on your instrument. You really know how to pound those skins. Me, I'm just messin' around up there."

"That's not true. You drive men crazy."

"You think so?" She looked at me uncertainly. Honey Bare, shimmering icon of desire, barefoot in a print dress in my garden, had no more confidence onstage than I did off.

"Maybe we'll see each other again," she said, putting it more as a question, I thought, than a declaration of fact.

"I'd like that."

Honey laughed and turned away. "Gawd. My pussy is so sore. And I smell like Mentholatum all over."

We showered together, then I drove her to the club so she could try to sneak into Louise's rooming house out back. Luckily Louise was at Mass (she went every day).

Monday nights, the club was dark. When I came to work Tuesday, I passed Jack the bartender, setting up his station. He gave me his knowing junkie smirk and said, "So how was she, kid?"

"Great," I said distantly as if it was none of his business, or something I'd practically forgotten by now. Yet, even saying that much, I felt I'd betrayed an intimacy. I realized then that I really did want to see Honey again.

Before work, Louise showed us a publicity shot a photographer had taken of Honey and the band for the local papers. In the glossy eight-by-ten, Honey Bare poses in her buckaroo outfit, twirling fake six shooters, flashing a pile of cleavage. Remo, Art, and I stand behind her in our white tuxedos, grinning, arms thrust wide, as if presenting the Texas Bombshell to the world.

During the strip that night, Honey and I shared few looks. Our encounter seemed to have turned us paradoxically shy. It wasn't so much what had happened in bed but afterward, out on the porch, in conversation. Our few words seemed to have unmasked more than the hours of sex. Now our performance—the strip, the drums, the dance, even the lovemaking—seemed the true disguise. Maybe taking it off was just a way of putting it on.

After the second show I went backstage to find her. I had no plan; I just knew she'd be leaving for an engagement in Reno the end of that week and I wanted to be with her again. I opened the door to the dressing room. She was already dressed and gone.

Back out on the club floor, I found Eddie, the second bartender, closing up the registers. When I told him I was looking for Honey, he nodded in the direction of the side door.

I hurried over and opened it in time to see Jack the bartender guiding Honey to the passenger side of his Chevy Impala.

I stepped back into the doorway so they wouldn't see me, burning with humiliation and disappointment. What had I expected? That she'd meant it when she said she wanted to see me again? Clearly I didn't understand something. Maybe I'd waited too long. Jack had just hustled her away from me.

I stood alone in the empty parking lot, as I had a few nights earlier, smoking and looking desolately up at the waning moon. Ridiculous, I told myself. She's just some stripper, come on, you've already had her. But Honey must have touched something in me, more than anyone else I could think of. The embalmed world of suburbia; the contests and talent tests and marching bands; the evasions and subterfuges of family and school life; the icy, daunting literary Brahmins I was apprenticing to. I'd never felt much human contact in any of it, let alone unabashed, guiltless delight in pleasure. Watching the taillights of Jack's Impala disappear down Milpas Street, I felt wildly bereft.

"Hey, Antonio."

Remo Bono was beside me, holding his trumpet case in one hand, pulling off his bow tie with the other.

"Guess what? There's two new broads comin' in next week. One, I seen her, Fatima. Used to dance for King Farouk. She's a contortionist, with a body like you never seen. She can suck her own snatch, ferchrissake. And Jenny Lee's comin' in. The Bazoom Girl. Miss 44D. A legend in the business. We're gonna have a double strip show. Louise must have cut a deal with the cops. How 'bout that?"

Remo shoved his bow tie in his tux pocket, then reached up and pulled off his "toop." He held the grimy headpiece in his hand, his slick pate gleaming in the moonlight.

"The hits just keep on comin', don't they, kid?"

As Remo walked off to his car, I saw a figure hovering in shadow against the building up front. Stepping out into the neon glare of the *UKE'S *UPPER *LUB sign was the girl with the violet lipstick and bangs who came in alone every night and watched me play. She turned and blew smoke from a Parliament into the colored light, her dark, doleful eyes steadying on me.

I hesitated for a moment, then walked toward her.

The road into Coldwater Canyon begins at Sunset Boulevard just east of the Beverly Hills Hotel, not far from where William Holden fell into Gloria Swanson's clutches that fateful night his car broke down in *Sunset Boulevard*. Behind the hotel's palm-framed pink stucco redoubts lurks yet another pool I used to swim in while my father met in the bungalows with Greer Garson, Charles Boyer, or whoever Jimmy Durante's guest was to be that week on the CBS show Dad produced and directed. Lately, since my return to L.A., I've begun to envision my childhood as a succession of immersions in strangers' swimming pools: vertiginous thumpings of diving boards, nubby towels over shivering shoulders, chlorine-withered fingertips. Adolescence would change my water world from fresh water to salt: beachfront, boardwalk, waterfront dive; surf, turbulence, sex; and insatiable wanderlust, stirred by the infinite prospect of the horizon as seen from the California strand.

On a Sunday near dusk, I trail scant traffic past the green park and the fire station at the base of the canyon, the two-lane road's curving contours as intimate as breath. Contemporary stucco-and-lath homes crowd newly subdivided lots among the statelier older ones. A warm wind rushes down the canyon from the valley side, buffeting the car. I ride a corridor of memory, jogged by scrapbook sessions with my father. But what do I hope to find?

The Greek poet Simonides was possibly the first practitioner of the memory palace, a mental construct to house elements of recollection. Parts of speech were assigned rooms in an imaginary building, to be called up later. Interest in the device peaked in the sixteenth century, then fell out of favor. Today the photograph is our mnemonic spur, storehouse of memory if not of perception itself. The albums on my father's lap contain glittering nuggets of recollection imprisoned in the photo's fixative bath. If art is commemoration, an attempt to rescue experience from time, these days Kodak ads ritualize memory, Hollywood demonstrates the art of the kiss and the kill, porn flicks instruct us in sexual technique.

But "the recurrence diminishes the original, replaces it, falsifies it," the writer Tim Parks has said. "An old photograph may be considered as stealing something of its original." Driving toward the old childhood home, I wonder if my memories of Coldwater Canyon have any physical reality apart from the family snapshots, slides, and home movies of it. Am I traversing a fictional construct, seeking an illusory anchor in a real world that no longer exists or indeed never did? Am I feeling nothing more than a nostalgia for the virtual? Is it Sunset Boulevard I'd driven to get here, or *Sunset Boulevard*?

The distance to Cherokee Lane, an epic journey to a Little League first baseman lost in the plush red leather seat of Dad's Buick, is far less than I'd remembered. It looms suddenly on my right, sporting a stoplight now. Wending up the narrow street overhung with towering eucalyptus, I realize Cherokee Lane is coded in memory not by nature or architecture but by celebrity names: to my right, where there used to be a dry creek, the old Western actor Ward Bond ("Nice guy, Ward") had lived; Shirley Temple Black ("Had her on my show once") lived in the corner house where Beaumont Drive cuts in; forking right onto Hazen

Drive, I instinctively glance left at the small colonial where Ginger Rogers ("Danced with her at a party") had lived with her mother. This was the map of the world my father had drawn, which was of course a portrait of himself, what he identified with. He'd limned a Map to the Stars' Homes—not unlike the ones hawkers flog to tourists along Sunset Boulevard—inside his son's head, stocking it with private anecdote and recollection. In this star-studded topography articulated by my dad, Coldwater Canyon—like Egypt's pyramids, the Loire Valley, Kyoto's temples—commemorated the dwellings of Myrna Loy, Sonny Tufts, Peggy Lee, the Durango Kid. I can still point out where every one of them had lived. In my father's memory palace—and in mine too, I realize dishearteningly—they still do.

The narrow canyon road fills with shadow. Rolling the window down, I catch whiffs of honeysuckle, sage, pine.

"All these sensations," St. Augustine writes, "are retained in the great storehouse of the memory, which in some indescribable way secretes them in its folds." Memory, Augustine surmised, is a faculty not of the mind but of the soul. Drawing ever closer to the old home, I like that idea, with its suggestion that my life of fitful wanderings, passages through art, and succession of spiritual disciplines, resembles a journey of purification: stages of disentanglement from the imposition of received memory—of family, country, human history itself. If only I could be sure.

Twilight deepens. The gated driveways widen. The homes more resemble estates. Turning right up the little cul-de-sac street, the car emerges suddenly back out into light. There, on the eastern slope, basking in the day's last rays, stands the house.

I pull over at the foot of the driveway and turn off the engine. My eyes run up the ivy bank, past the curved green sward of lawn, to the Spanish-colonial edifice, looming in grave silence on its hillside, its white stucco façade eerily bright in the dying light.

It looks smaller than I'd remembered it, of course, though the surrounding trees have grown much larger, the magnolia by the front door rising higher than the roof now, its great white blooms like nested egrets. The once skimpy firs soar, the oleanders bordering the lawn have rounded to the size of rooms, and the southern bank of eucalyptus trees towers over the house.

I open the car door and step out. It's still warm here, the little cleft in the canyon retaining the day's heat. I smell damp soil, fresh-mowed grass. All is quiet but for a battery of sprinklers on the sloped lawn, shooting rainbow-flecked plumes into the inert sunset air. I planted this ivy bank one young summer, cutting by cutting, at my father's insistence, for a pitiable allowance. These flagstone steps that form the long path from street to house I helped cobble into this hillside of decomposed granite.

Water trickles down the steep, fir-sentineled driveway where Mom, in her cups, had spectacularly crashed the station wagon; and where I'd skidded off my Schwinn bike over and over, incurring scars that still illustrate my flesh. A gardener's truck parked beside the open gates is the only other vehicle on this tiny dead-end lane. Next door, inscrutable behind its Southern Revival columns, stands the house where neighbor Betty used to invite me in for our eroticized afternoon television viewings. Who living there now could summon the penumbra of sense echoes lingering in that shuttered den? Turning, I notice that the only other house on the street—a postwar ranch-style home where a kindly couple had proffered food and safety when neither could be found at my house—sports a second story now.

I gaze back up at my old dwelling. Impossible to tell if anyone is inside. No cars in the driveway, the three-car garage door shut, the opaque windows along the front reflecting the crimson sun. Darkness advances up the steep lawn like a tide, lapping at the base of the house.

It was from this bastion of desolate splendor that I took my first forays into the greater world: the Hitching Post movie house in Hollywood Saturday mornings to ride with Hopalong Cassidy; summer camps at Big Bear to catch butterflies and swim in the icy lake; baseball competitions on the city's sandlots; anxious schoolyard confrontations. From here the kid drummer took his paradiddles and ratamacues onstage. And it was on this wide sloping lawn, along these hillside paths of scrub and yucca and tumbleweed, among those great lonely rooms, that I began to hollow out a space within space, filling it with language, music, Eros: a parallel world of escape from the one I was marooned in.

Beyond the house, at the top of the hill where the light still holds, the red tip of a radio station's transmitting tower blinks against the hard blue sky. One summer day my friend Bobby and I hiked through underbrush to a cement bunker beneath that tower to visit Ace the Deejay at KKUL-FM, Radio Cool, holding forth in his air-conditioned capsule, spinning platters high above the city. He sat us in swivel chairs next to the console, let us wipe clean the shiny acetates with black felt and place them carefully on the turntables. "Hole's in the middle of the record, kid," Ace joked, with his pockmarked face and scabs up his inner arm, playing his vinyls, drifting on Anatolian smack, wafting the sweet sounds of Mantovani, Percy Faith, and "A Summer Place" to the freeway dreamers below. (Years later, I'd learn that it had been Ace who'd given Bobby his first snifter of the ethereal poison, recruiting him into the ranks of the stoned purveyors of easy dreams, marking him for OD death at twenty-four in a Pontiac Bonneville in the desert outside Palm Springs.) That same afternoon, Bobby and I had sneaked onto a property down the mountain and, peering through a crack between poolhouse blinds, watched a cowboy actor ravish a starlet against a mini-fridge. Afterward, in the bushes, jeans around our ankles, we'd enacted that boy's rite forgotten until now, conjoining us to a new secret world of lust. (Santa Ana breeze rustling the oleanders, smell of suntan oil and semen . . .)

The lawn sprinklers sputter and cease. In the silence, I hear the distant rush of traffic, a leaf blower buzzing down in the canyon somewhere. Closing my eyes, I feel a torpid peace enfold me, inseparable from perfect terror. I imagine throwing myself upon this ivy bank, coming to rest here in some permanent manner, the sprinklers washing away my flesh, merging it with the topsoil on its descent to the sea.

I open my eyes. Halfway up the driveway, a Mexican gardener, spooling his turquoise hose in the dying light, is looking at me. I feel suddenly furtive—a voyeur, a thief of memory, an illicit lurker in my own childhood. Hurriedly I get back in the car, start it up, and drive off.

Farther into the canyon, I turn up a onetime fire trail that wound behind the old house. It's paved now and has a name. I pull over against a bare slash of granite hillside and turn off the engine. Across the road, a chain-link fence borders the back line of the property.

I can see down the precipitous slope, through a stand of eucalyptus, to the rear of our old house: red tile roofs, arched leaded windows, walls trellised with shoulders of bougainvillea. A jolting familiarity to the scene causes me to catch my breath. The wood stairs leading up through the ice-plant bank to this fence are still there. In the leveled backyard, where an iron armature once held two leather swings and a teeter-totter, a clutter of bright orange, blue, and red plastic toys glints through the trees. An oval swimming pool shimmers indigo in the twilight, its diving board a slit of negative space. On a raised brick platform, patio furniture flanks a barbecue rig.

Two black Dobermans fidget by the back door, chains dragging on the flagstone tiles. Catching my scent, one sets up a doleful howl, echoed by the other. I step behind the trunk of a pine tree.

Beyond, the view extends across the roofs of the houses, past azure-tipped mountains, to the sky over the Pacific, still light, salmon-mottled in the fading day. In the canyon below, lights are already coming on. A few crickets start up, quickly joined by others, commencing the evening chorale. At least the insects survive, I think, if not the rattlesnakes, coyotes, raccoons, and deer that once populated this canyon, providing a boy with a firsthand nature manual.

Below, in the gathering dark, a faint luminescence seems to hover around the house. I hear a muffled woman's voice. A light goes on in the kitchen. Children's laughter rings out. The back door opens, and a pair of little silhouettes tumbles out into the patio—a boy and girl of six or seven. A man's voice joins the woman's in the kitchen. Clatter of plates, dinner preparations. The sounds rise into the air, the words indistinct but the voices clear. The man has an East Coast accent.

The scene before me lights up by degrees, like a stage set: dining room, hallway, patio. In the moonless dark I glimpse, through the eucalyptus grove, fragments of the unfolding tableau. The kids' sounds of delight chime up the hillside. Here, on the cusp of a fresh century, a young family, new to California, bobs in the tiny vessel of their lives, invisible currents bearing them downstream toward an unseen sea.

A dog howls somewhere up on the mountain. The restive Dobermans answer. The children hurry inside for dinner, slamming the door behind them. A breeze flutters up the canyon, bearing the sting of chlorine from the pool.

Unimaginable, that these raw interlopers could know anything of what transpired in those rooms a half-century earlier: when Uncle Bing, Uncle Bob, Aunt Peggy, and Uncle Jimmy gathered around the spinet, stilling time with song, while natty Jack Ross kept time with his Slingerland sticks. Scenes of gaiety and laughter, forever lost: the stars and parties, the maids and butlers in Dotty Lamour's grand house, which was our house too; postwar California still fresh to itself, America's future incarnate—space shots, Cold War triumphalism, Elvis, and incipient doo-wop—tomorrow spreading away like a virgin tract of beachfront, tendering its infinite promise. This ingenue quartet, its clanking silverware cantata rising up the hillside on a current of night-blooming jasmine, can't remotely access the ghosts that inhabit their own dwelling—the wisecracking gag writers, the svelte ladies in suits and hats and veils, Mom and Dad kissing beneath the mistletoe hung from the great crystal chandelier in the marble hallway as clock chimes tolled time-lapse freefall into a less shining fate.

No, something is wrong with the scene below. Too little has changed. The family at the table glimpsed through slatted blinds repeats our lives and doesn't know it. The house hasn't been razed to the ground and replaced with a contemporary one but still stands, much the same. Coldwater Canyon, if built up, still hosts the same trees and plants and insects, sounds and smells. Same landscape of desire, same cradle of flawed hopes. California, avatar of the ineffably new, accretes a history.

An oleander branch brushes my face, its pointed leaves sharp, acrid-smelling. The crickets' din crescendoes and begins to throb. In the spaces between the now indiscernible mountains, colored lights run across the city below like the bloodstream of some irradiated beast. Desultory sounds of dinner talk ride up toward me on the night air.

It's the same! I think, swept with feeling. *The same!* I want to cry out to the little family behind the shutters: *Watch out! Hearts will break! The future you imagine will never arrive!*

Soon, I think, my father will die. I will take his place. In turn, the little boy in that dining room where I used to sit moves onto the endless turning wheel: to bittersweet loves that await, discovery and betrayal, journey and return—all that will one day form *his* memory palace. Each life an arc across time: no more or less futile than these crickets', whose pulsing serenade will last until dawn, then cease?

Or does a consciousness move through us, reaping light?

On the dark hillside, a figure lurks unseen at the fence above the house, tears running down his face, bestowing unheard blessings upon an anonymous family.

A sudden panic grips me. I realize I'm communing with ghosts, and in doing so setting a course toward them. The dead reach out to capture the living, wafting the elixir of memory. This is what it is to grow old, then: to die into history, the way a spent plant is absorbed back into soil. For the first time I understand how my father constructed his memory palace, and now he is disappearing into it.

Suddenly I don't want to be here, on this street, in this canyon, in this city. I want to be back across the border, out along exile's edges, where sun is sun, air air, and history and memory the province of others.

I turn and run back to the car, knowing I'll never come here again.

I speed down Coldwater Canyon in the dark, as if running before a blaze. The hills and trees and homes seem to close around me. I'm thirteen again, fleeing the bonfire of home.

At Sunset I turn west toward the sea, driving too fast, desperate to reach open horizon.

Two

"Strictly speaking, one never understands
anything from a photograph."

SUSAN SONTAG,
ON PHOTOGRAPHY

He poses for me in memory, a bearded cadaverous figure in a torn overcoat standing outside the American Express office on rue de l'Opéra, beating his tattered mittens against the cold.

"You just get in, brother?" he says, springing into sound and motion.

It took me a few moments to place him, then I got it: Greenwich Village the September before—Geno Foreman, a street poet and scene-maker (shortly to be memorialized in a documentary film before dying reportedly of an overdose).

"Yeah," I said. "So how's Paris?"

"Man," Geno said, shaking his head sadly, "Paris ain't what it used to be."

I passed on through the tall glass doors and took the steps down to the mail-pickup line, Geno's elegiac verdict clinging to me like a weird curse. What did he mean, that Paris ain't what it used to be? Since a few weeks earlier, when he got here? By the time Gertrude Stein and Joyce arrived? Was Gide's, Cocteau's, Proust's Paris dead, finished? The Paris of Voltaire, Racine? There'd been a centuries-long cultural orgy, and now it was over. It was the winter of 1961, and I'd arrived too late, missed it all.

At the mail window the clerk examined my passport, retrieved an envelope, and handed me a letter from home. I tore it open, fumbling for the check I'd asked for—the last of my drumming savings. Instead I found a brief note from my mother, a letter from my old girlfriend Sandra—and a notice from the U.S. government telling me to report for induction at the U.S. Army base at Orléans, outside of Paris, a few days after New Year's.

I emerged onto rue de l'Opéra steeped in gloom.

"Hey, you wanna score some shit?" Geno Foreman crooned, steam bursting from his cracked lips. Grinning through shattered teeth, he fished a rumpled nickel bag of pale Lebanese hash from his overcoat pocket.

Before graduation that June, I'd been offered a scholarship to Cornell to study for a doctorate in literary criticism. Far too restless to take it, I'd hung around L.A. and San Francisco most of the summer, dogged by the threat of army induction, playing intense, free-form jazz with other young musicians deep into Ornette Coleman, Sun Ra, Stockhausen, Monk. I'd stayed at my parents' house for a while, but my passions, confusions, and nighthawk ways clearly disrupted their cooling, routinized existence; so, when a friend asked if I wanted to crew on a yacht sailing from the Virgin Islands to Spain in September, I jumped at it. For weeks I memorized the parts of ketches, sloops, and yawls, then crewed on a forty-footer from Santa Barbara to Ensenada for practice. In late August, I answered an ad to drive a woman to New York in her new Cadillac Seville.

Since taking up drums at the age of eleven, I'd never been away from them. Each new town or school had a scene, a milieu in which drumming conferred acceptance, companionship, sustenance: a self. When I left California late that August with only a backpack and a blank notebook, I felt barren, underequipped, a naked stranger on the road. Nothing could have suited me better. Las Vegas, looming out of the desert, exemplified the tawdry American surface materialism I was ready to disavow. In a Nebraska motel, I began a notebook that would spawn years of them, full of truths and lies. Sipping midnight coffee in a Howard Johnson's on the Pennsylvania Turnpike while the woman slept in the back of the Seville, I felt release from all that lay behind me.

By the time I got to Manhattan, a storm was brewing in the Caribbean, delaying the sloop's sail date. I slept on the floor of a dancer's apartment in the Village, phoned St. Thomas every morning for a hurricane update, passed the days walking the streets of the city where I'd been born. Nights I spent at the Village Vanguard listening to John Coltrane play until his mouth bled: creation at full intensity, both sacrificial and prayerful, loosening the bonds of form, heralding a new age. Listening to Elvin Jones's incendiary percussion tumult, I felt I'd arrived at some holy shrine on that journey begun back in Dick Monahan's drum shop.

My dollars shrank; the tropical hurricane lingered teasingly off the Yucatán coast; awkward visits with East Coast relatives I barely knew came to quick, uncomfortable ends. With the possibility of an army draft notice hanging over my head, I was unable to wait any longer; I booked cheap passage on a German freighter leaving Norfolk for Hamburg.

Eight days later, I stepped off a tugboat onto the cobbled Dutch streets of Tenheuzen, elated to feel something old beneath my feet. A retired German boat captain who had made the crossing offered me a ride to Bremen, stopping every few miles in bars to drink schnapps and beer. I fell asleep in his house beneath a goose-down comforter, drunk and wildly happy.

A few days later, in Hamburg, I drummed at a Reeperbahn club with young English rockers playing American blues with more energy than skill, several of their mop-topped mugs soon to festoon the world's magazine covers, then stalk our days forever. The next week, in a small, crowded Copenhagen club, I played with a Danish hard-bop quintet. Afterward the leader asked me to stay and work with them, but it was too soon: I had money left and wanted to travel more. Still, I'd learned that drumming was a currency that crossed borders.

In West Germany, American jeeps and troop-filled khaki trucks thundered down the autobahns. Crossing barren East Germany into Berlin, where the Wall had just gone up, only heightened the growing tension I felt, a reminder that any day I'd be called up for induction. Seen from the clattering elevated train to East Berlin that stopped running at sundown, West Berlin was a lavish Technicolor movie giving way to a black-and-white neo-realist one of cold gray rubble.

In Innsbruck I climbed an Alp with an unapologetic Nazi, shared a bag of pale Moroccan *kif* with a wasted English poet in Switzerland by Lake Lugano, jotted in my journals. South of Genoa, I fell in with a blonde German student hitchhiking the same strip of road, and that night, in a field outside of Civitavecchia, we fumbled at love. Three days later, in Pompeii, we argued over the gross attentions of Neapolitan men and split up. In Rome I stayed with Vanessa, a folksinger I'd known in California, her keening renditions of old lefty songs soon to bring her inexplicable fame in Europe, and played a weekend in a Via Veneto club with a jazz group headed by Benito Mussolini's son Franco. In a Florence hostel, felled by fever, I missed home and family for the first time, even as I realized I'd never again find succor there. By the time I crossed the border into France in early December, weakened and lonely and confused, my money nearly gone, I was barely able to recall the exultant inception of my three-month drift across the Continent. Tunneling into the bare, chill reality of a derelict European winter, I had few resources left, inner or outer, to protect me.

A Citroën ride from Lyon discharged me on Paris' Boulevard Raspail, where, at a table at La Coupole, I found Rafe, a bearded Spanish-American sculptor I'd met in Berlin. He offered to share his room at the Hôtel Dieppe, a stooped, barely lit, unheated walk-up with a single cold-water tap on rue de l'Ancienne Comédie, a few blocks from the Seine. I dropped my luggage off there, then walked across town to American Express (a supplicant's path I'd beat many times that winter), to receive Geno Foreman's equivocal benediction and the draft letter tolling my fate.

The army induction was to take place the week after New Year's. Two weeks before Christmas, Rafe headed south to escape the cold, leaving me alone in the cheerless, icy Hôtel Dieppe. I lay in the narrow, sagging bed, swaddled in street clothes beneath skimpy blankets, reading Knut Hamsun's *Hunger*, Kafka's *The Trial*, Sartre's *No Exit*, Camus's *L'Étranger*, Otto Rank's *Art and Neurosis*, Lorca's collected poems, and *Tropic of Cancer*—or simply staring up at the peeling, bare-bulbed ceiling. Henry Miller had merrily proclaimed freedom along these very *rues* and *allées* that to me, facing a two-year army stint, seemed only dreary, disheartening corridors of doom. Lying among the rumpled bedsheets, the narrow, stained walls closing in around me, I felt everything unspoken and dissimulated in my early life erupting through my pores: Mom's alcoholism, Dad's poisonous ego difficulties, the deathly vacuity of postwar American suburban life, my own terrible confusions.

Why were we drafting people? America wasn't at war. Who was the enemy? The Soviets, as I'd been raised to believe? Surely not those pathetic troops I'd seen patrolling East Berlin. An American GI I met at a crêpe stand on rue Contrescarpe said that inductees were being sent not to Georgia or Germany or Japan but to South Asia to fight a new war there. I knew my enemies lay within, not in some remote paddy field.

Paris winter dream . . .

I'm in California with Sandra in the backseat of a car near the stream in the canyon below my parents' house. We've just made love. I'm leaving to go on a trip but can't find my shoes. My father has hidden them somewhere in his house and won't let me have them back. I'm looking under the bed, in the closets, behind the couch. A panic fills me. I rush toward Dad, pummel his chest.

"Give me my shoes!" I shout.

He won't tell me where they are. He says there's a condition to getting them back but he won't tell me what it is. I feel trapped, suffocated.

"What is it?" I cry. "What do you want?"

"Love me," he says.

"I can't!" I shout. "It's the one thing I can't do!"

I woke up in an icy sweat, my chest heaving. . . .

In between readings and nightmares, I filled my notebooks, hating the words that came. How dare I lift a pen before the weight of literary history except in a critical capacity? Twenty-one, unknown, unpublished—indeed, unwritten!—Rimbaud had already revolutionized literature and decamped to Zanzibar by my age!—I felt paralyzed by my father's early admonitions about "talent," and by the very education that was to have freed me. What flowed easily in sound seized up on the page.

Letters and postcards arrived from Rafe in Tangier with images of palm trees, harbors, and camels, inscribed with his surreal colored-pen filigree and cryptic cadenzas, full of veiled allusions to *kif, majouun,* hashish, and a mad scene of Arab and European writers, musicians, and painters. These sunny, libertine missives were a torture to me, stuck in chilly Paris staring into the hungry jaws of the imperium. Clearly I was a man with no future, mere cannon fodder for the dogs of war.

Some nights I'd clamber out from beneath the blankets and go to the live jazz clubs nearby—Le Caméléon, Club Huchette, Le Chat Qui Pêche—and hover along the walls, clutching a beer, too dispirited to ask to sit in. Back out in the streets, I was accosted by hustlers, drug dealers, cruising homosexuals. One night in Le Caméléon, I hung up my overcoat on a rack with my passport inside and came back to find both coat and passport were gone. Another night, at a club bar, I ended up talking to the precocious, light-limbed daughter of a Vietnamese diplomat, home on holiday from a private school outside Paris. She came to the Hôtel Dieppe and stayed with me that night, and nights to follow. Hai Yen and I seldom spoke or went out; only the language of sex was available to our unhappy, unformed selves.

Church bells rang through the quarter on Christmas Eve, tolling my misery. Alone and far from home, and Hai Yen in Neuilly with her family, I had crept out to buy a bag of *frites* when I ran into Petrus, an impish, goateed Dutch pianist I'd played with in Copenhagen. Excitedly he dragged me off to Le Chat Qui Pêche to hear an intense group of New York musicians from the touring company of *The Connection,* an American play about junkies. Before the last set, I asked to sit in.

Sitting in is always a delicate matter. The bandleader is obliged to make a judgment on the spot, often based on little or no evidence. Club owners tend not to like it. If the musician isn't good, everyone suffers; on the other hand, sitting in freshens the music, invites discovery. A white drummer asking to sit in with a black band is forcing the odds: it's assumed he won't be any good. The tenor player, probably thinking I was French and it would be rude to refuse, warily said yes.

I took my place behind an unfamiliar Gretsch drum set, picked up a pair of new sticks that felt too light. I hadn't practiced or played in months. I adjusted the position of snare, bass drum, and high-hat cymbal to accommodate my limbs. I tapped the snare a few times, loosened the tension knob to make the sound less brittle. Abruptly the pianist counted off "Cherokee" at a lightning tempo—a quick way to weed out a bad drummer, and a move I could take as hostile.

Sketching the tune's frantic pulse with my right hand on the large ride cymbal, I divided it into twos and fours with my left foot on the high hat. And suddenly there it was: the groove, jazz's global constant. Miraculous, that strangers from half a world apart can assemble such a complex musical creation on a moment's notice. Hands and feet responded, whether from the pent-up desperation of recent weeks, or in response to the New York nights absorbing Coltrane's tumultuous innovations. I dared the music out along thought's edges, inciting the players. Though the other musicians were black, shared American griefs and certainties, both grave and joyous, took us to the marrow of this music as intimate to us as breath. The pale French listeners fell rapt. By the third chorus we'd achieved that state of controlled abandon Duke Ellington meant when he described jazz as "an accelerated lack of concern."

Sometimes when I was drumming I'd think of my father. Across the divide of a generation and sensibility, the love of music remained our one shared pleasure. Dad had regaled me so often in childhood with snatches of his favorites that, when he hummed some long-forgotten Jimmy Dorsey, Jack Teagarden, or Jerome Kern phrase, I was compelled, like Pavlov's dog, to join in on cue, slightly embarrassed for us both. Surely I was the only person on earth who could enact this rite with him. Yet he'd always seemed ambivalent about my drumming, sanctioning it but careful to shape it in my eyes as a mere youthful hobby, a pleasure to be put aside one day. He liked to dredge up the tale of his first boss at Paramount Pictures calling him into his office and saying, "Do you want to be a bad musician or a good producer?" The next day Dad had sold his C-melody sax, as if putting childish things behind. I knew I'd never do that: my commitment to music ran far deeper.

Still, I wanted to look out from some bandstand and see Dad watching, tapping his foot, pleased and proud. It would take me a long time to understand that his own faded dreams and regrets bore in upon him so heavily it was difficult for him to celebrate another's attainments, most of all his son's; and that the special wounds he bore dictated that I mustn't become too good. By surpassing him as a musician at an early age, I'd broken faith, taking on the color of the enemy, betraying the aura of self-importance he'd labored to weave around himself, and by which he measured loyalist or foe. This of course presented me with a terrible dilemma: advance, or hold back for my father's sake? There could only be one possible outcome.

When "Cherokee" was over and the applause in the smoky

cave had died down, the musicians' tight nods let me know it had been good. Afterward some were going to the Blue Note, on the Right Bank, to hear the brilliant, disturbed piano icon Bud Powell, then living in Paris. Having no money for the cover charge, I went instead with the bassist, the tenor player, and a few girls to the nearby Hôtel Louisiane, where in a turreted room we sat around drinking wine and sharing a joint. When the subject of my draft induction came up, the saxophone player said, "Saigon, man. They're shipping the brothers over there to fight. Always the first sign war is coming." I received from those assembled counsel on various classic methodologies for avoiding the draft—going as a dope fiend, appearing in drag, simulating psychosis—until the fierce Afghani weed silenced all but the sound of "Blue Monk" on a stereo bleeding through the wall from the next room.

Just before New Year's, I received a letter from home containing the rest of my drumming money, and my lone remaining hope: a letter from an allergist attesting that I had asthma, and another from an osteopath who had treated my trick basketball knees in high school. Rafe wrote again from Tangier, exhorting me to bring his Triumph motorcycle down from Paris to Spain as soon as I got out of the draft, then we'd head south to Marrakech to hear the Gnaoua drummers who played all day in the square. His postcard left me heartsick.

On New Year's Eve, I worked with the band from *The Connection* at Club Huchette, coaxing the revelers into an uncertain, nuclear-clouded 1962. Afterward Hai Yen and I huddled in my freezing bed at the Hôtel Dieppe, drinking flat champagne from a bottle, too dispirited to make love.

On January 3, I trudged through the snow to the American Embassy on the Champs-Élysées to get my stolen passport replaced. In a photo studio a block away, a hooded man behind a box camera snapped a photo of me in a cheap black sweater over a tee shirt, unwashed hair curling around my bare neck. Blemishes mark my face and cheeks from tension, lack of sunlight, and a diet of *frites,* crêpes, and baguettes. I gaze sidelong into the camera, doleful and untrusting, the embossing ripples from the U.S. Embassy stamp distorting the expression of my mouth into either a scowl or a plea for help, depending upon how the light hits the laminate.

On the day before my induction, the *International Herald Tribune* headline announced: U.S. BREAKS RELATIONS WITH CUBA. That night Hai Yen, Petrus the pianist, the musicians from Le Chat Qui Pêche, and my folksinger friend Vanessa—en route from Rome to London to record her first album—came to my tiny, cold room at the Dieppe. We drank cheap Burgundy and I said my goodbyes.

Morning dawned cold and gray. Out my window, snowflakes clung to the stairwell. My appointment at Orléans was at eleven. The draft letter said to bring clothes and a toothbrush and expect to be sent directly off to basic training.

I took the metro to the end of the line, then a local train to Orléans. The U.S. Army base was set in woods a small distance from the town. A pair of armed sentries stood at attention behind high barbed wire before a somber complex of cement buildings. A massive billboard proclaimed PEACE IS OUR PROFESSION, first in English, then in French. I showed my fresh passport and the induction letter to the guards, who looked me up and down with ill-concealed disgust, then waved me through.

Walking down polished hallways, I drew dead-eyed looks from passing soldiers, their pressed uniforms, shined shoes, and scalp cuts making me conscious of the apparition I presented: wild-eyed and pasty, hair trailing over my shoulders, stained flea-market jacket and battered shoes—the very scourge these corn-fed boys had come to Europe to protect the Free World from.

I took a seat on a bench in a corridor outside an office. I seemed to be the only inductee, which boded ill: a tasty morsel for the war machine on a slow day? Sunk deep in the despair I'd inhabited for the last month, I rehearsed stratagems of indifference, resignation. Practice being a piece of meat, I thought, because that's all you're going to be for the next two years—if you survive it.

I was given forms to fill out. A male nurse beckoned me inside and told me to strip to my underwear. I was measured for height and weight; I peed into a cup. The letters from the two doctors were taken from me. An X-ray machine was wheeled in and lowered to the level of my knees. I was instructed to stay still and not breathe. Then the nurse X-rayed my chest.

In another room I waited shivering on an examining table. After a long time a young, bespectacled, pipe-smoking doctor breezed in, his smock open over his officer's uniform, a stethoscope dangling from his neck.

He held up my chest X-ray. "When does the asthma bother you?"

"At night. Or when I run. Or dance."

"Dance." He smiled.

"Or play."

"Play?"

"Drums. I'm a drummer."

"No visible lung damage," he said, peering at the X-ray. "We have lots of soldiers with asthma. We control it with medication." He tossed the X-ray aside. Then he picked up the knee X-rays. "Both knees?"

I nodded. "Basketball."

He grunted. "There it is. The spur."

I craned to see the gray-blue transparency he held up against the fluorescent ceiling light. It was in front of my right tibia: a floating piece of cartilage about the size of a marble. I knew it well; it often slipped around, hobbling me for hours, sometimes days. The little irritant seemed to have conveniently drifted front and center for the X-ray.

"You have problems with this?" the doctor said.

I nodded gravely. "All the time."

"When you dance, I bet," he said. He put the X-ray down. "You'll need to stand at attention for long periods of time. Or march. Especially in basic. This could be a problem." He looked at me. "How do you feel about the army?"

"Feel?"

"Well, do you want to be a soldier?"

Was this a trick question? Desperately I tried to read his intent.

He waited, puffing on his pipe.

The week before, my father had written me a letter telling me about how he'd been too old to be drafted in World War II, and he hadn't volunteered either. Instead he'd directed some radio shows for CBS to help the war effort, one a drama about the partisan uprising against the German invasion of Czechoslovakia, another a live broadcast from Paris hosted by Edward R.

Murrow. He still had the old 78 rpm air checks around the house. In his letter he'd asked me to consider if I'd regret later in life not having served my country, implying that he did.

I couldn't remotely imagine this. Among the tangled blankets at the Hôtel Dieppe, I'd been reading Graham Greene's novel *The Quiet American,* so eerily prophetic of the fatal American embroilment in Vietnam. I saw only futility and disaster in U.S. Cold War meddling in Indochina, indeed anywhere in the world at that point. A childhood of duck-and-cover drills, McCarthyism, loyalty oaths, and missile gaps had left me dubious of war in any form, though I hadn't yet raised it to the level of principle. More viscerally, I'd escaped the constraints of home and country at last and now wanted Marrakech, not boot camp, even if it meant misery and destitution.

"Look," the doctor said. "You're borderline. I can classify you 2-Y, something where you don't have to be on your feet a lot. After basic you drive a jeep. Or a tank. Or a desk job. The other possibility is 4-F."

The magic, coveted status—4-F and you're out!

The doctor folded his arms over his white coat and looked at me. "So which will it be?"

I felt blank, paralyzed. I couldn't believe he was offering me the option.

"I think for now," I murmured, "4-F would probably be better, sir."

Shrugging, he scrawled something on the form. "This doesn't mean you won't get called later for retesting." He held the paper out to me. "But probably not for a year or two. If ever. Show these papers on your way out."

I raced back down the same corridors I'd trudged up, indifferent now to the soldiers' glares and cracks. At the barbed-wire entrance I waved my papers at the sentries, then hurried down the long, tree-lined path until I was out of sight of the Orléans base. I veered off into the bare winter woods, stumbled to a deserted spot, and fell to my knees in a snowbank.

"I'm free!" I shouted to the scattering crows. "My life is my own!"

As if it were that easy.

The next day, I reserved a seat on the overnight train to Barcelona, then checked Rafe's 650cc Triumph motorcycle out of the garage where he'd stored it. I pushed it through the snow back to the Hôtel Dieppe to collect my luggage. A black Citroën limousine with diplomatic plates was parked in front, a liveried Vietnamese chauffeur waiting at the door. I found Hai Yen in my room, sitting on the edge of the bed crying.

"I missed my period."

I looked at her, dazed. "There hasn't been enough time."

I tried to calculate the days and weeks. She was eighteen and tended to histrionics. I knew she didn't want me to leave Paris. Even if it were true, what could I possibly do about it? How could she have the baby? We hardly knew each other.

"If it's true, your father can arrange for an abortion," I said. "It's France, after all."

"If he finds out," she wailed, "he'll send me back to Hanoi."

"How late is your period?"

"Two days."

"But that's nothing," I said.

The limousine driver honked outside.

She threw herself into my arms. "Will you write to me?"

"Of course."

"If it's your baby will you come back?"

"I promise."

We hugged goodbye. From the window I watched her emerge into the rain—a tiny, huddled figure in a black coat and chapeau, looking like something out of Jean Rhys or Marguerite Duras—and disappear into the massive limousine.

I never contacted Hai Yen, of course. A long time would pass before I'd think about her again. When I did, I'd wonder if she really had been pregnant, and if by chance she'd kept it. I strongly doubted it. Still, as years went on, and I had my daughter, and she grew, sometimes I'd lie awake wondering if somewhere on earth she has a secret half-brother or -sister, spawn of a young, foolish, drifting, unknown father.

Early June 1999. An offshore breeze whips spume off wave crests. Barefoot I trace the beachfront from Venice to Santa Monica at sunset, glancing wistfully toward the horizon, plotting new escapes, as the century dies on me. Grounded among L.A.'s Gobi of suburbs, I serve my time.

At seven this morning Nell called. "Your dad has had another stroke." Paramedics had come. He was in Santa Monica Hospital, Room 822, "resting comfortably." I slipped into my clothes and jumped in the car.

Riding up in the hospital elevator, among wheelchairs, orderlies in their green scrubs, and the smell of sickness and disinfectants, I thought how I'd seen my grandfather out in this same hospital, then my mother. Here I was again, a crowd of one, my own achieved life unseen or in abeyance, unimportant here. Looped back to this null point of repetition, hopelessness, expiration, I am the designated mourner who does not grieve, the reluctant actor unsure of his lines, the mop-up boy: Tony boy.

I found my father propped up in bed, strands of silver hair matted on his damp forehead, a plastic ID tag around his wrist, machines hooked to his flaccid arms. He didn't seem to know where he was. Behind a half-open curtain in the same room, an Asian man lay on his back, his mouth open like a fish.

"Hiya, honey," Dad greeted me slurrily.

He'd never called me that. Did he think I was my mother, dead seventeen years now?

The dying day reddens. My flying feet tattoo the dark, wet sand, picking a path among tangled clumps of rubbery kelp. Some days the littoral is strewn with shells, stones, driftwood. Other times the sand is smooth and clean, the water is green and glassy at low tide, the gulls' reflections are visible as they cruise low. Once, after a Malibu fire, everything the conflagration had disgorged down charred gullies to the sea washed up on this beach, forming a trash city miles long: window frames and Styrofoam, boxes and bottles, Tampax dispensers and toilet plungers—detritus of canyons, effluvia of an age.

History moves west, following the sun, someone once said to me in a town whose name I can no longer remember. Travelers fling such assertions around like loose change; still, it had always comforted me to think that my earthly wanderings somehow mirrored the drift of the species. "The rejection of the call," Joseph Campbell wrote, "will wall the Hero up in boredom and dread." A round-trip ticket to somewhere stuffed in my pocket always served as an amulet against entrapment.

My father always fancied himself an adventurous sort. Back in early radio days, he'd barnstormed with the shows, directing some of the first network live broadcasts from ballrooms around the country. "And now, live from the Ambassador Hotel's Coconut Grove Ballroom in Los Angeles! Freddy Martin and his orchestra!" In the photos, bandleaders in white dinner jackets and slicked hair pose, batons in hand, before polished orchestra units—Artie Shaw, Ellington, Whiteman, Charlie Barnet. "All the greats," as Dad would say. Bonuses and perks came with the shows he produced and directed, and so, throughout my childhood until well into the 1950s, complimentary wooden crates of Coca-Cola arrived at the house weekly simply because Dad had once plugged the drink on the *Jimmy Durante Show.* As a result, my sister and I were constantly being trotted off to the dentist to have cavities filled. From time to time, Dad would pull a snowy-white wide-brimmed Stetson out of a box, a gift from some live radio broadcast at a Houston rodeo with "Uncle" Paul Whiteman. A cigarette sponsor provided years of free cartons of the Chesterfield Kings my mother smoked to her early demise. An inscribed stopwatch with a fancy fob, a gift from CBS, took pride of place among my father's memorabilia, along with the Durante calabash pipe.

Whipsaw dislocations back and forth from New York to L.A.—I attended a dozen different schools, from posh Upper East Side preps to L.A. blackboard jungles—were never by choice, simply part of Dad's work cycle. On his own, he was no traveler. A car trip with Mom to New Mexico took on epic proportions, generating an oft-repeated tale about trying to take some photos and upsetting the Taos Pueblo Indians. The summer I was thirteen, the family journeyed in the Buick Roadmaster through the Pacific Northwest, a quarrelsome misery never repeated. Dad went to Europe once, in his fifties, when my mother expressed a wish to revisit the Paris of her teens; and there was a voyage to Japan to visit me when I lived there. After the big shows ended, Dad would fly to New York once a year to visit the head office of the ad agency he worked for, and to see relatives and old friends. Odd that my mother never went along, since she so loved New York. Did he visit old flames, or new ones? In later years, Dad confessed he envied me my wanderings and adventures, but I think what he really meant was my erotic life in an era when women were more accessible. His clubhouse humor embarrassed me not because it was lewd but because it was lame, relic of a hornier age, when only prostitutes and "sluts" were easily available to men.

In the six weeks since my return, things have unraveled at Dad's house. Angela the caretaker has fallen ill; pale and weary, she hemorrhages and must go for tests to determine if it's something serious. She has no health plan, so we'll pay. Her work permit didn't come through, and new forms must be filled out, guaranteeing an employer's support for the next year. One of Nell's grown children has money problems. How do I refuse this old family friend who sheltered my sister and me in our childhoods? Dad's bank account, intended to last his span and provide a legacy for his grandchildren, withers. I am its custodian. What if Angela and Nell can't maintain? Does Dad go to a nursing home? Where, and when? If I were to send him directly to one after this hospitalization, Medicare would pay all expenses for the first six weeks. There's one in Santa Barbara, which means my sister's family could bear some of the load, freeing me to leave at least for a bit, resume work on my new book. Selling Dad's house in this boom real-estate market should subsidize the rest of his life in a home. Of course, Angela and Nell would be devastated, feel betrayed. Would Dad too, or would he notice? Where are my loyalties here?

My wife, Masako, and I keep tabs by e-mail, talk once or twice a week by phone. Working out of our Mexico house, she nears the end of shooting photographs for her book. We miss each other, yet there's no good reason for her to come up and join me. Are you able to write? she asks. Certainly not on the new book my publisher awaits, because I can't travel anywhere. We've talked of my taking a break, getting away for a few weeks, but my father's new stroke puts an end to that. Nothing to do but wait and see. My own life elsewhere seems distant, half remembered. Indeed, all the world beyond this place dims, leaving me yoked to memories and identities I struggle helplessly against. I feel like a man pinned beneath a safe.

Yesterday Masako asked how long I'd be here. For the duration, I answered.

What does that mean?

"Dad."

The nurses have cleaned and dressed him but haven't put in his teeth. The Asian man behind the half-curtain is gone. I know without having to ask that he died during the night.

Dad turns away from the soundless golf match on the overhead television monitor. "Tony boy," he gums.

He seems to know where he is today and where we're going: home. After four days, he's regaining some of what he's lost, as after earlier strokes. Indomitable.

The drawn-in knitted lips, the caved cheeks, the jutting grizzled jaw. I've seen him before without his dentures, but it's still a jolt. This once vain, preening man, a figure in his day, looks like the geezer sourdough in old Western movies.

Feebly he beckons me to his bedside. Reaching out his hand, he mouths something.

"What's that, Dad?"

"I love you," he says.

I recoil, don't quite know what to say back. He's never said that before. Does he think I'm my mother again? I smile uncomfortably, squeeze his crusty hand, let it go.

How easily I'd always unmasked my father in secret; now age cruelly abets the task publicly. Seeing him lying there, helpless and stripped, so little of him left, I think how facile I'd become at critiquing the gap between his self-presentation and how he really was. This left me with a harsh, unforgiving view of him. Yet I've never admitted there might be a breach between my perception of him and the reality. If his vision of himself is flawed, perhaps mine of him is equally so. James Baldwin said of a white man's perception of a black one: If I am not who you thought I was, then you are not who you thought you were. If this is true, both images must yield, shift, come into alignment at the end. Or else I will bear a false perception not only of my father, but also of myself, beyond his grave to my own.

For a moment I think I glimpse a slow, subterranean shift, a thaw in the endless Dad-watch.

To his family back east, Dad was always a hero, the glamour guy who made it big, hobnobbed with the stars. A terrific guy— a swell, as they used to say. But I suspect he was always better in long shot; in intimacy he often fumbled, missed the mark. By the time he told me the facts of life at eleven, I already knew them. By the time he wanted to have a heart-to-heart, he'd already lost mine. A few days ago, my sister sent me a letter from one of his relatives back east, saying what a grand and beloved figure our father was. At the end Meg had scrawled, "They didn't have to live with him!"

My sister had always seemed so consonant with Dad, the one more like him, his advocate and fan. I'd felt alone in my views, the rebel son, the betrayer who'd jumped ship. Had it been different from what I'd thought? Meg visits seldom these days. Did Dad lose her along the way too? I feel a sudden, surprising tenderness toward this lonely, diminished man.

I notice on the window ledge, among a faxed get-well note from Meg's family and cards from Nell and Angela, a bouquet of flowers. Drawing closer, I read the note card: "To dear Philip. Get well fast, honey man. Love and kisses, Kitty."

Kitty was a classic Dad item, a onetime showgirl who'd allegedly been married to a studio head's son—a fact Dad was always quick to mention, as if this marginal credential raised her in others' opinion, when in fact it only made the whole thing more absurd. It reminded me of another time he'd been in the hospital, and the one thing he seemed to draw comfort from was that a celebrity, the old actor Pat O'Brien, was in a room down the hall—dying, it turned out.

Five years ago, at a stoplight on Sunset Boulevard, Kitty, idling in her car, had noticed Dad in his old brown Mercedes, and tossed her business card through his window. She knew a potential sugar daddy when she saw one. "Sometimes it gets lonely for me," Dad would say by way of explaining how he'd called Kitty, taken her out to dinner, begun spending time with her. There are so few left who remember his career, his cronies long gone. Kitty was an echo, however faint, of the glamour days, assuaging his hunger for attention. Sheepishly yet with pride, he showed me a picture he carried in his wallet taken at Chasen's, the old Hollywood stars' restaurant, Kitty kissing him on one cheek and some busty girlfriend of hers on the other.

Kitty lived in a small apartment in Brentwood on some slender alimony, picking up odd gigs in retirement homes as some sort of "entertainer." I first met her at a dinner Dad had ceremoniously arranged at a West Side watering hole. Cheerful and good-looking, in her early fifties, Kitty was an unapologetic dyed-blonde floozie, a party girl. Why object, when the extent of Dad's favors seemed to be meals, telephone chat, a gift once in a while?

Dad kept reassuring me in confidence that they didn't have sex, an unnecessary disclosure at his age. If Kitty was reaching her hand into Dad's pockets, I figured it wasn't for that. Then, a couple of years into their friendship, I was visiting him in L.A. when he floated the idea of having Kitty move in—which I took to mean he'd already asked her. My sister and the grand-daughters, meanwhile, had gotten wind of the mystery woman. Meg saw her half of the inheritance, such as there'd be one by the time Dad had finished running the table, flying out the window. Our mother, according to Meg, had warned on her deathbed, "Watch out for your father and the ladies."

The climax came at Dad's ninetieth-birthday party, to which he'd invited Kitty, along with his few remaining family, friends, and neighbors. Over chocolate cake and champagne, Kitty made off-color cracks, openly flirted with me, and con-fided a stunningly inappropriate physical intimacy about my fa-ther to Meg. "She has gold digger written all over her," my sister hissed furiously in the kitchen.

A few weeks later, at the behest of the women in the fam-ily, I sat Dad down and told him that, though it was his own business whom he consorted with, he should know that Kitty had laid an egg, and there was risk of disaffection within the family if she moved in. I told him about a friend of mine whose family had been irreparably sundered by the arrival of a younger, controlling girlfriend late in his father's life. But it wasn't until I mentioned Groucho Marx, to whom this had fa-mously happened—the celebrity angle always worked—that

Dad started to pay attention. The next time I saw him, he confessed that, yes, he'd already asked Kitty to move in but she'd turned him down—at least for the moment.

Surely what drove Kitty off in the end was the arrival of Nell, who'd been at the ninetieth-birthday party and gotten a good look at her. When Nell moved in the next year, Kitty's presence tailed off dramatically. I suspect Nell simply wasn't letting her calls through. Among my father's papers I came across a ten-thousand-dollar handwritten bequest to Kitty, but a year after Nell moved in he halved it, then dropped it to three thousand dollars. "Kitty never calls or visits any more," he complained. Eventually Kitty was stripped to nothing—a bum rap, I think, because she'd given Dad attentions when it mattered. But my sister was dead set against her ever seeing a dime.

Dad nods toward the bedside table, where a set of dentures floats in a glass. He gestures to his mouth.

I've never done this before. "What do I do?" I ask.

He points to a tube on the table.

I rinse my hands in the bathroom sink, take the cap off the tube. I lift the upper denture from the glass of water, dry it off, then squeeze a hefty glob of gel on—as if laying toothpaste on a brush—and spread it around with my finger.

Dad has had bad teeth for as long as I can remember. Epic sessions with a Beverly Hills dentist for extractions, bridgework, and implants had been as regular a part of his life as golf, or the constipation that confined him to long sessions in the bathroom Sunday mornings.

Inserting the upper denture between Dad's quavering lips, I recall him coming out of Rothschild's barbershop in Beverly Hills, immaculately crimped and coiffed, saying hello to everybody, pressing a coin in the palm of the black shoeshine "boy," who was in fact an old man, me a little kid scurrying to keep up with the dapper producer and director, man about town, the VIP whom everybody seemed to know and like.

But many years before Dad dated Kitty, he'd become one of those guys you fall into conversation with in a waiting room or on a plane who tells you how he once knew Bogie or Bacall, Benny or Berle.

"Was he always so . . . dim?" Masako asked me gently one night, driving home after yet another wearying, interminable dinner with Dad.

"No," I said, leaping to his defense. "In his heyday he was quick, decisive, a good leader." I pictured him in script conferences with Uncle Jimmy Durante, trading wit with the gag writers, directing his live nationwide show in the CBS studios at Sunset and Gower.

I was surprised to hear myself sticking up for him so vehemently. I guess I wanted Dad still to have it.

I work the upper bridge into his mouth until it settles onto the metal implants. I must have put on too much gel, because it bubbles out between his lips like some awful distemper or a sci-fi affliction. I wipe off the excess with a tissue.

"You ready, sir?" An orderly is standing at the door with a wheelchair.

"Almost," I answer for my father, reaching into the glass for the lower denture.

"Dad," I shout into his ear. "You're going home."

A soft Atlantic breeze swept the ferry deck. Behind us, Gibraltar's sere scarp shrank away. Ahead, a white city spilled down its hills to a crescent harbor.

"There it is," Rafe said.

Approaching the dock, the Algeciras-Tangier ferry reversed engines. I looked down into the roiling waters, feeling a languid indifference to my fate.

Mid-April 1962. Three months since I'd left Paris for Barcelona, where in a hotel room off the Ramblas I'd found Rafe, the cheery, bushy-bearded sculptor I'd first met in Berlin, transmuted into a wild-eyed, disheveled *sadhu* in army-surplus jacket and sandals, beard and hair effloresced into gnarled extrusions. Grinning, Rafe had emptied his bags onto the floor, revealing amulets, stones, potions, *kif* from Morocco's Rif mountains, hashish from the Congo. Tales tumbled from his lips. Marrakech, he crooned. But first there are caves in the Canary Islands, three days south by boat from Cádiz, where we can live for free. After Paris and the release from the draft, I was ready for anything.

We'd set off down Spain's east coast on Rafe's big Triumph, each day a windblown epic, each night a series of strange investigations trigged by the pale Moroccan weed and dark, disorienting Congo hashish. Soon our own minds began to frighten us; the days took on a harsh glare, presenting endless obstacles; we became delicate, daunted, skittish. Surely Franco's draconian *guardia civil,* patrolling the roads in their stiff khaki uniforms, were staking us out. We reached Cádiz, a paranoid wind at our backs, and hurriedly boarded the boat for the Canaries.

Three days later, on the island of Tenerife, we found the caves above a black volcanic-sand beach. A month passed there, the derelict days coming to resemble each other. Distant affairs of continents arrived as Spanish headlines glimpsed in the lone village café. Letters from California to *poste restante* questioning my actions and future plans went unanswered. My reminders to myself that I was a free man now struck a hollow note. I kept waiting for the exultant release I'd expected after Orléans but felt only dread and despair. One day an American drug dealer dropped a pistol on the main street of the village and it fired off, grazing a local child. Police began rounding up foreigners of his acquaintance. We hastily buried our illicit substances in the floor of the cave; but Rafe's bushy beard and army-surplus clothes resembled too closely Fidel Castro's, and my shoulder-length hair and wispy mustache Che Guevara's, to suit the wealthy cigar-makers who'd recently immigrated to the Canaries from Havana. We were expelled from the islands as suspected Cuban agents.

Now, as we stepped off the ferry onto Tangier's wharf, Arab guides accosted us with offers of drugs, arms, sex, currencies. Climbing from the harbor up into the old *medina,* I followed Rafe through a maze of narrow, shaded alleys until, deep in the quarter, he knocked on a low, oddly shaped wood door. An ethereal blonde girl of no more than five opened it, smiling silently.

We followed her through a warren of whitewashed rooms of different heights, sizes, and shapes. I smelled the sticky, sweet aroma of mint tea and *kif.* In one room a bearded European was curled up on a mat; in another, an Arab in a djellaba and skull-cap was cutting up *kif* leaves on a flat wooden board, the little round seeds rolling across the tiles. There was little light and no furniture. In a long central room strewn with pillows, a half-dozen Europeans and Arabs sat around smoking *kif* from pipes, sipping mint tea, and talking in low tones.

Rafe introduced me to Galen, a small, rumpled American in his thirties, who offered us an empty room to sleep in. His Russian wife, Tatyana, drifted in and out of rooms pouring mint tea and tending to their two little blonde daughters.

Galen was an amateur scholar and drug aficionado, who from his little house in the Tangier *medina* corresponded with European and American doctors, drug connoisseurs, and academics across the world—Leary; Huxley; the Swiss physician Albert Hoffman, who first synthesized LSD—all committed to a revolution in Western consciousness. Alcohol was belligerency, dope pacific; war was straight, peace high. Cannabis, LSD, peyote, and psilocybin would transform the lethal Strangelovian American Cold War vision into a kinder, gentler one. To these serious drug romantics, history was a seamless, stoned epic in which every important historical figure from Sophocles to Napoleon to JFK owed his accomplishments to the use of some transformative substance: opium, hashish, mushrooms, *yage*, laudanum, *ayahuasca.* President Kennedy was getting high, of course, and soon the entire youth of America would be smoking pot and taking acid—assertions that seemed preposterous to me that spring of 1962 but would be borne out, though hardly ushering in Galen's millennial change in consciousness.

Characters of every nationality and description drifted in and out of Galen's house at all hours: dealers and hustlers, poets and scholars, sociologists and artists, heiresses and aesthetes. What united them was dope: a cult of *Cannabis sativa* and hallucinogens.

I found this messianism peculiar. I'd never thought of drugs as ends in themselves, or as instruments of social revolution, but at most as aids to creation. Certainly among musicians the aim of getting high was to enhance performance—though Huxley's *Doors of Perception* had proposed psychedelics as an instrument of widened consciousness.

When the wild speculation, bad poetry, and flurries of paranoia at Galen's became too much, I'd slip out into the alleys of the Casbah, hallucinatory in themselves. A freewheeling, glamorous international free port and banking haven until Moroccan independence a few years earlier, Tangier had settled into a seedier version of the same. Considered irredeemably corrupt by most Moroccans, abandoned by the West, it floated in its own brackish backwater. I'd hike up through the crumbling *medina*, willfully lost, unable to separate the effects of the *kif* from the dreamlike reverie of the city. I'd stop for sweets and mint tea in a Socco Chico café, scribble furtive indictments in my journals, or simply watch the passing parade of Arabs and foreigners to the hypnotic pulse of dumbeks, tambourines, and plangent ouds spinning out of the bazaar radios.

Sometimes I'd cross the Socco Grande into the old French quarter, and take a table at the Café de Paris, where an international crowd met to read the journals, smoke, and conspire. Among the habitués was a tall, pale American writer whose small novel, written ten years earlier, had been pressed upon me by a writer staying at Galen's. I'd read *The Sheltering Sky* in a sitting, enraptured by its lucid, unflinching gaze into the void. It had left me with a hunger to travel farther south, into the desert, the tale's primary landscape. Sometimes I'd see Bowles's writer wife, Jane, distractedly trailing an Arab woman through the streets. One night she appeared at Galen's house in an agitated state, claiming a spell had been put upon her. Allen Ginsberg and Tennessee Williams had just left Tangier, as had William Burroughs, a writer unfamiliar to me; but at Galen's I came across two small, interesting pamphlets—Burroughs' *Exterminator!* and *Minutes to Go*, which employed an experimental, cut-up method of writing that seemed to mirror perfectly my own fracturing consciousness. His novels *Naked Lunch* and *The Soft Machine* had just come out in Paris and were much talked about, though nobody in Tangier had copies yet.

Each day the Algeciras ferry discharged fresh voyagers from Europe. Once a week the *Yugolinea*, a cheap freighter from New York, arrived bearing poets, painters, and lapsed Manhattan ad executives to join the stoned throngs. Days, weeks, or months later, they'd set out for Europe or America laden with drugs and philosophy. Meanwhile, at Galen's, there was talk of a big crackdown. We were being watched by Tangier authorities and Interpol; nobody was to be trusted. Once, in the middle of the night, Tatyana roused us without warning because Galen had had a presentiment that a huge bust was coming. Potential betrayers were evicted on the spot. The rest of us struggled into our clothes and wandered through the city like aimless ghosts until dawn and the danger—real or imagined, it was impossible to tell—had passed.

At a party at the Woolworth heiress Barbara Hutton's Casbah villa overlooking the harbor, Paul Bowles, lean and elegant in a white suit, smoked hashish through a cigarette holder, paying great attention to the musicians in attendance. I wanted to talk to him about both his book and his ethnomusicological interests (a composer as well, he'd recently made a series of field recordings of Moroccan music for the Library of Congress), but the *kif* rendered me shy, speechless. Jane Bowles, entering dementia, cowered in the corner with her lover Cherifa. The rooms pulsed with local oud orchestras, hermaphroditic dancing boys, *joujouka* trance drummers from the Rif mountains, a Ghanaian dance troupe en route to Paris to perform at the Olympia. Ahmed Yacoubi, a Bowles protégé, painted water colors *in situ* while dancers whirled and pipes were refilled. Nearly everyone I'd seen in Tangier was there, and by midnight the saturnalian revelry had reached a fever pitch.

"I'm going to Marrakech to hear the Gnaoua drummers," I heard myself say to Bowles.

"Oh, they play in the plaza every day this time of year," he said pleasantly, sounding no less strange than any of us. He seemed good-humoredly indifferent, neither kind nor unkind.

I told him I'd found *The Sheltering Sky* remarkable and wanted to buy a copy.

"Out of print, I'm afraid. As is all my work," he said. "But let me know how you find the Gnaoua when you get back to Tangier."

I promised I would.

At some point I must have fallen asleep on the cushions along the wall, for when I woke up, to insistent, repetitive drumming, half the party had left. I climbed up to the roof, my head throbbing.

It was a starlit night. There was one other person on the roof—a hulking, dim German known around the Socco Chico as Mad Ludwig. His mind deeply furrowed by drugs, Mad Ludwig had stopped talking several weeks earlier and now only communicated by tapping on a little clay hand drum, nodding and leering, or occasionally writing a few words on a pad.

Mad Ludwig stopped playing and looked up. His idiotic, obsessive noodling must have produced some kind of expression of distaste on my face, for he scrawled something on his notepad and handed it to me.

"You think you're the drummer," it said. "But which one of us is playing?"

I stumbled downstairs, fled the villa, and followed the winding path to the harbor. Dawn was breaking over the Straits, the low mountains of Europe still veiled in mist. I paced the sand in torment. Is a drummer who doesn't play still a drummer? No, Mad Ludwig was right. Perhaps I was a writer, then, like Bowles. Yet clearly the stoned rants flooding my notebooks were of no possible merit. What was I, then?

Despairing of any solution, I climbed wearily back up into the *medina* and fell asleep on my narrow straw mat at Galen's.

The scene was dissolving into a miasma of fear, conspiracy, unreason. Rumors flew. Some carried guns and knives, others were simply flipping out on the streets. A Belgian poet we knew had run naked through the Arab quarter until finally he was arrested trying to set fire to Barbara Hutton's villa; now he languished in Tangier's insane asylum awaiting repatriation. The hothouse dementia of the *medina* was turning toxic. Rafe and I decided we had to get away.

Inside Marrakech's high, crenellated walls, in the great Djmaa el Fnaa square, a troupe of black Gnaouans made a visceral thunder in the rising red dust of sunset, surrounded by a wide circle of onlookers. Wearing loose white robes and colored babouches, they loudly beat wood drums, hung from shoulders straps, with curved mallets wrapped in goatskin. Others played metal hand cymbals, chanted, and danced. An old member of the troupe and a boy sat to the side, making mint tea and filling the pipes.

Individual drummers improvised variations against a surging, repetitive rhythm—a six-eight pattern with accents on one and four—sustained by the others in unison. Chanting and dancing surged, then subsided, as the pulsation shifted. This drumming resembled less the hypnotic repetition of North African Arabic percussion than something blacker, closer to what I knew as jazz. I stood mesmerized at the edge of the circle, borne on the throbbing current, until nightfall, when the drums finally faded into silence.

As we walked away from the darkened square, Rafe said, "I've never seen you look this happy."

The next day, the Gnaoua drummers began midmorning and didn't stop. When one drummer or dancer tired, he sat down for tea and a pipe and another replaced him. Even the old man played for short periods, and then the boy was allowed to join in. Before long the drummers, realizing my special interest, beckoned me into the circle. I sat sipping mint tea, supremely content, a drummer among drummers. I knew I could play with them, were I to ask, but I wasn't here for that.

Inside the vital Gnaouan circle of drumming, I was linking up disparate bits of musical teaching, connecting threads running back through those tonic rhythms that had first stirred me in youth: Jack Ross's vaudeville licks on my father's piano top, the thunder in Dick Monahan's drum shop, Gene Krupa's maniacal poundings, bop drumming's quicksilver polyrhythms. Here were the cadences, figures, and motifs I'd heard Elvin Jones play in New York with Coltrane, embedded within a continuous culture: drumming as conversation, healing, and sustenance. Preserved through exile and slavery, the Gnaouan drummers still exorcised and entertained in the markets and oases of southern Morocco. The rehabilitating energies of the drums acted directly upon me, assuaging months of drifting and doubt. Emotions rose and receded, mixing with tears and smiles. I felt restored, filled with a new desire to play. I'd arrived at what I'd come south to find.

Back in Tangier, we found Galen, fearful of repressive new worldwide government conspiracies, preparing to flee with his family to Europe. Mad Ludwig was rumored to be holding an English girl hostage in a room at the Hotel Carlton, drugged, a sex slave. I went to see Paul Bowles, eager to report on my encounter with the Gnaoua, but he was up in the Rif mountains with the painter Yacoubi. I left him a letter, initiating a correspondence that would last many years.

Rafe had begun hatching a plan to run *kif* up into Europe, a venture owing less to Galen's quixotic belief in pot's power to dismantle the Cold War than to the fact that we had no money left and no evident way of getting any. Rafe's army-induction notice had come, and his draft board, unlike mine, insisted he return to the States for testing. One run, he figured, would pay our way to Paris, buy him his plane ticket back to California, and keep me going until I could find work drumming.

Since January, Rafe and I had been getting in and out of difficulties, enduring each other's sometimes alarming changes in mood and mental condition. Rafe's easy, anarchic charm enabled him to meet the world head-on, negotiate his way past barriers and scrapes; whereas I, more oblique and skeptical, needed to take the world into my cave to digest. I'd come to trust Rafe's ability to prevail against odds, but the idea of running dope unnerved me. The Tangier guides were rumored to be collecting payoffs from Spanish authorities at Algeciras customs for tipping them off; the week before, a Scot we knew had been arrested coming off the ferry in Algeciras and sentenced to seven years in prison.

The trick, we decided, was to board the ferry quickly and surreptitiously, early in the morning, before word got out among the guides.

"Prueba," said Mohammed, a tall, beaked Bedouin, squatting on Galen's floor in his djellaba, inviting us to inspect the fat gunny sack full of dark, uncut hashish brought by caravan all the way from the Congo. Over mint tea, we concluded a price.

The next day, Rafe and I walked to the French quarter and bought some used clothes: tweed jackets, slacks, old Arrow shirts, cheap leather shoes. On the roof of Galen's house, Tatyana cut our hair short and divested us of our beards. In our shabby new garb, we looked like fresh-faced graduate students from some Eastern-bloc country.

Galen's little girl, Maya, betrays her age in the skewed snapshot she took of us that day—mostly sky, showing only a slash of our newly shorn heads against a tilted minaret.

All that evening and the next day, we lined plastic sheets with the Congo hashish and Moroccan *kif,* stitching them into body suits. But there was far too much, so that afternoon Rafe bought a padded Moroccan stool from a merchant in the

Casbah, stuffed it with the remainder of our cargo, then packed it and left it with Galen to mail to him in Paris.

We set off before dawn the next morning to catch the first ferry. During the crossing, we stood wordlessly at the railing, too terrified to speak. Our bodies ran with sweat from the plastic bags beneath our clothes. We could have been set up by anyone in Tangier—Galen, Mohammed, the proprietor of the Socco Chico café, Interpol, the U.S. Consulate, one of the numerous guides—for any reason. As Gibraltar loomed, I noticed a trail of *kif* dribbling down Rafe's pant leg and sent him to the bathroom to repair it. He came back out just as the ferry bumped against the Algeciras pier.

We followed the disembarkation line into a low Quonset customs shed. Our luggage was examined, our passports were scrutinized. A customs officer asked a few questions in Spanish that we professed not to understand.

Then he waved us out of the line.

We waited in a small, locked room, gazing miserably out through a barred window at the two-lane road running north to the waiting Madrid train. I rehearsed the call home to California to my crestfallen parents, envisioned the trial, the years of jail.

Two customs officers arrived and asked us more questions. They conferred behind our backs while we waited in silence. Then they told us to stand up and marched us out of the room.

We were pointed toward the barrier gate. At first, we didn't understand but the officers kept waving us on. The gate lifted. We walked through and started up the road, streaming with sweat, expecting at any moment to be hailed from behind, ordered to halt, or shot at—even after we rounded the bend out of their sight.

On the train north to Madrid, I sat by the window, watching the stony fields of southern Spain flicker past, wondering why we'd been let go. Why had we been detained at all, then? Had we just been lucky, the guards distracted at the end?

The truth was not yet within my power to discern.

Though I'd never see Bowles again, we'd keep in touch through the years. Chatty letters, typed on thin blue aerogrammes with odd little Moroccan postmarks and stamps, would arrive full of droll news of Ramadan, police crackdowns, Arabs and foreigners amok in the *medina*. Bowles was essentially a forgotten figure; his books were mostly out of print until a revival began in the mid-1970s. In 1977, he sent me a story to include in an anthology I was editing. By the time of his death in the spring of 2000, he'd become a literary icon.

Meeting Bowles probably marked the beginning of my life as a writer. In him, I found an American of my father's generation who'd neither compromised his life for commerce nor lived in the United States. His novels, short stories, essays, and letters became steady companions. If my literary training had left me impatient with the Beat writers' lack of rigor and restraint, I found in Bowles a writer who combined formal calm with radical vision. Through him I understood how a musician might also write, a path I was on without yet knowing it. More deeply, I sensed in him someone who, as another writer would later note, "retained, everywhere, the singularity of a stranger." I was beginning to understand that I had no true home and might be fated never to find one, but that I might become one of those equally at home everywhere and nowhere. Through

Bowles's example, I gleaned there were other ways of being American, alternatives to the suffocating vision promulgated by my father.

In Tangier at that time, a week seemed like a year. Artistic and human investigations were undertaken at a high cost: dementia, visions, death. It might be said that in a sense, the next stages of artistic and social development in the West were prefigured in Tangier during that brief time. Galen's mad prophecies would soon become everyday American realities, his colleagues culture heroes. For years, I'd run into poets, artists, musicologists, editors who shared Tangier as an abiding reference—a slightly disturbed force field that included many things, of which Bowles was inevitably one. (Soon after I left, Galen was expelled from Morocco and fled with Tatyana and the children to rural England, then Amsterdam. Later he wrote a few books—quaint artifacts of the era—on the revelatory powers of drugs.)

Bowles would remain as I first encountered him, the calm eye of the storm while those around him went variously mad. Writing under a steady dosage of *kif,* he was the only seriously good writer I'd meet who managed to work well stoned over the long haul. His writings opened us to the Arab world and brought us to the desert, though in truth he has many British and German precursors (including the remarkable Isabelle Eberhardt, whom he translated). But it is in his lean, luminous style and fearless existential vision of emptiness that his work endures.

Sometimes in his letters I'd hear sadness. Jane had died in a nunnery in Spain, the theater of Tangier and Morocco had passed, his output had slowed. I returned to Morocco a number of times over the years but out of reticence never visited him in his little flat in the Iseta Building (there was no telephone; you simply showed up at his door).

I never did like Tangier except for its setting; it's one of the most corrupt, claustrophobic places I've ever been. But that first day I arrived on the ferry and entered the Casbah, I was changed. As Europe liberated me from America, so did the Arab world release me from the West. On later trips I'd stay a night in Tangier, then move on, feeling a great sense of relief when I crossed the High Atlas and got the first whiff of the silent desert Bowles wrote about so unforgettably.

Late spring, and the Paris streets were alive, the clubs brimming with jazz and blues, the cinemas unfurling new Antonioni (*L'Avventura*), Buñuel (*Viridiana*), and Bergman (*Through a Glass Darkly*), the bookstore windows bright with new titles. This was the Paris I'd come to find the winter before; and in fact on my second day back I ran into Geno Foreman, that barometer of cultural temper, skulking along Boulevard St.-Germain, hair flying, proclaiming that "Paris is happening again, man!" If it ain't what it used to be, at least it was something.

Re-established in our old room at the Hôtel Dieppe, Rafe and I let it be known around the quarter that we were dealing some good dope. We assembled little matchboxes of Rif-mountain *kif* (five francs) and Congo hash (ten francs), while keeping aside hundred-gram and kilo bags for the serious buyers. Rafe booked his ticket home to California, expecting to pay for it with drug earnings, and I looked for chances to drum. The nickel and dime matchboxes flew out of our hands in the cafés and *allées* as word spread, but the profits took us little further than rent and the day's meals. We needed to find bigger customers.

I didn't think of myself as having become a dealer, just a small seller of enough to get along. Carrying *kif* from Morocco was like bringing jade from China, or rugs from Turkey, wasn't it? I wasn't ready to admit to the aesthetic allure of crime, or to transgression as inseparable from the embrace of my own despair.

While we hunted around for the big score, I haunted the bars along St.-André-des-Arts and rue de la Huchette, listening to the fiery new Blue Note jazz releases—Jackie McLean, Dexter Gordon, Lee Morgan—blasting out of the speakers. On nights I could afford it, I'd descend into the *caves* to hear live music. The drummer from *The Connection* I'd met the winter before was working at Le Chat Qui Pêche with a new band of expatriate New York players, and he invited me to stop by and play.

Perhaps it was simply release from the haunted life I'd been living, but that night my limbs coursed with energy. The sticks did whatever came to mind, the drum heads chattered, the cymbals flared like heat sources. Gleanings of Gnaouan motifs from the square of Marrakech tricked jazz's four-beat constraints, opening up space, letting in fresh improvisatory air. Rafe, who'd never heard me play, was there that night, and years later would chide me for having ended up a writer and not a drummer. He couldn't understand how someone could so love something and do it that well, then choose not to (though "choose" always struck me as the troubling word). Afterward the musicians wanted to know where I'd picked up all this new stuff. Africa, I said. They thought I should be working around Paris, but nobody seemed to know of a gig.

This left me flogging the little nickel and dime boxes in the cafés of the fifth and sixth *arrondissments* for enough francs to eat *prix-fixe* meals at the Algerian couscous restaurants on rue de la Harpe—which is where Milt Mezzrow, a black American photographer (son of the fabled hophead clarinetist and memoirist Mezz Mezzrow) took the photo of me standing in front of the food display and Arabic lettering of the Café Fez, hands jammed in my trench coat, looking hunted, desperate.

The Brentano's on rue de l'Opéra stocked William Burroughs' books in their plain green Olympia Press Travellers' Companion paperback editions, still illegal in the States; and every minute I wasn't dealing or in the clubs I was reading *Naked Lunch,* or *The Soft Machine,* or *The Ticket That Exploded* in a state of high perturbation and excitement. I felt I'd found the first literary artifacts of the new age, writing's equivalent of Coltrane's form-bursting jazz—a path beyond Joyce's culminating, valedictory artifacts of modernism. Burroughs' bleak hilarity and visionary vaudeville scatology, collaged into musical routines and riffs, exposed the roots of language and mental activity, spinning off a cold, fractured poetry tinged with beauty, nostalgia, and pain. Here, I thought, was that exact juncture of language and music I'd sought.

Burroughs was living a few blocks away at number 9 rue Gît le Coeur, better known as the Beat Hotel, where Ginsberg, Gregory Corso, and the poet Harold Norse, whom I'd met in Tangier, stayed as well. The prospect of possibly encountering Burroughs quickened me. Who else among his readers was absorbing the entirety of his intent as deeply, as perfectly, as I? My daily life as a small seller of drugs, in which everything and everyone was suspect, every level of reality a potential con, every transaction fraught with black comedy, eerily mirrored scenes and characters in *Naked Lunch.* Making furtive contacts on street corners and in cafés to sell off the little boxes Rafe and I had prepared in our room, I lived in constant dread.

The fierce Congo hash, which hadn't been seen around Paris, became the rage; our traffic grew. Pot was still regarded in France as near-synonymous with heroin; the penalties were severe. Regularly the police descended upon the cafés in the quarter where drugs were openly sold and hauled dealers off to jail, sending tremors through the scene. The *flics*, on edge from terrorist attacks and bombings as the Algerian independence struggle reached its climax, were in no mood to be tolerant. Rafe and I tried to deal only to people recommended to us, and never in public establishments. But who could be trusted? I felt no pleasure in these maneuvers, only a dull sense of inevitability and a curious resignation to the possibility of getting caught. Drugs had ceased to represent pleasure or enlightenment, only commerce and danger; I was far too tense and busy to get high myself any more. The whole enterprise was weighing us down. We were desperate to sell off the rest of the dope in one big score and get off the street. But everyone we met was small-time.

I played regularly in the clubs but couldn't seem to land a steady job. Was it because I, a white drummer, disturbed Paris's romance with Negritude? Out of desperation, I accepted a friend's invitation to interview at the *Herald Tribune* for a copy-editing job—Henry Miller's old gig, a time-hallowed Paris stop-gap—but, busy selling *kif,* I lost track of which day it was and missed the appointment.

One afternoon on rue de Buci, I ran into Leda, a tall, red-headed Bard College dropout and aspiring writer I'd met in Tangier. She'd left the week before and had news: Galen and Tatyana had been expelled from Morocco, Mohammed the Congo dealer had been knifed in a Casbah alley and had fled south to the desert, and Mad Ludwig had smashed his drum to bits in the Socco Chico. Bowles was translating the stories of a Moroccan, Larbi Layachi (later to appear as *A Life Full of*

Holes), and Jane had passed out drunk in front of the Café de Paris.

Leda and I began spending time together, in cafés or her room, drawing on napkins, writing little fables, talking about books. She was advanced in her tastes, and we taught each other things: she gave me Hesse and Escher, I gave her Beckett and Burroughs. Some nights I stayed over at her hotel on rue Contrescarpe, finding respite from the street in her bed.

At last a potential buyer for the Congo hash surfaced through Rod Jackson, an American poet friend. A meeting was arranged. Carefully Rafe and I reweighed the three kilo bags of Congo, bound them, and stuffed them in a backpack. Rod met us at the Hôtel Dieppe after dark, and we walked down rue St.-André-des-Arts past a cordon of police (the night before, a junkie had overdosed in a room at the Beat Hotel, and his friends had carried him the half-block to the Seine and dumped him in; the body had washed up in Neuilly that morning, according to the papers).

Rod took us on a circuitous path past the *flics* to a cheap hotel, where we climbed six floors of narrow, creaking wooden stairs, then ducked into a low garret room lit by candles. Four unsmiling black Americans sat on pillows with their French girlfriends. Edwin, the buyer, scarfaced and glowering, neither said hello nor shook our hands. Instead, he proffered some nasty remarks about our race, our manhood, and the presumed quality of our goods.

Rafe undid a kilo bag of the cut Congo hash, filled a small Moroccan pipe, and passed it around. Edwin sucked deeply of the Congo. The bowl flared red, the tiny spent ash hopped onto the floor. Rafe filled another pipe.

Conversation ceased. Eyes grew red and watery. Heads slumped onto chests, the silence interrupted only by the spitting of the candles, the hissing of the smokers inhaling, the occasional cough. The fierce Congo was rapidly disassembling Edwin and his cronies. Rafe and I, having long since grown wary of its somber, soul-searching effects, always a hair's breadth away from a gut-twisting slide into shuddering fear and suspicion, had agreed not to smoke that night, even if it meant enduring the scorn of our customer.

Edwin sat in leaden silence, eyes closed, chin on his chest. One of the girls got up, drifted to the room's lone window, and reported that *flics* were in the street below.

Rafe slipped a rubber band around the neck of one of the plastic bags. "That was on the house," he said.

A small rustling ensued. Edwin opened one reddened eye and asked how much we wanted for the shit.

To my astonishment, Rafe quoted double the kilo price we'd decided on that afternoon. Madness, I thought. Edwin looked very displeased. The room tone shifted perceptibly. Rod glanced at me in alarm. I began to gauge the distance between us and the door. Surely Edwin and his friends had weapons. They might simply seize the bags, I figured—a preferable outcome, I thought, to walking back out into the *flic*-infested streets with a rucksack full of hash.

Rafe was all bluff; we had no other customer. He needed the money to get the plane ticket home for his draft physical. I needed it to live and be relieved of dealing. Now he'd blown it.

Edwin looked balefully at Rafe through bloodshot eyes. He reached in his pocket, pulled out a fat wad of francs, and began counting them off in the guttering candlelight.

Rafe handed the bills to me to count. It was the full amount he'd asked for.

We stood up, backed slowly out of the room, and closed the door behind us. We tiptoed down the rickety stairs, not daring to breathe. In the *allée,* two *flics* stood against the building across from us. We turned toward the Seine. The empty backpack felt deliciously light on my shoulders.

At the quai we settled with Rod, then walked silently along the river, the cool night air filling our lungs. Suddenly, at the Pont Neuf, Rafe jumped in the air and whooped with laughter. "We fucked them! The Congo took that bastard Edwin apart!"

We stumbled back to the Hôtel Dieppe, reliving our little victory, fending off the self-disgust we knew would hit us later.

It was early June, and I had enough money to last a month. I didn't want to stay around Paris scuffling in the clubs. Before leaving for California, Rafe had collected the additional dope we'd mailed ourselves from Tangier and shipped it to California to sell, an enterprise I was entirely willing to cede to him. After Marrakech, I only wanted to play music, seriously and steadily. London had a good jazz club, I'd heard. I began to think about heading there.

A few days after Rafe left, I ran into Arthur, a tall, thin youth from a wealthy London family who'd taken up with Burroughs in Tangier.

"Want to go meet Bill?" he said cheerily.

I followed Arthur the several blocks to the Beat Hotel. As we mounted the stairs, my knees began to shake. What would I dare say to a man whose books I'd been reading steadily for a month, from whose pages I could recite entire passages?

Burroughs opened the door dressed in a suit, looking sallow and gray, more like a bank clerk—the Hombre Invisible of his books—than an author. Entering his tiny, spare, orderly room, I saw notebooks, newspapers, and scissors arrayed on a narrow desk: the tools of his literary cut-up procedures. The walls were bare but for a black-and-white snapshot of him in overcoat and hat, standing behind a swarthy young man shooting a rifle at an amusement-park gallery. A radio, tuned to no discernible station, softly emitted static. When Arthur commented on this, Burroughs said dryly, "It's all I listen to any more."

Burroughs was curious about my recent stay in Tangier, where he'd written most of *Naked Lunch*. I told him what I knew of Paul and Jane Bowles, the party at Barbara Hutton's, the recent disturbances and arrests, Galen Andrews' flight. When Burroughs proffered a joint and lit up, I became uneasy: my own interest in drugs was fast waning, ironically in part because of Burroughs' substance-steeped work, which reveals drug experience as simply another delusory con game.

A knock came at the door, and an effusive, well-tailored man entered. I was introduced to Brion Gysin, Burroughs' visual collaborator. A discussion ensued concerning the two men's difficulties with their publisher, Paris-based Olympia Press (which had also published Beckett, Nabokov, Terry Southern, J. P. Donleavy, and an array of pseudonymous erotica), whose publisher, Maurice Girodias, was enduring a new wave of suits in France, principally because of Burroughs' books—which in turn was causing payment delays to its authors.

We adjourned downstairs to the small bar off the lobby, where Burroughs quickly downed two Pernods, then, alarmingly, ordered two more—a substitute, he explained, for the heroin he'd allegedly kicked with the aid of the drug apomorphine, about which he made much in his books. While Burroughs and Gysin conversed, Arthur and I stood silently by. Between the weed and the Pernod, the afternoon was swimming.

At one point Gysin left, taking Arthur with him. I found myself alone with Burroughs, who gazed intently at me in the late-afternoon light of the hotel bar. I realized, with rising discomfort, that "Bill" was regarding me as a sexual offering.

Burroughs' pale eyes bore into me. "Back upstairs?"

"I have to go," I said, flushing with humiliation.

"Well, then," Burroughs said, his gaunt gaze unreadable, "come by and visit tomorrow."

"Yes," I said. "I will."

His handshake was bony and cool.

I hurried out into the street, eager to get away.

That night, I lay awake, imagining what I might have said but hadn't. I was just a cipher, a boy, mere flesh to someone whose work I admired and felt I understood. If I went back the next day, would I be able to make myself clearer? How could I surmount the towering barrier of the books, secretly uniting yet separating us?

The next morning, I checked out of the Hôtel Dieppe, left my bags at Leda's hotel, and wandered the quarter all afternoon, until dark. Twice I circled past the Beat Hotel but didn't dare go in.

The following day, I left hurriedly for London.

15. The Exile of Return

An early-summer morning in California. I kick open a Persian *kilim* I haven't seen in twelve years and spread it on the hardwood floor of the Venice cottage. Dust clouds swirl in the inert foggy light pouring through the windows. Ducks honk and ruffle in the narrow canal outside. I slide a Japanese tansu chest against the wall next to my writing desk, arrange a couple of wicker chairs on the little sunporch to face the water. In the hovering mist, the two men who live next door row past in their canoe, their golden retriever in the prow.

"Marine layer," the weather people term this southern-California haze that blankets the coastal area most nights and mornings in June. Or "early-morning low fog, clearing by noon," they say, though often it doesn't. When this happens, Venice falls prey to a mood, desolate and poignant. Scant, featureless specters trudge across the sand. The ubiquitous monkey palms become ghostly sentinels. Foghorns moan.

I seem to have fallen into a strange haze of my own, suspended between worlds, neither a grown self I recognize nor the boy I once was here. As that filial tug that every culture has a name for draws me deeper into this tangled, rueful re-engagement with a place and a family I'd left—a landscape in many ways as exotic to me now as distant places I fled to in youth—I feel a sense of suspension, hiatus. My life slows to the pace of my father's fading heartbeat. Old possessions and scrapbooks emerge from storage boxes: irradiated objects, symbols of rootedness, closure, entrapment. Mired in the exile of return, I grasp for affirmations of transience. Early this morning, a small tremor rippled forth from its epicenter off Catalina, setting off a cacophony of car alarms across Venice, louder than the dogs' howls, summoning Caltech wizards onto local TV channels to divine the seismographic scribbles. It brought an odd pleasure, this reminder of loose underpinnings, tectonic motion, the idea of traveling while staying still.

Amid complications and lulls, my father's relentless fade accelerates. He isn't ill or in pain—never has been—just vastly decrepit. His conversations have become surreal, incoherent, astounding. He hasn't left the house in weeks. His daily routine has crumbled; he sleeps late, skips dinners. I am the lone remaining family member who visits regularly.

My face floats into view in the window—gaunt, intent, ever mysterious to its owner. My eyes, reflected in the glass, seem to regard me with a question, one I suppose I've tried to answer with the act of my life. Still my own image backs me down. A writer who presumes to read character in others, I can no more read my own visage than a book in an unknown tongue.

Outside, the dissolving fog exposes a collage of low, rickety rooftops. Rinsing off a few dishes, I remember how this area was once an enclave of beatniks and welfare cases. Underage kids, we'd drive to Venice to find winos to buy us beer. Junkie musicians I used to jam with lived in tumbledown cottages like this one. Now gentrification has applied its rote coat of charm to these canal homes, sheltered from the waterfront hubbub a few blocks away, to form an exotic redoubt, a touch of "color" or "character" in a city famously devoid of it. These days Venice Beach, thronged with bicyclists and Rollerbladers and tourists, touts itself as "the second most popular tourist attraction after

Disneyland." These few surviving canals, relic of a quixotic 1920s real-estate scheme shamelessly invoking the Adriatic original, were built by a booster and essayist named Abbott Kinney, who survives in the name of a nearby boulevard.

I open a folder of my work, neglected for months. I look at the introductory pages to *Turista*, the new travel memoir I'd begun before my father's decline drew me back here. Some *turista*. How can I write about travels not taken? I feel the cheapest sort of ill will toward my father, as if his aged condition is willfully blocking my way.

But it's all too fitting somehow. He'd never been a friend of my writing. It was only after years of struggle that he even recognized I wrote. When had I passed the "talent test"? Probably never; but I do remember a morning when a friend of his called and told him my first published novel was one of the *New York Times* Notable Books of the Year and I heard reluctant pride in his voice.

Soon after that, I was driving him to a doctor's appointment and told him I was working on another novel. He said, "You know, some guys only have one book in them. Are you sure you've got it?"

The bastard, I thought. He can't abide my small success.

When I was twenty-nine, I'd given Dad a draft of *White City*, the first novel I'd written. After he read it, he phoned me and said, "I wouldn't have this piece of crap in my house. I wouldn't let your mother read it. It's sheer pornography." He'd taken umbrage at some sex scenes.

When my third novel was published, he said to me, "I'm sure you're anxious to hear what I have to say about the book." Hardly. I was forty-three years old by then, and my father's opinion of me or my work had long ago ceased to carry much weight. In his heyday as a producer and director, he'd been discerning about "material," and I granted him that, but his tastes in fiction were common, outdated. I dreaded hearing his views. Still, I knew I'd have to sit through it.

Over lunch at a local deli, he proceeded to tell me where he felt the book failed, came up short, went off track. I found myself feebly defending its success—the good reviews, the outsized paperback sale, the foreign editions. Meanwhile, I'd already heard through my sister that Dad was bragging to the relatives back east about his son's authorial achievements. At the end of lunch, he asked me to sign my few remaining free copies to send to them.

He just couldn't help himself.

This morning my sister, Meg, called. We talked awhile about our father, as always—a fact that would please him, we often note with bleak humor. The others in the family, or our own lives, barely get a word.

Then Meg told me about a dream.

"I had this one all through childhood," she said. "A nightmare, actually. I still have it once in a while. I'm alone in the backseat of the car on a steep hillside. The car begins to roll. The doors are locked, the windows shut. I'm small, I don't know what to do. The car picks up speed. I feel terror, panic. I begin to scream. I wake up in a sweat, terrified."

"You're kidding," I said. "I had the same dream for years."

"Isn't that weird?"

"I guess it's obvious what it's about. The family out of control. The adults not in charge."

"Do you think it's just a car thing, and everybody who grows up in California has that dream?"

"Maybe in another culture it would be a chariot, or a horse. Or it's just modern life, at the mercy of machines."

"No," Meg said emphatically. "It's about our family."

Meg was born when I was four years old. Resentful of the shift of attention away from me, I'd greeted her entry into the world by trying to throw her out our apartment window in Manhattan. As we grew, and I bore the brunt of my parents' difficulties, Meg remained the innocent, it seemed. She appeared to fit seamlessly into the family fantasia of 1950s suburban existence—a teenager who liked surf music, parties, and boys—while I stayed in my room immersed in Coltrane and Lorca, cultivating art and disaffection. Meg even recorded a hit doo-wop record with a group of high-school friends and flew back to Philadelphia to lip-sync it on Dick Clark's *American Bandstand.* She married a guy from high school, moved up the coast, had a couple of kids, and settled in. If her suburban life didn't seem very exciting to me, I can only imagine how I—the wandering, indecipherable, shape-shifting, lost older brother—must have appeared to her.

Meg had seemed to adore my father, seeing him as wise and benign. To me, he'd conned her with his charm act, chucking her on the cheek, telling her how pretty she looked in pink, leaving me in sole possession of unspeakable family knowledge. Later, when Dad and I began to clash, I'd think about my sister and wonder: How could two people grow up in the same house and come out so differently?

Then I'd think: But what if I've been wrong all along and Meg has it right? If so, then I was a monster, a scourge, an angel of darkness visited upon my own family. I'd hate myself, doubt my perceptions, harbor suicidal thoughts.

I was a remote brother and uncle to Meg's kids, seldom around. Visiting her reawakened all my discomforts about suburban life and family. Meg stayed in touch with her friends from youth, had reunion parties, vacationed in Las Vegas. I was inclined to think she'd settled into an unquestioning, unexamined American life.

Gradually, over the years, reality entered Meg's life as it did mine: divorce, health and money stresses, problems with her kids. As my life slowly coalesced along lines of work and love, hers unraveled a little along its borders. Chastened by experience, she became a less artificial person to me—and, I expect, to herself. Her idealization of our father necessarily came under scrutiny, something he unknowingly abetted in his elder years by revealing himself in a far less flattering light. She looked to him for less. The approval she sought from him as a grown, capable woman she came to see he could never grant: he just wanted pretty in pink.

Across the seventeen years of my father's widowerhood, Meg and I have come to love and respect each other. We laugh, we commiserate. I feel less burdened, less alone because of her. Our fond, open relationships with our own children are so different from ours with Dad. In speaking frankly about my father, I've probably furthered her disillusion. She recognizes the irony that I, who liked my father less, have become the central figure in his late life.

Meg visits Dad seldom these days. She finds it painful, and I understand. It grieves her to contemplate the reduced hero of her youth. "I wish he'd died the same time as Mom," she said to me once. "Then I'd remember him at his best."

Recently Meg surprised me with a memory she had of my mother, drunk, saying: "I can't stand your father. I wish I could leave him." I was shocked; I'd never heard anything like this. Meg would have been around eight at the time.

Maybe she hadn't grown up so innocent after all.

Later, thinking about this little revelation, I wondered: Did my mother transfer an unspoken bitterness toward my father into me?

"So how far has Dad come back from the stroke?" Meg asked on the phone this morning.

"Halfway, maybe. He doesn't leave his bed much."

"Does he still think he's in Chicago?"

"He's in his childhood home in Meriden now. 'Upstairs,' wherever that is."

"He's not in any pain?"

"No."

"Everything under control at the house?"

"Seems to be."

A pause. "I really appreciate what you're doing," she said, her voice tinged with remorse. Then she said, "You know, he always spoke so highly of you when you weren't around."

Sure, I think. To the extent it brought him credit in others' eyes.

How I hate bearing this cynicism so late in all our lives! I'd rather think that when Dad said "I love you" in the hospital it was directed to me and not some figment. But in my sister's voice I hear a message: the family aches for father and son to reconcile, find peace.

I open a carton sitting beside my desk in Venice, one of those unearthed from storage. It contains things of my mother's that came to me after she died. I've never looked at it. I find stacks of notebooks from lectures she attended at the New School in New York during the war—a young mother with a tiny child, me, studying European history with eminent émigré scholars. A second batch, of small brown leather ones, documents, in her tiny, immaculate hand, her studies at UCLA on psychology, mysticism, Jung, Egyptology. Another notebook tracks lectures on contemporary architecture: Le Corbusier, Moholy-Nagy, Neutra, Schindler. Always trying to improve herself, shore up an identity separate from the family.

What accommodations lay at the heart of their marriage? When she was dying and my father looked to me for attentions after years of distance, I began to feel the heat of his relentless need. How had my mother borne it? My sister and I have asked each other this question often.

In the same carton, I come upon stacks of letters, postcards, and aerogrammes from my travels, bound by rubber bands. She'd kept every one. Opening one, I flinch: how opaque, how dissimulating, how little revealing of what was happening! "Saw some beautiful African art at Musée de l'Homme," I write from Paris around the time Rafe and I were dealing drugs at the Café Odéon.

Afternoon sun beats down on the roof of the cottage. I lift from the bottom of the carton a pair of drumsticks. The red lettering along the striated wood shafts has long faded from these sticks Jack Ross left behind on Dad's piano top half a century ago, the ones a boy picked up that morning, tapping fate. But I can tell by the feel they're Slingerland 5A's.

Among the crinkled, scored photos laid out on the hardwood floor in Venice, one remains mysterious to me. There's no date, but it would have been June of 1962, or close. Jacob and I are standing in front of his old Citroën on Hampstead Heath, dressed in narrow dark suits and wraparound sunglasses, looking a little like half of the Beatles. If this image doesn't resolve easily, it might be because I recently saw Jacob again after all these years.

Jacob, who lived in a sunny flat across the street from the site of the photo, was studying theater and art at London's Slade School of Fine Arts. Petrus the pianist had given me his name and number before I left Paris. Jacob was Dutch, exactly my age, twenty-two, to the day. We were the same height and weight, and we even looked a little alike. It was uncanny. His father was a nuclear physicist working on top-security bomb projects outside of London, and his mother lived in the Amsterdam suburbs. Neither he nor his roommate, Ravi, seemed to mind if I shared their flat for a while in exchange for a little rent money.

My second night in London, I headed for the city's one good jazz club, Ronnie Scott's. Free of Paris and the drug scene, I was ready to establish myself in England as a musician. I stood at the bar listening to a tightly rehearsed English big band run through a few standards—"Out of Nowhere," "Tenderly," "April in Paris." Dull, predictable, light-years behind. I was told to come back on Sunday afternoon, when there were open jam sessions.

On the way out, I passed a poster advertising the imminent arrival of the tenor saxophonist Dexter Gordon. Since his recent release from a lengthy jail stretch in California for heroin possession, Gordon, John Coltrane's primary influence, had recorded a thrilling series of new albums for Blue Note I'd heard blasting out of the *boîtes* of Paris that spring.

Checking out other clubs around London that evening, I found the scene mired in Dixieland-style "trad," "skiffle"-derivative white-boy blues. It wasn't even worth asking to sit in.

In the nights to follow, I drank with Jacob and Ravi and their actor schoolmates in cheery pubs. After months among demented wanderers, weird cabalists, jaded drug merchants, and petty criminals, it was a relief to tipple pints of Guinness with clever, vain, naïve students my age who laughed brightly and imagined glittering futures for themselves. It helped me pretend I was still one of them.

Sunday afternoon at Ronnie Scott's I jammed with energetic Caribbeans, European strays, and local talent. Afterward the owner, a decent saxophonist himself, suggested I stick around London, wend my way into the local scene, perhaps do the odd night at his club. I told him I needed to work full-time. British labor laws, he said, made it near-impossible for an American to get a work permit unless he was contracted for a fixed appearance.

"Does Dexter Gordon have a drummer?" I dared to ask.

"Kenny Clarke's coming over from Paris," he said, ending the conversation. Clarke, one of modern drumming's great innovators, had left New York for Paris some years ago and now worked regularly with Bud Powell at the Blue Note.

My plans to drum in England were adding up to little. Soon I'd run out of money again. I was desperate to find a way to survive in Europe—anything to avoid returning to California and some meaningless straight job, as my father in his letters was exhorting me to do. I began to think of Copenhagen, where I'd played when I'd first hit Europe, as my last hope. Dexter Gordon would be going there after London, I'd heard; maybe I'd catch up with him after all.

The next evening, Jacob arrived back at the flat in a state of giddy excitation. An actor friend at school was making a lot of easy money, he said. The deal was simple. Every afternoon, lonely matrons and dowagers came to a venerable London hotel across from Hyde Park to take tea and make contact with young men. His friend was plying this escort racket—an old Slade standby among male acting students—to great effect. Having burned through his semester's allowance from his father, Jacob, looking for ways to stay in London that summer, proposed we try it.

In Paris I'd seen the movie of Tennessee Williams' *The Roman Spring of Mrs. Stone,* in which Warren Beatty plays the handsome, cruel young gigolo to aging, pathetic Vivien Leigh. What exactly would we have to do? Merely serve as companions to these women? Or did you have to sleep with them too? It depends, said Jacob. If you don't want to go to bed with them, you don't. Obviously he didn't know.

There's real money to be made, Jacob insisted. Besides, it would be an adventure, a lark. I was dubious. It was less the moral issues involved—I seemed to have already crossed that line with room to spare—than that I, wildly shy, uncertain, and sunk down inside myself, lacked Jacob's preening, extroverted theatricality. I couldn't remotely imagine romancing a woman as old as my mother. Anyway, I didn't have the clothes for it, I pointed out. Jacob ran to the closet and pulled out a second suit, shirt, tie, and shoes—all of which fit me perfectly, because of course we were the same size.

The next afternoon, dressed as the young escorts we were to play, we drove in Jacob's old black Citroën sedan to Hyde Park and left it around the corner from the hotel. Crossing the elegant lobby, suffering the desk clerks' derisive stares, I regretted having agreed to this.

Beyond, in a hushed, chandelier-hung anteroom, teatime was commencing. We were seated across the room from an array of powdered, bejeweled women of a certain age, sitting alone or with lady friends. A pair of waiters moved about with silver trays bearing teapots and platters of biscuits, serving as go-betweens, Jacob's friend had said, conveying messages from the ladies to the objects of their interest on the tea trays.

"We're the only guys here," I whispered to Jacob.

"All the better," he said coolly.

Ordering tea, I felt the women's scrutiny. Most, richly attired and heavily made up, looked to be on the far side of fifty. The apparent pathos of their situation—reduced to such devices for companionship, attention, or sex—found little in me to mirror their need: not scorn, or charity, or a need to be mothered, or vanity in being the object of their furtive gazes. I only felt ashamed, and began scheming routes of escape.

"Why would a fancy hotel like this allow this to go on?" I said under my breath when the waiter had left.

Jacob looked at me pityingly. "Tony, you are such a nice innocent boy from California."

The room seemed eerily quiet; there was only the rattle of teacups, clinking of spoons, patter of the waiters' feet. Jacob sipped his tea calmly, a napkin on his crossed knee. I felt rising panic. The more I tried mentally to project myself into congress with any of the women sitting opposite, the worse it became. They all became variations of my mother.

Jacob was nodding toward a jowly, pink-powdered lady with a frozen coiffure. "I think she fancies you. Definitely."

The rotund lady fished in her jewel-encrusted purse, extracted a notepad and a small gold pen, and jotted something. She tore the paper out, folded it carefully, and flagged the waiter.

The waiter crossed to our table and proffered his silver tray with the lady's note tucked discreetly among crumpets.

Jacob took the note and unfolded it.

"I would like to invite the handsome gentleman in the blue tie to my suite for a cocktail," it said, giving a room number on the fifth floor.

Jacob glanced at his blue tie dangling from my neck.

Across the room, the woman stood up and walked to the elevators, casting a slight glance back in my direction. I watched her commodious derriere disappear into an elevator.

"Definitely rich," said Jacob.

I looked back over at the tea tables. One woman, a late arrival, sat reading a book. Simply dressed in tweeds, she looked intelligent, interesting. Perhaps sensing my gaze, she glanced up over her bifocals, then back down at her book.

"What about her?" I said. "You go with the rich one."

"She isn't here for men. Can't you tell the difference?" Jacob nudged me. "Go ahead. She's waiting."

The waiter arrived again, this time bearing a note for Jacob.

Riding the elevator to the fifth floor, I thought of Betty, our married neighbor in Coldwater Canyon whose swaying breasts

I'd coveted at thirteen, and our silent, vaguely erotic afternoons before her television set. I'll talk with this lonely woman for a few minutes, I thought. No harm in that. She's just lonely. Then I'll excuse myself and leave.

The elevator door opened onto a hushed corridor. Pale floral wallpaper and peach-toned carpet stretched off into the silence. The aroma of cut flowers in a vase on a polished wood table thickened the cloistered air.

The room was halfway down the hall, the door ajar.

I hesitated, my mind racing. Was she already in negligee, awaiting my affections?

No, I can't do this, I decided. I started to turn away when I heard, "Come in, please."

Numbly I walked through the door. She was sitting on a settee in the middle of a large bedroom, a handkerchief clutched in her fist, looking as nervous and distraught as I was. She gestured to a tall plush chair opposite her.

I sat. The woman gazed worriedly at me in silence. Up close, her large blue eyes seemed rather kind. I watched them fill with tears.

"I'm sorry," she said, weeping into the handkerchief.

"I'm sorry too," I said.

"You're a lovely boy. You remind me of one of my sons. You shouldn't be here. Please go now."

Sobbing, she took an envelope from the table and handed it to me.

I placed it back on the table and stood up. I slipped out of the room, closing the door behind me.

Down the corridor, the elevator was still open; it made its soft bell sound as the doors closed around me.

In the lobby, there was no sign of Jacob. I walked back

through the tearoom without glancing at the waiting women. As I crossed the floor, the doors opened before me, letting in a heartening blast of fresh air from Hyde Park opposite.

I found the Citroën around the corner, where we'd left it. Jacob wasn't there. I stood against the car, lit a cigarette, and drew deeply. It was I who'd abased myself, I thought, not the woman. She caught herself in time; I'd already crossed the threshold.

I'd smoked the cigarette nearly down when I heard my named being called. I looked up to see Jacob running toward me, his jacket tails flying.

"Thank God," he said, breathlessly.

"What?"

"They didn't tow it."

I looked up at the sign. We were parked illegally, a ticket on the windshield.

Then we were inside the old Citroën, sweeping along with the traffic circling Hyde Park. I asked Jacob if he'd gone with a woman. He just said, without much conviction, "We'll come back tomorrow. The selection will be better."

We drove back to Hampstead Heath in the advancing evening, chatting and laughing about anything but where we'd just been. When we got back, Ravi took the photo of us that survives: Tony and Jacob, in near-identical narrow-legged dark suits and dark glasses, cigarettes dangling from pale digits, looking cool and svelte: a couple of matching young jerks.

The next day, I told Jacob I was leaving for Copenhagen. He offered me his Citroën to drive as far as Amsterdam and drop off at his mother's house. He wanted to stay on in London for the summer and couldn't afford to keep it up.

With a car at my disposal, I decided to stop off in Paris to pick up mail and see Leda. I'd brought no drugs into England, having left the remaining kilo bag of Congo hash with her in Paris. Still, every border crossing was a journey into fear, and on the ferry crossing to Calais, the gripping paranoia that had been a steady fact of existence since Tangier abated only after I'd passed without incident through French customs.

I arrived in Paris late that night to find Leda at her hotel, frightened and stoned. There'd been arrests across the Continent, she said. Interpol was closing in. Anyone who'd been through Tangier was marked. Galen was hiding out in Sussex somewhere. Dan, a guitarist I'd first encountered in the Canary Islands, then again in Tangier, had been arrested here in Paris. Leda, eager to get out of the city, asked if she could come with me as far as Amsterdam. She was a questionable companion under any circumstances, a magnet for attention: lanky, braless, neurotic, and embroiled in a complex pharmacopoeia of dubious palliatives. Okay, I said, but no drugs. You mustn't bring any drugs with you. She promised.

We took off in the old Citroën the next morning and reached Chartres by midday. The cathedral's luminous geometry soared before us but, drawn back into the conspiratorial alter-world of Tangier I couldn't seem to shake, I was far too agitated to enjoy it. A few hours later, we reached Brussels and parked downtown to buy food, planning to reach Amsterdam by nightfall. Passing a large department store, Leda said she needed to buy a couple pairs of underwear. She disappeared into the women's department while I waited outside.

When she emerged back out on the busy street, police suddenly surrounded us. I was shoved against a wall. A man in a business suit ranted at Leda in Flemish. A policeman grabbed her purse, opened it, and began removing nylons, underwear, lipstick, and a bottle of perfume—their price tags intact.

We were marched to our car. The policemen opened the Citroën and began rummaging through it. One opened Leda's suitcase and lifted out the plastic kilo bag of dark Congo hash I'd left with her.

This is it, I thought. We're finished.

The cop looked at the bag, held it to his nose, and sniffed. Then he put it down on the backseat, in full view, and continued searching the car.

The car was impounded; we were taken to the police station. For several hours we sat handcuffed on a bench in a corridor. I didn't dare say a word to Leda for fear of screaming at her.

Finally we were led into an office where a police captain interrogated us in English, his contempt merging with all I felt toward myself.

We were left alone again. There was a murmured consultation in the hallway, then the captain returned. The department store was willing to drop charges, he said, if we'd make restitution—and be out of Belgium by sundown.

By sundown. It sounded like a line from a John Wayne movie.

Quickly we agreed to both conditions. Our handcuffs were removed, Leda paid for the petty goods she'd taken, and we were led downstairs into the police garage. The Citroën sat with its doors open, the bag of dope on the backseat, exactly where the policeman had left it.

It made no sense. Unimaginable that the Belgian officials didn't know what it was. Why let us go? What indecipherable game was in play?

We drove to Holland in stony silence. In downtown Amsterdam I opened the door and told Leda to get out. She asked me for two cigarettes, which I gave her. "I'm sorry," she said over her shoulder, then disappeared into the night, taking my last kilo of hash with her.

I called Peter, a friend of Jacob's who lived on a houseboat on the Amstel. He offered to put me up for the night. When I arrived I found Dutch kids arriving in droves, drugs in tow. Peter, thinking to be hospitable, had invited all his friends to come over and meet me and get high. Nothing could have been more unwelcome. I felt tainted, trailing some terrible dark shadow.

The next morning, Peter said, "Is somebody following you?"

I peered out a porthole. Two men in windbreakers stood beneath a tree, eyeing the boat.

I had to get off the houseboat somehow, try and get the Citroën back to Jacob's mother, and leave Amsterdam. Swimming wasn't an option, so I simply grabbed my bags and walked ashore. As I passed the stakeout men, their eyes followed me but they didn't move. Once in Jacob's car, I circled around the canals to make sure nobody was trailing me, then drove to Hilversum, the suburb half an hour away where Jacob's mother lived.

She opened the door, a thin, querulous woman, her eyes full of fear. "Police have been here looking for you," she said. "What have you done?"

I tried to reassure the poor woman that I had done nothing and there must be some sort of mistake. I felt wretched: I'd stayed with her son in London and used her car, and now I'd brought her this trouble. I gave her news of Jacob, then declined the frightened woman's offer of dinner and hurriedly left.

It was growing dark. The train station was only a ten-minute walk away. After a few hundred yards, I turned and looked back down the street. Two police cars were turning into her driveway.

I ran to the station and caught the next train back to Amsterdam. Sitting by the clattering window, I wondered why they didn't just arrest me and get it over with, unburden me of this sickening pressure. I'd become a liar, a dissembler, secretive, and untrustworthy, all in a few months' time. If I got out of this, I vowed, I'd make a fresh start in Copenhagen.

At the Amsterdam station I hurried outside and took a taxi to the highway running east to Germany. I fashioned a cardboard sign that said ALEMANIA and stood in the dark by the roadside, my thumb out.

A German in an Opel picked me up. At the border checkpoint a guard asked for our passports. He took them and went inside his booth. While we waited, the driver offered me a German cigarette.

The guard walked back to the car and peered in the window. Glancing sharply at me, he handed back our passports and waved us through.

A few years after I left London, Jacob would achieve passing fame in a Jean-Luc Godard film. But before that, while I was still in Europe, he'd visited California and stayed with my family, frightening them with his vain intensity and unsettling stories of their son amok in Europe. He hung around California for a while, then worked his way back to Paris and roles in films. News would arrive by way of the travelers' circuit that Jacob was in Cap Ferrat with a rich woman and had a painting studio, or shooting a new film in Ibiza, or back in London acting in underground films. Somewhere around the end of the 1960s, news faded and I lost track of him.

Last fall, en route to an International PEN writers' conference in Warsaw, I arrived at my hotel in Amsterdam to find a note that "Jacob" had called. Could it be him, after all these decades? And how on earth could he know I was here?

The next night, I called California to inquire after my father. Nell told me that a few nights earlier Jacob had called from Amsterdam. Apparently feeling sentimental, he'd called Los Angeles information and discovered to his surprise that my father was still alive and living in the same house. To his greater amazement, Nell had told him that by sheer coincidence I was just arriving in Amsterdam, and she'd given him my hotel number.

I was ambivalent about calling him back; it stirred so many ghosts. I assumed Jacob—handsome, educated, multilingual, variously talented—had gone on to do interesting things in the intervening years: act, direct in film or theater, perhaps establish a career as a painter.

He called and left a second message. Finally he called a third time, when I was in. It was odd but not unpleasant to hear his voice. I suggested we meet and go have dinner somewhere. "I hope you've got money to pay for it," he said. "I don't."

That night, I waited for Jacob outside my hotel. He drove up on a rickety bicycle in a torn pea coat, a cardboard tube under his arm. His hair was long, gray, and unkempt; some of his teeth were missing. We embraced warmly and walked to a *ristoffel* restaurant nearby. Talking fitfully, popping an array of pills— "for high blood pressure," he said—Jacob painted a picture of a life of buying and selling antiques, running sports cars in from

Germany until his partner ripped him off, opening a bicycle shop for a while only to have all his bikes stolen when he forgot to lock the door. His physicist father, cancerous from his own nuclear-radiation lab experiments in England, had shot himself years ago. Recently his mother in Hilversum had died, leaving him a small inheritance. Broke and in ill health, with an array of children, ex-wives, and lovers scattered about Europe and the U.S., he was counting upon Holland's prodigal welfare benefits to keep him afloat.

We moved on to a bar and drank and talked about such people as we'd known and what had happened to them. We talked about my misadventures after I'd left London in his Citroën. But we never said a word about that afternoon at the London hotel when we tried to be gigolos. At the end we exchanged addresses, though it felt like a formality.

Before we parted, Jacob removed from the cardboard tube he'd brought a pastel drawing of the lighthouse at Cap Ferrat, and gave it to me. "1968," it said in the lower right corner.

"My best year," he said.

August 1999. The white stucco walls along Pacific Avenue flare
brick-rose in the late day. We're driving to my father's house—
my daughter, Maya, and I—for a Sunday-night dinner to celebrate Nell's birthday.

"So what's your take on Poppa?" Maya asks, using the
grandkids' name for him.

"His short-term memory is shot. Since the stroke he can't
remember ten minutes ago."

"They say goldfish have such small brains that each trip
around the bowl is like the first time. Poppa's like that now."

"He lives in a sort of eternal Connecticut. But he still con-
nects with things from way back. Real or imagined."

"The photo albums are still big."

"Yes."

"And flowers. He loves flowers." Sadness creases Maya's
face. "He says he can't remember being married."

Maya cherished her grandparents, who often filled in for
her peripatetic parents when she was a kid, sharing that grace
that sometimes blesses alternating generations. Appreciative of
that, I'd always tried to hide my tensions about my father, but
had failed, and we both know it.

Salt-spume smell floods the car. Ripple of salmon sky, surf,
abdominals along the beach. Sometimes I wonder how it is for
Maya, watching the elders go, one by one. She's known all four
grandparents and at least three great-grandparents here in

California, not to mention step-relatives. Hardly the cramped nuclear quadrangle I knew, the relatives all "back east." Still, Maya at thirty-two seems as unsettled as her father. Beautiful, bright, and interesting, she doesn't seem to be growing roots either. She produces state-of-the-art digital attractions for theme parks, the ones tomorrow's children will wander through. If my father's heyday of Jolson, Crosby, and Whiteman seems creaky and distant to me, I can only imagine what it looks like from her warp-speed perspective. Do my obsessions with writing, music, and travel seem as antique, a relic of the decades that spawned me?

"I called the house the other day," she says. "Nell sounds tired. They both do."

"Nell had an eye operation. Angela was sick but she's better."

"What if they can't maintain?"

"We may have to move Poppa to a nursing home."

I feel Maya flinch. "He's always said he wanted to die at the house," she says.

"There's a home in Santa Barbara, near Meg and the kids. I told his doctor last week I'm thinking about it."

"What was the reaction?"

"Nobody wants it." The light changes. Sunday beach traffic drifts forward. "I think Nell is lobbying Dr. Smith against the idea."

"Do you think Poppa would notice?"

"He doesn't know where he is half of the time. Some days he doesn't recognize Angela or Nell."

"But he always recognizes you."

"So it seems." I, reluctant protagonist, have ended up the central figure in this endless drama. That which you resist you become. Will I be the last person my father remembers before the lights go out? Or will I too become dim wallpaper, nameless and unrecognizable at the end?

Roller-bladers, backlit by the flattening sun, glide past against silvery palms. Crossing Santa Monica, I recall a visit home from college at nineteen, in sullen existential rebellion. Dad was in the driveway washing his new car, bought at a discount because Chrysler was a client of the advertising agency where he worked. I believe I made some smart-ass crack about his being a company man. He began telling me how after radio died he could no longer find work producing or directing in television, so he'd taken the job with the ad agency as "entertainment consultant." One day he'd had to go onto the set of a live television show and help rearrange a food display for a commercial in front of some big stars he used to direct on radio. He was trying to describe that humiliation—it must have been a bitter moment—perhaps to let his arrogant son know that sometimes in life you have to do things you'd rather not: to help your family, say, or put a son through college. I probably said in retort something like, "That must have been tough, Dad," feeling less pity than disdain at his confession.

What could I have done for this man? Offered more sympathy, surely, the understanding I myself craved but seldom received. Instead I punished him mercilessly with distance—often living in countries where, ironically, elders are cherished, honored, taken in, cared for.

"If Poppa goes to a nursing home, what would Nell and Angela do?" Maya asks.

"Nell would move back in with her kids, I expect. Angela would find another elder-care job. Or she'd go back to the Philippines. She has family there."

"They've done a lot for him."

True, I think. Before Nell and Angela arrived, I worried constantly about my father living alone: falling repeatedly, still driving his car to everyone's horror and consternation, preying upon strangers to assuage his aching loneliness. If Nell and Angela have brought aid and relief, now they're like family too, with needs and personalities to deal with. Some days it seems worse than before they came. My sister, Meg, always closer to Dad, will do anything to avoid coming to the house these days; there's strain between her and Nell, and now between Nell and me, since I turned down her request to support her daughter's business venture. Wednesday I went to see a doctor to be examined for cold sores, fever, swollen lymph glands. Stress, he said. In darker moments I think: Dad is dragging us all down with him. He should be in the hands of professionals now.

"Nell and Angela and the doctor probably think I want to move him to a nursing home so we can sell his house for money." I hear the defensiveness in my voice. "It's not about money," I snap. "It's about care."

"I know that, Dad," Maya says gently.

We get along easily, Maya and I. We talk about almost anything, have friends in common. How different it was with my parents. For all my absences or dereliction when she was young, Maya forgives and accepts me. She is more advanced in love than I, still disentangling from my father this late in life.

"Look," Maya says.

Ahead, traffic has slowed. Along the palisades a car has run up against a palm tree. Steam rises from the crumpled hood. The palm bark is black with scorch marks. A homeless man lies beside the car, curled up. A crowd runs toward the car, the man. The man slowly gets up, does a little dance.

"He's okay," Maya says, exhaling. "So's the driver."

Cars move ahead slowly along Ocean Avenue. I wonder: did I ever love my father? Maybe in early childhood. After that, there was affection, yes, when he was funny, kind, or endearing, even if his intent was to elicit praise or approval. When he listened to old music, innocence and pleasure filled his eyes, stirring my affinities. But somewhere around nine or ten years old, I'd sensed lies swirling in the air around us, obfuscations about who we were and what we were about. To enter our house was to ascribe to Dad's version of the world, an equation that never added up for me. *No, it isn't that way,* an inner voice countered. I'd set out, drumsticks in hand, upon a course of escape and correction.

The twist in the tale had something to do with origins, my mother's condition, things embedded in our lives long before that day when the Santa Fe Super Chief deposited our little nuclear family at Los Angeles' Union Station, fresh from New York. This opaque narrative, full of omissions and absences, had as its metaphor *suffocation.* We all smoked, coughed: Mom had asthma and emphysema; Meg suffered from nerves, skin rashes, had a breakdown in high school; I had asthma, hay fever, chapped lips, bit my fingernails. In our house full of smoke in a smog-choked city, anxiety was internalized in a fiesta of allergies and conditions. Everyone seemed diminished but Dad, hale patriarch, holding forth behind his newspaper, pipe clutched between his teeth, while Mom shriveled into isolation and sickness, Meg into an early marriage, and me into rage, rebellion, and flight.

There'd been no dialogue, no therapy, no forum to discuss my mother's drinking, my father's problems when his work world collapsed, the ghosts of their pasts that drove them so far from their own families. These were matters barely alluded to. The unspoken, the undisclosed, the unconfronted had to erupt in somebody.

The fresh air of college only confirmed the fraudulent nature of the family scenario. Through books I found ways to name it, denounce it. Suddenly I found myself among tribes of dazed youths exiting equally strange homes, caught in the dissonance between private dysfunctional family life and a public culture that sanctified it. I watched fathers replaced with Elvises, Kerouacs, James Deans. As sons rebelled against fathers, women began to rebel against men. Soon there would be no more isolated figure than the American father.

Dad's resistance was fierce. He contested and invalidated any new perspective—political, social, racial, spiritual—I brought through the door on visits home. At first I'd felt no need to go back in and challenge, enlighten, or rescue my family, only joy and relief at being away. But, relentlessly dismissed by him, I began battering back at his story, tearing it down. Violent arguments erupted around the dinner table, my mother wringing her arthritic hands, helpless to intercede. I challenged every view he held. I defended Mao, Ho, Castro, draft-card burning, psychedelics, revolt in any form.

Clearly the soil in which I grew up, half a generation deep, was going to offer little purchase. If the entry to the past was blocked by my parents, the way forward was wide open. I'd cede them that past, then, with its murky, freighted ambivalences, and set sail for the future, a place they couldn't go. I'd become an escape artist. I'd choose freedom over belonging.

Sometimes this drive from Venice to my father's house in Santa Monica Canyon becomes a sort of dream corridor. Passing the low-slung Spanish bungalows of Raymond Chandler's Bay

City, I think of Brecht's wartime stay here, which gave him his opera *Mahogonny* ("city of seduction and defeat, the antipode to critical intelligence," in author Mike Davis' description). Banking down into Santa Monica Canyon, I pass the street where, at Salka Viertel's table of exiles, Thomas Mann and brother Heinrich stood after a birthday meal to intone texts into the wee hours. Christopher Isherwood's house on my left stirs thoughts of him and Aldous Huxley and Igor Stravinsky driving in a top-down convertible to the Sunday bullfights in Tijuana, and how on their return Stravinsky was detained at the border as a suspicious alien. On a bluff to my right, a sleek Richard Neutra dwelling stands where a Polish sculptress my mother knew used to lounge topless by the pool; while I, at eleven, raptly watched her oil herself with Coppertone, observing for the first time the malleability of breasts.

Wisps of cultural anthropology, none of it mine. For me, growing up among august émigrés pushing supermarket baskets up aisles, my exile would have to be enacted elsewhere.

Canyon light deepens. Oak and pine trees become tall shadows. Sea breeze, pungent with salt and iodine aroma of kelp, floods the car.

"I visited Poppa last Sunday," Maya says. "There was this guy there in a toupee."

"Larry. The last of Dad's old cronies."

Eighteen years ago, at a Pacific Pioneer Broadcasters banquet at the Sportsmen's Lodge off Ventura Boulevard—Liberace was the emcee—Larry had presented my father with a Lifetime Achievement Award. It was the year before my mother died, a sweltering summer afternoon, and it had taken all she had to attend.

We'd sat at a round table among the old-timers, the guys

who started it all, who still call media "broadcasting." Their clubhouse and archive in the basement of the Home Savings Bank at Sunset and Vine is full of antique mikes and memorabilia, signed black-and-white glossies of George Raft, Dorothy Lamour, The Shadow, Red Skelton, Milton Berle, the names still sweet magic among the duffers, a half-century of new cultural movements but dust on yesteryear's great golden statuettes. *I got a million of 'em,* as Uncle Jimmy would say. When my father dies I'll donate his old air checks, wire recordings, wartime scripts, 78's, and photos to them.

I looked around the room at plaid jackets, golf caps, aging dolled blondes, flashing bridgeworks, and rust-colored hairpieces plopped over silver temples. Applause rippled across a sea of white tablecloths as Dad rose to receive his award, napkin still tucked in his shirt, crumbs at his chin. I lightly pulled away the napkin; my mother dabbed at the crumbs. Dad looked down at me, shy and proud. *Knuckle grazing my chin, forged celebrity autographs, a short-pants kid dribbling vanilla on the wine-red leather seats of the Buick Roadmaster...*

We all stood in unison to applaud Dad's last hurrah.

Oh, hell. Maybe I do love him.

I turn up the winding canyon road to my father's house, a drive I'll soon make for the last time, after years of reluctant revisits for Christmases, birthdays, fêtes, and illnesses, arguing with him in my mind or aloud, feeling that same knot in my stomach my sister feels now. Called back to the original scene of confusion, contention, and boredom, I suppress the urge to turn and speed off. Soon we, his weary descendants, will withdraw at last from this spot in space that held for forty-five years.

Lately I feel more like a doctor making a house call, enacting a somber but not unredeeming duty, my task clear: to offer, in lieu of unforced love, its symbolic and functional substitute—proximity, empathy, aid. Perhaps even burdens become comforts with repetition, I think.

When he goes, I go. Or so I figure. I never wanted to plumb secrets, puzzle out why it was the way it was, rummage through family baggage, extract meaning. Meaning lay anywhere but behind those dull doors. I bore the place no grudge; it had gotten me up and out. Wasn't that enough to ask of home? I only wanted the one thing my father never wanted to cede me: release.

How much energy has this inner struggle taken? What will replace it? When the end comes, will I feel the liberation I expect, greater even than the day I first left home for college? Or have I been so shaped by this burden that I'll unconsciously seek to reproduce it, find another, similar conundrum to attach myself to? Or perhaps, my nemesis vanquished, I'll merely slip into sloth and apathy. Has our tortured dialectic so thoroughly and irretrievably wound itself into my personality as to be inseparable from me? The thought makes me shudder.

We round the last curve and pull up before the wide lawn. Turning off the engine, I look up at the cracked redwood beam along the front of the garage. My mother's 1959 Ford Fairlane station wagon sat in that garage for fifteen years after she died. Dad kept the insurance up on it, as if maintaining a grave plot. Finally, two years ago, he let my nephew have it, bestowing upon him this great family heirloom.

Suddenly the front floodlights come on, illuminating the tropical hydrangea, birds of paradise, Hawaiian palms.

"Did you see that?" Maya says.

I look at my watch. Six-thirty on the dot. "It's on a timer."

So are we, I think, Dad's obsessive promptitude still driving us.

"Let's try and make it cheery," Maya says we get out of the car, gifts in hand.

Crossing the lawn, I throw my arm about her shoulder. We laugh, matching long strides.

Do it till you get it right, I think, as we reach the front door, already slightly ajar in anticipation of our arrival.

I arrived in Copenhagen in early July 1962, tired and frightened and broke. Without enough money to rent a room and still eat, I began sleeping nights on benches in the central train station. Policemen rotated through the place every twenty minutes, and though I'd try to remain sitting up, inevitably I'd drift back down and curl up, only to be startled awake and upright by a rude rap on the soles of my shoes. I'd slump back down, and the cycle would continue until dawn, when the station flooded with light and the cafeteria across the square opened. I'd order a cup of coffee and a pastry and jot or draw in notebooks, trying to stay awake until it was warm enough to find a grassy spot in one of the city's parks. Sometimes I'd go into the cafeteria bathroom and fall asleep sitting on the toilet.

I had a blanket a bum had discarded, and I hauled it around with me—hungry, unshaven, homeless, a derelict myself. I kept my backpack in a coin-operated storage locker in the train station, filched cigarettes from public ashtrays, hovered outside bakeries scrounging for stale throwaways. Abject, stripped of all self-regard or ability to act on my own behalf, I was indifferent to what happened to me as long as I wasn't arrested or sent to jail. Fearful of drawing attention—in fact, bent upon erasing myself from existence—I was dropping out the bottom of the world.

After some days and nights of this, I decided to go to the

Vingarden, the club where I'd drummed the fall before, during my first weeks in Europe. Palle the trumpet player was still there, though Niels, the young bass player, had moved to a bigger jazz club, the Montmartre. Palle, looking visibly shocked at my appearance, invited me to sit in. I thought I played well, considering how little drumming I'd been doing, but Palle kept looking at me as if to say: What's happened to you? Are you all right? The fresh-faced American drummer who'd thrilled him last September had resurfaced as a tattered wraith.

I hadn't realized my condition was so visible. I knew my clothes had become worn and too large, and I had to keep cutting new holes in my belt, and I hadn't washed properly in days, since there was no place to shower or bathe at the train station. I'd glimpsed my visage in the bathroom mirror at the cafeteria a few times, and my eyes did seem to stick out, my skin pale and jaundiced, my cheeks hollowed.

After the set, I waited around for Palle to offer me a job, or at least invite me to come play again. When he didn't, it frightened me: my drumming ability was the one thing I'd always been able to count on.

I was standing at the bar trying to sort this out when a young American in a trench coat sidled up and asked me if I knew where he could score some dope. Why me? Was it that obvious? Did I look like someone who would know? Was he an agent? Terrified, I shook my head no and fled the club.

That night I was told I was no longer welcome at the train station. I began sleeping in doorways or stairwells. Surely there was free lodging to be had somewhere in socialist Denmark, yet I was too beaten down to go find it. The summer nights were cold but endurable. I'd wander the streets until late at night, then huddle in my blanket on a stoop or in a stairwell, or move to another if I was chased off.

On the day I realized I was down to my last fifty-dollar traveler's check, I wrote my father a panicky letter asking him to advance me money for a plane ticket home, then tore it up. At American Express, after cashing the check, I went to the mail counter on the chance there might be a letter from home with money—though I couldn't recall when I'd last written, or if I'd asked for money, or if I'd instead chastised my parents for trying to restrict my freedom and holding my behavior to account.

There were two letters, one from Jacob in London, another from New York bearing no return address. I skulked away from the mail counter, feeling the old fears flood in. I imagined police having waited days for me to come pick up these incriminating missives, and now I was playing right into their hands. I stuffed the letters unopened in my pocket and walked outside. Glancing behind to see if I was being followed, I traced a tortuous, haunted route by way of various parks and boulevards back to the cafeteria.

I opened Jacob's letter first. Police had come back to his mother's house in Hilversum after I'd left and taken the Citroën away "for inspection," he said, returning it later without explanation. He wanted to know what I'd done; his mother was a nervous wreck and imagined her son to be some kind of criminal drug czar. He added at the end that Petrus, the Dutch pianist I'd played with in Paris, was in Copenhagen working at the Jazz House Montmartre.

I still couldn't understand why I hadn't been picked up in Holland. The Dutch police would have found traces of Leda's drugs on the floor and seats of the Citroën, easily enough to make an arrest in those times. I could only figure I was being spared by design, later to be picked up, charged, and given a jail sentence. Looking around the semi-deserted cafeteria, I wondered if even now I was being watched.

The second letter was from Leda, a drifting monologue telling me how her parents had sent her a plane ticket home from Paris, enrolled her in NYU, and gotten her into psychotherapy and onto tranquilizing drugs. No mention of the kleptomania in Brussels, only the hope that I was well, making music, and writing. (All summer I'd receive eerie, dense letters from Leda; then they'd stop. A few years later, I'd learn she'd hanged herself that winter in her mother's bathroom in Rye.)

Hurriedly I left the cafeteria and traced an elaborate route to the Nyhaven docks. There I tore the letters into bits and cast them on the water. With my remaining fifty dollars I got a haircut, had my shoes resoled, and bought a clean shirt.

I found the Jazz House Montmartre that night, on a quiet side street, slipped inside, and stood at the bar in back. The tables were packed with attentive Danes. If Paris had been the first to welcome American jazz artists fleeing racism, economic oppression, and indifference, now other European cities had thriving clubs as well. The Montmartre was heading into its first great jazz summer.

On a small stage in front, Petrus was etching his witty, Monkish stylings with the precocious Niels on bass and a local drummer. After a few tunes, two Americans mounted the stand: Bennie Bailey, an expatriate trumpeter living in Berlin, and Herb Geller, a quicksilver altoist from California whose work I knew. Their solos sizzled and soared. After the set, Petrus spotted me at the bar and introduced me. On his word, they invited me to sit in.

I mounted the stand gingerly, my confidence-sapping experience at the Vingarden still fresh. I sat down, weak from hunger, behind a worn Ludwig kit. The sticks were, reassuringly, Slingerlands, with the new plastic bubble tips that made them last longer.

Bennie called off "Night in Tunisia," Dizzy Gillespie's artful piece of bop exotica. I made a pattern with cymbals and tom-toms, blending echoes of the Gnaoua rhythms of Marrakech. To my relief, idea and act coalesced: the music leaped forward. Blood rushed to my head as I drove the tune through its sustained release, setting up the solos. Bennie flew through his choruses, riding time's current; Herb sliced the air with flashing thought. After Petrus bounced and clumped through his solo, I exchanged four-bar solos with each in turn—then eights, sixteens. At some point the others had stopped and I was playing alone, time flowing through my hands, gripped by that sensation when the mechanics drop away, rhythm accesses something beyond itself, and you feel as if being played, not playing.

We rode the tune out to waves of applause. Bennie and Herb were grinning and shaking my hand. I felt shaky, dazed. Petrus was rubbing his goatee mischievously, as if to say "See?"

At the bar, Herluf, the bearded Dane who owned the Montmartre, said, "That was great. Come and play again."

"Yes," I whispered. "Thank you. I will."

Then I was out in the cold night again, alone.

In the days to follow, I wandered the streets until nightfall, living for the hour each night when I'd sit in with the band at the Montmartre.

Finally Herluf proposed I work alternate nights with the local Danish drummer. When I told him I didn't have a place to stay, he offered me a room upstairs at the back of the club. I didn't ask how much money I'd get, and I didn't care.

My tiny room had a bed, a sink, and a light to read by. After the streets, it was paradise. At night, when work was done, I'd eat leftovers in the club kitchen, then go upstairs and fall happily asleep. I'd awaken around noon and meet Petrus for pastry, *smorrebrod*, and coffee, then go to the nearby baths for a soak. Afternoons I'd practice on an old drum set in the Montmartre basement, putting my technique back together. Sometimes I'd walk the city, past parks I'd slept in, or down along the Nyhaven docks, where I'd wandered nights with a blanket, looking for a doorway. The relentless undercurrent of agitation that had been with me since the draft physical in Paris began to abate. I began reading again, writing in my notebooks.

One afternoon, walking through a neighborhood of wide streets, I came upon a crowd of young Danes demonstrating in front of the U.S. Embassy. A few, recognizing me from the Montmartre, looked up at their placards sheepishly: "Cuba Si, Yanqui No!" The newspapers had been full of little else but the nail-biting nuclear standoff. As much out of curiosity as conviction, I joined them in protest. Afterward we went off to bars to drink Tuborgs.

The next day, a photo of the demonstration, one of dozens all over Europe, appeared on the front page of the *International Herald Tribune*. I am crowded in among the chanting Danish youths, several rows back, looking past the camera at my embassy, my mouth open, as if mouthing the vocable "a" of "Cuba" or the "Yan" of "Yankee." The photo probably found its way into some FBI or Interpol file. I cut the picture out and folded it into my notebook, meaning to send it to somebody back home as a wry statement—a triangulation report on position and place—but I forgot to do it. Years later it resurfaced, crumpled and faded, at the bottom of my drum case when I took out my last snare to sell it.

Long midsummer nights exploring the ruminations of Thelonious Monk, the weightless skywriting of Charlie Parker, the abstract interstellar voids of Miles Davis. Surely art redeems. The revelations in performance, the telepathic convergence of improvising minds, the listeners' responses—all that later, in writing's solitude, I'd miss most.

The musicians changed continually as new artists booked in for a week or two, or others passing through Denmark sat in. The little drug activity around the club I ignored; only the music mattered now. I wrote home and asked my father to ship my drums to Copenhagen.

Drumming is, almost by definition, a tool of seduction—I'd learned this long ago, that first night at the YMCA dance—and soon long, pale, pretty Danish girls, lost in crushes from their seats at tables in the club, would find me at the bar between sets, or come see me afterward. Sometimes they'd stay with me in my little room above the kitchen, or take me the next day to their favorite cafés or parks in the city.

One Saturday night in late July, I came offstage to find Dexter Gordon sitting at the club table in back where the musicians gathered, a saxophone strap hanging from his neck, suck-

ing on a reed. We were introduced; then the tenor legend unfolded himself—all six and a half feet—from his chair and
walked to the bandstand. Niels and I followed.

He counted off a familiar standard tune. After a clear statement of the melody line, he began his improvisation. His invention unfolded like a Japanese scroll, one line woven
flawlessly into the next, each chorus more fluent than the last.
When an idea completed itself, Dex, as he was called, would
hang near the tonic note, vamping with his fat sound, until
picking up the next wave of thought and spinning another long,
lucid line, rich with emotional logic. He played more than a
dozen choruses. It was the most commanding jazz performance
I'd heard (excepting Coltrane's in New York, which was of another order).

Dex was thirty-six at the time, recently released from ten
years in prison in California for heroin possession, and about to
take up a fifteen-year residency in Copenhagen, with the Montmartre as his base. If Coltrane had taken his influence to the
next level of possibility, Dex, a bridge from 1930s swing to "bebop" ("Such a trivial name for such a serious music," he'd say),
was content to range richly within the standard repertoire.
Musically, he was at the height of his powers. Bearing a vast
musical encyclopedia inside his head, he interlaced his improvisations with quotes, allusions, and witty asides from every
imaginable musical source. Niels, Petrus, and I were his rhythm
section, the carpet on which he rode, and we had to be attentive
and unflagging so as not to break the spell.

Offstage Dex was witty, ironical, veiled. Even with a fresh
start in clean Denmark, he hadn't licked heroin (nor would he).
Drug dealers from Germany would hover along the walls of the
club, happy to provide. Sometimes after his solo, Dex would sink

slowly into a crouch, eyes closed, until I'd wonder if one of us should rush forward and grab him before he fell offstage. Then he'd slowly rise back up to his full height, his horn finding its way to his mouth, and enter on cue and execute perfectly.

With Dexter Gordon installed at the Montmartre, every great jazz figure touring Europe that summer—Horace Silver, Cannonball Adderley, Wayne Shorter—stopped by to visit and sit in. I played with them all. I couldn't believe my good fortune.

One night I looked down from the stand and saw a familiar face sitting at a table alone, nodding to the music. It was Marcus, whom I'd met in Tangier the night of Barbara Hutton's party. I liked Marcus, a black anthropology student from Boston who'd dropped out of graduate school to travel; but anyone from Tangier was a dissonance, an unwelcome apparition here in my musical haven.

After the set, we stepped outside and talked. Marcus was on his way to Stockholm to visit friends and had happened upon me here, amazed to find me drumming in such company. Through a friend at the U.S. Consulate in Tangier, Marcus had learned more of what had happened: Mad Ludwig had stopped tapping on his drum long enough to finger every foreigner he knew, culpable or not, to Interpol. Rafe and I, small fish not worth bothering with, had indeed been spared arrest in order to tag larger dealers across Europe. We hadn't proved out, except in the instance of Edwin in Paris, apprehended with the Congo hash a few days after Rafe and I sold it to him and given a long jail sentence. Others we'd known in Tangier had been picked up and were in jail elsewhere. Even now our whereabouts were surely known, Marcus said, each border crossing noted and reported, warrants sitting on desks waiting to be activated.

Suddenly talking together like this seemed dangerous. We

shook hands and said hasty goodbyes. Marcus vanished into the night.

Walking back into the club, I thought how the paranoid conspiracies of Interpol were far more byzantine and deluded than the ones of those they pursued. The fact that Rafe, Leda, and I, merely foolish young travelers, were seen as part of some grand narcotics cabal was exactly what had rescued us from our own incredible stupidity—caught, then let go in Algeciras, Paris, Brussels, and Amsterdam in the hopes we'd lead them to bigger fish!

Word came that my drums from California were waiting down at the customs docks. I claimed them, set them up in the Montmartre, and began practicing with a vengeance. Each night with Dex the music rose another increment; and lurking around the club bar were other good drummers from New York, Chicago, or Paris, waiting to move in if I faltered.

I'd been playing at the Montmartre almost a month when Herluf the owner drew me aside and told me the piano legend Bud Powell was arriving from Paris to play the first two weeks of September, alternating sets with Dexter Gordon. Herluf wanted me to back both artists—a prospect beyond my wildest jazz dreams.

That summer at the Montmartre, far from home and lost to it, I was challenged, exhilarated, happy. With barely enough money to eat, I worked every night at a strenuous level of performance with artists of supreme emotional and technical intelligence. After drug dealing, border crossings, and brushes with dementia and jail, the long days and nights of playing and listening, reading and writing, seemed like a reprieve, a wild gift, patterning a possible adult artistic life to be attained.

During this period I received a letter from my father scolding me for my aimless, dissolute existence. It was time, he said, for me to come home and take up my responsibilities. There was no mention of the work I was doing, the musicians I was playing with, or the fact that I was making a living, however slight.

I fired off a furious, aggrieved retort. What responsibilities? I asked. Why should I return to bury myself in some mediocre job? And to whom do I owe these responsibilities you speak of? Is someone ill, needing my support? I was certain I heard envy in his voice, and betrayal. I was living a free life, working with greater musicians than he had, violating implicit boundaries he'd set to make sure I'd never surpass him.

We'd disappointed each other yet again.

The week before Bud Powell arrived at the Montmartre, I came downstairs one morning to find a girl cleaning the club kitchen. Eva was nineteen, an art student, just back from London, where a relationship with an English musician had gone bad. Herluf had given her a job in the club while she figured out what to do next before art school resumed.

Eva was part Inuit, with wide cheekbones and sloe eyes beneath jet-black bangs. Smart, inward, and alluring, she had no shyness. Our first lovemaking, in a friend's apartment where she was staying, was frank and guileless—so different from the tortured, ambivalent sexual battlefields of my American youth.

The Montmartre had been buzzing with the imminent arrival of Bud Powell, scheduled to debut the following Tuesday.

Then, during our last set Sunday night, Dex unexpectedly announced him from the stage.

From my seat behind the drums, I watched him emerge from behind the bar in back. He was wearing a beret, an overcoat a little long at the sleeves, a suit and tie beneath. He looked to be about forty (he was thirty-eight), stout, with a mocha complexion and a thin, trimmed mustache. He strode deliberately through the club toward the bandstand with an expressionless mien, his left arm swinging slowly at his side, seeming to part the applauding audience like water (a space-altering effect celebrated in Thelonious Monk's tribute "In Walked Bud").

Of course I knew his work from the legendary recordings of the late 1940s and early '50s, flights of conceptual fluency and drive that modeled the language every jazz pianist since had been obliged to use. Only Charlie Parker rivaled his improvisatory powers. His early difficulties were part of jazz lore—epic tales of art and betrayal, martyred genius, alcohol and drugs, asylums and jail, mental breakdowns, heroic performances ("Were you there that night at Birdland when Bud Powell played forty-four choruses of 'Cherokee'?"). The mordant titles of his compositions—"Dance of the Infidels," "Oblivion," "Glass Enclosure"— suggested a mind off in its own strange corner. He'd moved to Paris in the late 1950s—a shadow of his former self, some said— and often worked with his trio at the Blue Note.

As Bud Powell stepped onto the Montmartre stage, Petrus, with a genuflecting flourish, relinquished his piano seat. Dex called off "Celia," a lyric, graceful Bud Powell composition, and Niels and I slid into an easy groove behind Dex's shapely choruses.

Bud Powell began his solo in a welter of lapses, flubs, fluffs. Slowly he gained footing and moved forward; still, I heard only an echo of his recorded brilliance. At best, he sounded like a slightly fuzzy Bud Powell imitator. From time to time he looked balefully up at Dex or Niels or me, lost in a distracted cloud, it seemed.

We finished up the tune to polite applause. It was an awkward, disturbing, unpersuasive debut.

I laid my sticks down on the bass drum, my mind full of questions. Perhaps Bud's seeming flatness was an illusion. Had his disciples so thoroughly imitated and absorbed him that the original sounded weak? Maybe the next generation, into freer forms, had buried the mainstream bop innovators' message beyond recognition. Yet Dexter Gordon was from the same era, and his intense, integral improvisations still commanded; Miles Davis' still thrilled.

Backstage I found Bud sitting with his hands in his lap, a puzzled, bedraggled expression on his face. A large black woman in a hat was standing over him.

"That's it for you, Bud Powell!" she railed. "I'm leaving!" She turned and stormed out.

Buttercup, Bud's common-law wife and court-appointed caretaker, furious that Herluf had given Bud an advance (which he'd used to get drunk) instead of turning it over to her, left for Paris that night, taking Bud's suitcases with her, leaving him with nothing but the clothes he was wearing.

Herluf quickly appointed Petrus Bud's caretaker. Nothing could have suited the pianist better, since only Monk was equal in his pantheon to Bud Powell. Each day Petrus went to Bud's little apartment near the club, saw that his lone suit and shirt were pressed and that he was shaved and ready for work, then fetched him a taxi to make sure he arrived at the club on time.

Weeks passed in creative ferment, each night brimming

with intense beauty and peril. I drummed with the ad-hoc Dexter Gordon Quartet (me, Niels, Petrus), then the Bud Powell Trio (me, Niels), then Dex again, then Bud. My recent troubles seemed insignificant beside the heavy behavioral baggage Dex and Bud bore, and its effects in performance—the oxygenating flights, the sudden sickening dips. Aware of the extraordinary circumstance I found myself in, I practiced daily, wanting to live up to the music each night.

The Montmartre was packed every night. Musicians and fans, drawn by the great double bill, arrived from all over Europe. Louis Armstrong's band stopped by, and the musicians from Art Blakey's and Horace Silver's units. Sometimes I'd think about Drew and Chaz from high school, or Art the pianist from the strip joint, and wish they could share this. I'd think of my father watching me play too, but tried to block it out, suspecting he'd be compelled to belittle it. Mostly I felt a growing distance from my past and thought of it as something cast off now, skins I'd shed.

Bud Powell, delivered from Buttercup's constant harangues, gained consistency in his playing, and some nights there were glimpses of the old inspiration. When this happened, luxurious inventions of purity and force poured forth from some clear, unnameable source outside of ordinary time.

Bud's playing always exuded a sense of danger, as if at any minute the entire web he was weaving might collapse; or as if he were (that comment often made about genius) struggling to translate from some language no one else heard. Sometimes a solo fractured into incoherence, and we'd be left plowing through shattered glass, bar by bar, limping to the tune's battered end. One night Bud stopped dead in the middle of a solo, hands upraised a few inches above the keyboard, staring into space—as if the transmission from the home planet had simply dropped out. Niels and I glanced at each other in alarm, continuing to vamp, play time. The audience began to stir. Just when we'd begun to wonder if we should simply stop and escort Bud off the stage, he reconnected and tore through the rest of the performance.

Offstage, Bud could do little for himself. In between tunes or backstage, he'd sit very still—blank, passive, in some impenetrable haze—only his fingers moving in his lap. Sometimes he'd hum snatches of favorite Beethoven themes. When he did wander out into the club between sets, it was usually to coax a beer from a stranger—a ploy he'd cultivated in Paris, since Buttercup never gave him any money. (Bud's flat, wheedling "Buy me a beer" had become legend across Europe.) He reacted terribly to alcohol, which collided with Largactyl, one of the ferocious tranquilizing drugs he'd been prescribed after his New York incarcerations. One beer and Bud was stumbling.

"Hey, Tony. Buy me a beer."

"I can't afford it, Bud."

"Why not? How much do you make?"

"A hundred kroner a night less than you make."

Bud looked puzzled. "How much do I make?"

All of us at the club were touched by Bud. Speculations on the mystery of his condition dominated conversation. I knew he'd been a prodigy, absorbing and performing in recital most of the classical and jazz repertory by age ten. Then, when he was nineteen, a vicious clubbing at the hands of police had left him with headaches, blackouts, disorientation. Mental hospitals had followed, and a panoply of dubious treatments—electroshock, restraints, experimental drugs—that only worsened his condition. Intermittently he'd emerge to stupefy the jazz world with

epic, nerve-shattering performances, extending the strato-
spheric reaches of high bebop, then drift back into the medical
twilight. To visitors at Creedmore, in upstate New York, where
he spent several lengthy periods, he'd complain, "They're de-
stroying my mind. I can't compose."

Dexter Gordon was as bedeviled by the riddle of Bud as the
rest of us. One night we were sitting backstage between sets
with some visiting musicians from New York. Bud sat blankly,
hands in his lap. Suddenly Dex said, "Bud, why don't you stop
with this 'crazy' act of yours? You're not fooling anybody but
yourself. Back in the States pianists are making fortunes off
your innovations. Why don't you pull yourself together, go back
there, and claim what's yours?"

The room grew uncomfortably silent. Bud gazed steadily at
Dex with his large, damp eyes. The two went back to 1940s New
York and the musical revolution they'd forged; both knew its
human cost in drugs, drink, madness, and death. Then Bud said,
in his flat, affectless voice, "Dexter, are you a junkie?"

It was a withering retort. Dex, a confident man, wasn't easily intimidated. Trying to make a clean life in Europe after
years of addiction, he was failing. Bud had said the one thing
that could hurt him, and in front of us all.

Dex stood up and walked out, shaking his head.

(In a twist of fate, years later Dexter Gordon would star in
Bertrand Tavernier's jazz film *Round Midnight,* playing a character modeled on Bud Powell.)

Another night, I was sitting quietly beside Bud between sets
when he suddenly took my hand in his and began stroking it
gently. Looking deeply into my eyes, he said, "Tony, I love you."

I was caught completely off guard. Emotion welled up.
Bud's declaration, so open and childlike, collapsed all the dis-

tance between us. It was as if some broken thing in him parodied or imitated the "normal" world of feelings, which he was very far from by then, and came out as an attempt to talk to us in our emotional language. At the same time, it felt perfectly pure and sincere. I felt stripped bare, as if Bud had seen to my very core.

"I love you too, Bud," I said, fighting back tears.

That night, Eva and I lay awake in my room above the club, speculating about Bud. Maybe he's just a reflection of ourselves, Eva said. What we love, what we fear. What they call in the East an avatar, I said—someone whose passage through life reveals others to themselves.

On one of his last nights at the Montmartre, Bud suffered one of his lapses mid-solo and simply stopped playing. Niels and I, used to this by now, just kept playing time, waiting for him to resume. Bud remained gazing into deep space, his mouth open, his hands suspended in space over the keyboard.

Minutes passed. The audience grew restive. Finally we just stopped playing. I stood up, walked over to him, and whispered "Bud." Gently I took his arm and led him offstage.

He sank onto a chair backstage. I'd never seen him look so sad, so beaten, so collapsed. Herluf the owner arrived and called a doctor. It looked as if Bud was finished for the night.

I walked out into the thronged club. A couple of New York hipsters were standing at the bar in back in dark sunglasses and cool clothes, loudly disparaging Bud. He's finished, they said, washed up. They mentioned several younger, imitative pianists whom on a good night Bud would have devoured.

No, you're wrong, I wanted to protest. *Bud can be as good as he ever was.* But on the evidence, these guys were right. It was so sad.

Music arose from somewhere in the noisy club. I noticed that the crowd up front had quieted down. I saw Bud sitting alone at the piano.

He'd begun to play a ballad, "I Remember Clifford," written in memory of the trumpet genius Clifford Brown, who'd died in an auto accident at twenty-five—the same crash that had taken the pianist Richie Powell, Bud's younger brother.

The noise in the room subsided. The bartenders stopped making drinks. The waitresses froze along the walls. Bud rendered the stately, dolorous dirge with full command, filling the room with a deep, aching beauty.

When he finished, the club was silent as church. There was no applause, only soft weeping, blowing into handkerchiefs.

It was the saddest, loveliest, most beautiful performance I'd ever heard.

Bud stood up and walked slowly offstage. I looked over at the hipsters, their heads bowed in contrition.

I hurried backstage to the kitchen. Bud looked lost, drained. Petrus was helping him on with his coat. "Today would have been his brother Richie's birthday," he whispered.

In the photo above my desk in the Venice cottage, Bud peers into the camera, a fixed, forced grin on his face. His round, soft, beautiful hands rest on the keyboard. Niels and I are out of focus in the background—tall, skinny white kids in dark slacks and white shirts. Bud looks intent, distracted, as if trying to contact the person or spirit inside the camera and convey some urgent truth. The glossy press photo from some publicity session at the Montmartre seems as empty of affect or meaning as if it were blank: Bud Powell, impersonating a "piano player." His frozen gaze seems to ask: "Where are we? Is this all a joke?"

Bud was scheduled to leave for Paris by train on Monday. Sunday night, before work, Herluf said, "Bud, I want to buy you a going-away present to celebrate your wonderful time with us here. What would you like? How about a suitcase?"

Petrus and I looked at each other, trying not to laugh. We knew Bud had nothing to put in it: Buttercup had taken everything back to Paris. Naïve Herluf had been in the dark about this.

Bud looked at Herluf, deadpan, and said, "Yeah, I'd like that, Herluf. Thank you."

The next afternoon, we gathered in front of the club to wish Bud goodbye. He came walking slowly toward us in his lone suit, hat, and overcoat, his eyes flat and looking straight ahead, his left arm swinging softly at his side, carrying in his right hand the expensive new suitcase Herluf had bought him. He bore it with great solemnity and care, as if it were packed with suits, ties, bottles of the best cologne. There wasn't a single thing in it—not a razor blade, not a handkerchief, not a pair of socks.

Bud gravely shook each of our hands. Eva hugged him and wept. We were all going to miss him terribly. Now he had to go back and face Buttercup's wrath, resume his gig at the Blue Note in Paris. (Three years later he'd be dead in New York, officially of tuberculosis.)

"How's the suitcase, Bud?" Herluf said.

"It's very nice, Herluf. I like it. Thank you," he said in his empty, polite voice.

The taxi pulled up. With what seemed an exaggerated show of dignity, Bud handed the empty suitcase to the cab driver, who, after a slight show of surprise at its weightlessness, put it in the trunk. Bud, betraying no expression, got in the taxi.

Petrus and I looked at each other, overwhelmed by love, sadness, confusion, hilarity, fighting not to bawl like babies.

"Goodbye, Bud," we all called as the taxi drove off.

Bud never looked back.

The days were growing short, the weather was turning cool. A Swedish unit was booked into the Montmartre for November. Dexter Gordon had left for an engagement in Germany. The great summer of jazz was over. It was time to move on—somewhere south, preferably, where it was warmer. Eva said she wanted to come with me.

Herluf had a new partner, an American named Harold who had owned a jazz club in San Francisco. Harold had this idea about opening a second Montmartre on the island of Mallorca, off the coast of Spain. His partner would be the great English poet and mythophile Robert Graves, who lived in the little village of Deya, about an hour from the capital of Palma, where the new Jazz House Montmartre would be. Graves, a jazz fan and amateur drummer himself, was apparently keen on this idea.

Harold proposed that I go south and set up the new club with Graves, then stay on as the house drummer. Acts would be cycled down from Copenhagen to stock the fledgling club. Graves, deep into middle age by then, would be the resident spirit, and I'd let the venerable poet sit in and flail away from time to time. I had a little saved up from the summer, which Harold supplemented with enough seed money to get Eva and me to Spain. He promised to send down additional funds and my drum kit as soon as I'd established myself in Palma. More interested in meeting the author of *The White Goddess* and *Goodbye to All That* than running a jazz club, I agreed.

A few days before leaving Copenhagen, I received another letter from my father, more conciliatory, offering to wire me money for an SAS polar-route flight direct to L.A. Instead I left Denmark with Eva, hitchhiking south through Germany, bearing my letter of introduction to Robert Graves.

"Peas?"

"No, *peace*," Nell says, smiling.

"Whazzat?"

"Peace, Dad!" I shout.

"Peas? No, thank you."

Laughter erupts. Dad sits at the head of the dining-room table in bathrobe and wheelchair, Nell to my left, Maya across from me. Angela is in the open kitchen readying food. Dad smiles sweetly. He doesn't mind being the butt of comedy as long as attention is paid him.

"I do think your father is entering a state of grace," Nell says, radiance flooding her face.

It's true that lately, as my father's grip on the outside world loosens, a residual childlike sweetness emerges in him. Intimations of calm settle about the house. We all feel it tonight and let each other know. Nell credits my being here with Dad's change in temperament; I'm more inclined to believe Nell's calm manner, her affinity, and her Hindu-Buddhist counsel have helped quell Dad's grasping, fretful ego at last. Still, there are moments when my skepticism kicks in, inclining me to recall how sometimes Dad just figures out which way the wind is blowing and plays to the crowd he has.

Nell, a student of yoga, lives much of the time on what she'd call "the spiritual plane," attuned to life's invisible qualities. She and I share certain understandings about this. Nell knows I studied Buddhism, and she's equally curious about Gurdjieff, Scientology, Sufism, anything having to do with mind or spirit. Knowing she reads the yogic magazine *Parabola*, my birthday present to her is a subscription to *Tricyle*, the Buddhist one. Sometimes, while Dad sleeps or gazes at the television, we talk softly of less temporal matters. Nell feels we are all one, indeed all is one; and though I have a slightly different view about that, we agree in many essentials. I've encouraged her to share her concepts of acceptance, the flow of life and death, with Dad, for so long earthbound and anxiously mired in the material, and I think he's taken some of it to heart.

When Nell first came to live here three years ago, she encountered a far different man from the dashing family friend she and her husband had known since swing-era days in New York. She wasn't prepared for Dad up close. On days when Nell wasn't sure she could manage it, she'd turn to me—of all people!—for counsel. "Play to his sense of humor," I'd say. "Refuse his endless demands. Draw boundaries or you'll go under." Gradually she became tougher with him, as was necessary, and when my father whispered to me one day, "Nell's a bitch sometimes," I knew she was going to make it.

Angela joins us in raising glasses to Nell. "Happy birthday!"

"Happy New Year," Dad sputters.

"It's Nell's birthday!" I shout.

"Happy Easter!" he burbles.

More laughter. He wants desperately to participate but refuses to put in his hearing aid; so, since he can't understand what's being said, he only responds with mutters or *non sequitur*s. We just talk around him until he gets so frustrated he bursts out with something, anything, to stop the show and get us looking at him. Tonight he knows something festive is happening and spirits are high. Cake crumbs stuck to his chin, he catches my eye, then nods toward the living-room piano. "Play," he says.

He always used to do the "Happy Birthday" song, but in recent years the task has fallen to me. I'd picked up a little piano in youth. On the music stand of the black spinet, the old songbooks are there—Rogers and Hart, Gershwin, Jerome Kern, and some sheet music of a song Dad co-wrote in 1929.

Angela wheels him over, Maya and Nell gather round. I hammer out a version in F, my best key along with B-flat. Dad moves his lips, unable to keep up with the words; but his benign expression tells me the music pleases him.

When we finish, Maya and I try in vain to get Nell to sing something. Once a lead singer with the great vocal groups of her era, she, unlike my father, has put her show-business days behind. A few years back, Dad was regaling a roomful of guests about old radio days and Nell, in an aside (asides were easy with Dad, what with his failing hearing and his self-absorption), said lightly to the rest of us, "Well, I was there and none of what he's saying happened. But so what?"

So what. I noodle the bass melody line of Miles Davis' tune of that name, which Dad wouldn't recognize—his jazz knowledge foundered at bebop—then drift into a slow blues. I move to the opening bars of the *Goldberg Variations*, the only part I can play without sheet music. He smiles with pleasure at the music, and probably at the idea that I'm making it, however badly. Chip off the old block, a second-generation hack pianist, my father's son after all.

"Not bad," he mutters.

If that's as good as I'll get from him, I can live with it.

Putting the piano lid down, I think: If I'd sent him to the

nursing home we wouldn't be having this little evening. I must try to keep him here until the end. If only the rest of us can hold on somehow. . . .

The photo albums are out. Maya and I sit on either side of Dad's wheelchair. In the background the local jazz station plays Sarah Vaughan's syrupy reading of "Lullaby of Broadway." Nell has retired to her room, Angela to hers. On Dad's lap, we're in the late 1940s in Coldwater Canyon. The four of us, plus my maternal grandfather, Bob, and flamboyant step-grandmother, Edwina, pose in bright sunlight, dressed and groomed to the hilt.

"Fancy job," Maya says.

"He must have hired some big-time photographer."

Indeed, the creamy black-and-white images on thick seven-by-ten-inch matte paper, the artful setups, bespeak an A-list Hollywood job. Why else, on a sunny L.A. afternoon, would the women be in fancy summer dresses and jewelry, the men in suits and ties, my sister in a ruffled little dress and Mary Janes, me gotten up like a little Eastern dude in pressed shorts with suspenders and a matching jacket I never wore? Nothing but the best in those days.

Turning the page, I gaze at my mother and me standing before the tall front door of the big house, my little hand in hers. She has on a stylish jacket over a blouse and skirt, a hat and veil.

"How beautiful she was," Maya says of her grandmother, whom she resembles.

I can't take my eyes off her either. I hadn't realized my mother was pretty until later in life. Now when I look at her image I get lost in the face—the cheekbones first, then the swept Nefertiti forehead. Finally I start scanning the expression for some sign of the anguish that would soon take her under. Was she drunk in this picture, from some gin bottle secreted beneath the Beautyrest mattress, assuaging the strain of hosting her wayward father and nutty stepmother on a visit from Manhattan? A fair guess, given that time.

Early incidents float into view: I am four and wander off from our house with another little boy. Mom runs down the street after me in a bathrobe, arms outstretched, crying hysterically, fearing that she'd lost me, that I'd been kidnapped, abducted. That must have been the first time I realized what I meant to her, and that I could hurt her by leaving. Another night, later, in the Coldwater Canyon house, Dad back in New York. A tall, mustachioed doctor with a black house-call bag visiting drunken Mom. He was always around in those days, it seemed. She had this inordinate adulation of doctors, scholars, men of learning. Meg and I would wonder years later if that doctor was a crush item, or more.

My mother, whose image radiates from tables and bookshelves and walls in this house, is the ghost in the drama, the linchpin. She was the one, I know now, who civilized my father, saved him from his worst impulses. When she died she left him rudderless, needy, exposed. She knew what was in store for us after she died. Years of attending to him have led me to understand her better; and sometimes I feel I know why she drank.

Different people leave behind different auras after death, not always what one might suspect from the lives they led. My mother's light burns ever more brightly in this family. The rest of us speak of her with near reverence these days.

What will my father's wattage be? Mine?

"Meg?" Dad says, stabbing at the photo.

"No, that's Mom. Mary Helen. Your wife," I say.

Dad frowns, looks fretful. "Where is she?"

"She's here, Poppa," Maya says softly.

Good answer, I think. Maya has my mother's compassion. Thank God, because I don't.

"Poppa, look," Maya says, turning the page. "Jimmy Durante."

Schnozzola's head is thrown back in laughter. My father stands opposite him in a pinstriped suit. They thrust unlit cigars toward each other as if jousting. This was at the supreme height of the weekly CBS hit comedy radio show, when at the end of every week's live broadcast my mother, sister, and I, sitting at home in the big house in Coldwater Canyon, would wait for the announcer to intone, "Produced and directed by Phil Cohan!" and then we'd applaud.

"Who?" Dad says.

"Inka dinka doo . . ."

Dad looks distressed. "No. No more pictures," he says. Agitated, he pushes the photo album away. "Angela!" he calls over his shoulder, honking the little klaxon attached to his wheelchair, signaling her to come and roll him to his room.

"I don't like to dwell upon the past," my father always used to say, when it was obvious to anyone that this was practically all he did. This time I know he means it. The footage has run off the reel.

Maya and I are left gazing into Dad's memory palace, which I suppose is ours now.

I shut the album and place it on the coffee table.

Dad lies against his pillow in the curtained bedroom. I sit in a chair beside him. The portable television set on his dresser is on, the sound low. Nell and Maya are in the living room talking.

Penguins swarm on ice floes. Waves crash against a steep Antarctic cliff. The penguins inch toward the edge. The first one waddles forward, hesitates, then jumps into the surf. The others follow en masse, flailing in space, wings whapping, alighting on the choppy waters.

My father lies with his hands folded across his chest, penguin images flickering on his retinae. "Tony boy," he whispers, reaching his hand out and squeezing mine.

He seems content, watching the penguins with me like this. Usually I'm too restless to sit and watch television with people. But penguins I could watch forever. If I hadn't become a musician or a writer, I think I might have become a marine biologist, maybe even gone to Antarctica and studied penguins.

Dad's new imperturbability is a surprise and a balm. Is it simply physical attrition, the inability to impose himself on things, that has softened him? Or is it *my* ego that has exhausted itself, crashing up against the shores of his, like those breakers battering the ice floes? Ill-at-ease across a lifetime, we're almost comfortable together now.

A penguin mom stands over an egg, jostles it into place between her feet to keep it warm, nudges it with her beak. My father murmurs something.

"What's that, Dad?"

"I'm ready to go now."

I look at him. "Go where, Dad?"

"Upstairs."

"Ah," I say. "Upstairs."

The penguin egg has hatched into a beaked, featherless

baby. The mother has lost many kilos of weight. The father returns to feed the mother mouth-to-mouth. Mom scoots the baby beneath Dad so she can go off and feed herself. Big gulls swoop down to try to snatch the raw little hatchlings during the transfer.

I turn and look at my father. Penguins and gulls flicker in his eyeballs. Then his eyes close, and the penguins are gone.

"Dad?" I whisper.

No answer.

He lies very still. Alarmed, I bend close to his mouth to see if he's breathing. The tiniest air stream hits my cheek. The sheet over his chest rises and falls, shallowly but evenly.

I remove my hand from his, get up, turn the sound down, and tiptoe out.

When I was a drummer, I never knew what the night held in store—where the music would go, who would come to hear it, whom I might go home with afterward. My brief encounters with daylight passed in that mute haze of anticipation every performer knows—a state akin to fear, near to rapture. My colleagues and mentors—expiring virtuosi and rising stars, strange geniuses and hoary legends—imprinted me no more or less than other madmen, criminals, and beauties who peopled my days and nights.

By the winter of 1962, I'd been drumming half my life—since I was eleven—in school bands and orchestras, at dances and weddings, in murky bars and jazz clubs, in strip joints and lounges, in cavernous rehearsal halls and muted recording studios, on outdoor bandstands and overlit concert stages. Drumming had shaped and defined me.

One day when I was twenty-nine I'd leave a recording session, drive to a drum shop, and sell my last set of traps. I'd never play again. Choice had little to do with it. The alternative would have been—so I was convinced at the time—death.

There were two incidents that prefigured the end of my drumming life, though neither explains it. The first took place that Christmas of 1962 in Barcelona.

In the photo, I'm standing in a plaza in snow. There's a Gaudi streetlamp behind me, and a wrought-iron bench. I wear a threadbare black sport jacket over a dark turtleneck sweater, cheap slacks, and worn, pointed Italian boots. A pair of scuffed drumsticks protrudes from one of my pockets, from the other a small leather-bound notebook. An arch frames a neon sign that says: CLUB JAMBOREE.

Beside me in the photo stands a young woman with round cheeks, sloe eyes, and dark bangs. Grinning, she beats her mittened hands against the cold. The fact that Eva is in the picture means someone else must have taken it: Memphis Slim most likely, or Guitar Murphy.

Turning the creased black-and-white snapshot over, I read: PLAZA REAL DECEMBER 21 1962, scrawled in light-blue ink. A week before my twenty-third birthday. The little snapshot had floated up from among my mother's things when she died.

A freak snowfall had hit northeastern Spain that week, I remember. Hawkers sold mittens and scarves along the Ramblas, shovels became sleds, and in the plazas children built their first snowmen. I was working the Club Jamboree, a *cave* in the Plaza Real off the Ramblas, with the blind Catalan jazz pianist Tete Monteliu and blues master Memphis Slim. Six nights a week, eight sets a night, I fueled Tete's sleek, witty bop investigations of "Stella by Starlight" and Monk's "Straight No Chaser," then laid down a backbeat for Slim's throaty vocals and rolling piano on "Kansas City" or "Goin' to Chicago"—a bruising double shift, pitting creative exhilaration against the body's exhaustion and the spirit's confusion. Underfed, underslept, overstimulated, I hovered on the edge of collapse. The slightest breeze from any direction would have pushed me over the edge.

This is the gaunt six-foot wraith with the bad haircut, bony face, and unreadable gaze I revisit in the snapshot.

It had been two months since I'd left Copenhagen, hitchhiking and taking trains south with Eva, bearing my letter of introduction to Robert Graves. We'd arrived in Barcelona, bought tickets for the ferry to Mallorca the next morning, then wandered up the Ramblas in search of a hotel room. We'd found one in the Plaza Real—by chance, across from the Club Jamboree.

The Jamboree was a cavernous subterranean dive with lava-like walls, graffitied columns, and Technicolor lighting—a kind of Roger Vadim film set for a beatnik movie starring Brigitte Bardot as imagined by Almodóvar. Eva and I had stood at the long, dim bar that first night, listening in astonishment to a blind piano whiz with cherubic marble face, little *putto* lips, and black wraparound glasses tear through the jazz repertoire, leaving his Swiss bass player and German drummer in the dust. Tete Monteliu, twenty-six then, still unknown outside of Spain, was about to establish himself as Europe's great jazz pianist.

After the set I approached him at the bar and asked if I might sit in. Tete, being sightless, relying upon instinct and not appearance—and the reassuring cachet of my recent employ in Copenhagen (like all pianists, Tete idolized Bud Powell)—agreed.

It was a Saturday night and the club was full. From behind a beat-up Spanish drum set I looked down upon a familiar scene: couples and groups clustered in the semi-dark around tables with flickering candles in bowls, uniformed waiters hovering along the walls, drinkers and hookers and night owls hunched along the sidelong bar.

Abruptly Tete clicked off Bud Powell's "Un Poco Loco," its percussive introductory figure memorably recorded by the great drummer Max Roach. We flew through the choruses, riding time's current. Joachim, the somnolent Swiss bass player, thunked his viol with new intensity. Tete's fingers chewed the

keys, flashing invention and wit. Our exchanges were incandes-
cent, our landings perfect.

Afterward, at the bar, Tete called the club boss over and told
him to fire the German drummer and hire me. I protested that
I was on my way to Mallorca. "No, man," Tete insisted in his
burry Catalan accent, tugging at my sleeve. "You stay and play
with me."

Suddenly the club start-up with Robert Graves that had
nudged me south was pitted against the offer of a real job with
a thrilling pianist. Eva said she didn't mind; she was along for
the adventure.

The next day the club owner, a local syndicate *capo* named
Carlos, found us a room in the Roma, an old Art Nouveau hotel
across the plaza from the club. I was given a small weekly salary,
a per-diem for food, and membership in the local musicians'
union. I began working as the drummer for the Tete Monteliu
Trio, my letter of introduction to Robert Graves yellowing in
my pocket.

Eva and I had stumbled into some rough paradise, it
seemed, and spent much of that fall making love in the wide
four-poster bed of our high, drafty room, observing our sport in
the tall beveled armoire mirrors. We peed in the scalloped sink,
shat down the hall, hung out in the plaza cafés afternoons for
warmth, and made our meals in the *tapas* bars. After hours we
ran with the flamenco dancers of the quarter, then ate breakfast
at dawn in the central market off the Ramblas before bedding
down. Eva, who'd never been south of Scandinavia before,
found intrigue in the *barrio* streets, sketching prostitutes, beg-
gars, musicians, and hustlers in her tall black notebooks with a
Rapidograph.

Nights with Tete at the Jamboree were exhilarating, full of

sudden turns and heady surprises. Still, I struggled with the terrible house trap kit, its flaccid snare funereal, its tom-toms lumpen, its cymbals trash-can lids. Desperately I wrote Copenhagen asking Harold to send my drums down. Meanwhile, we traded sets nightly with the house band, a lumbering sextet of tuneless hacks employed to fulfill union quotas by cranking out continental favorites of the day ("Eh Maintenant," "Cuando Calienta el Sol," "Never on Sunday").

In early December, the great American blues artist Memphis Slim pulled in with his sidekick Matt "Guitar" Murphy and no drummer. Carlos laid off the house band for the occasion, and from then on I drummed for both Tete and Slim every night from seven to two—an elating, exhausting regimen.

By midmonth, the Hotel Roma's pipes had frozen, coal deliveries had stopped, and Eva and I had taken to sleeping in our clothes. Our lovers' bliss was curdling into suspicion by then. Dark Spanish girls, lost in crushes from their seats at club tables, would find me at the bar between sets or afterward, and one night I'd had a drunken encounter in a *barrio* alley with one. Eva had attracted the attentions of a local dentist, who took her for spins on his Vespa. As Christmas approached, I was unmoored emotionally, losing musical focus, coughing and sneezing with pneumonia's onset.

A letter arrived from my father chastising me for having written home that I was living out of wedlock with a woman. My mother and grandfather didn't enjoy reading this news, he said, with shocking, disingenuous prudishness.

The day before Christmas, I was awakened from fevered sleep by a knock at the door. Chill white winter sun slashed through the tall windows. Eva had already gone out. I struggled up and opened the door. A familiar, unwelcome figure hovered in the hallway, fists jammed into the pockets of a long leather overcoat.

"What's happening, man?" Nick said, in his clenched way.

Nick was a character from the drama of the spring before, one I wanted desperately to end. Trouble rose off him like a vapor. I'd first run into him in the Canary Island village of Santa Cruz de Tenerife in March, a tense American in a slick three-piece suit, eager to share his Afghani hash, reveal his hidden weaponry, and boast of his gangster exploits. Admittedly, in the circles I'd fallen into, art bled imperceptibly into crime, and drug dealing passed as an art form. Still, people I tended to know didn't carry Lugers in their pockets, sport alligator shoes and matching black leather luggage, flash wallets fat with cash, or stay loaded on deadly substances every waking minute. Most could spell, and took an interest in things besides dope and women. Nick, raised in an industrial suburb of Buffalo, had ended up a GI stationed in England before drifting into the hustling life around Europe.

I suppose danger has the allure of mystery if you haven't grown up around much of it, a scent of truths to be plumbed; and so I'd allowed characters like Nick to orbit around my life during those months, imagining I was playing with the cultural anthropology of it all, while in fact merging inexorably into the objects of my study. Perhaps I saw Nick in pathetic terms, an inverted mirror of my situation—or, more darkly, as a necessary agent of my own unraveling.

Later that spring I'd come upon him in Paris, sitting at a table in the Café Dôme in a white silk suit with a tall, beautiful Swedish girl with honey hair and a sweet, wholesome smile. Greeting me unrepentantly, as if nothing had happened on Tenerife, he'd introduced me to Inge, a radiant young fashion model. What on earth, I'd wondered, was a nice girl like that doing with scum like Nick? Thereafter Nick seemed to turn up in every town I passed through, a weathervane of ill winds: in London at a party of actors dispensing substances from a little tobacco tin just before a bust; in Amsterdam climbing into a car outside a strip club; in Copenhagen at the Montmartre bar, talking up some girls. Then, in Barcelona, the week before, I'd looked down from the bandstand to see him sitting at a table with the radiant Inge, coolly nodding to the music. How had he known I was here? When I'd asked he'd shrugged, giving me that knowing hipster look that knows nothing. He and Inge were on their way to the island of Ibiza for a little vacation, he'd said.

Now he stood at my door in the Hotel Roma, nodding sly assent to some unasked question, his luggage slumping to the ground. I gazed into his green eyes, shiny pupils dilated behind some illicit mix, wide Slavic cheeks and frozen cheshire grin narrowing to a stiletto goatee, greased black locks curling around his ears.

"Where's Inge?"

"In Ibiza with friends," he said, patting his pockets and looking around. "Gotta go up to France for a few days. Okay to stash my bag here?"

Shivering in the doorway, I looked down at the fancy tooled-leather duffel. Assent seemed the fastest way to get rid of him and back to bed. "Okay," I said.

"Thanks, man." Nick slipped the bag inside the door. "See you in a few."

When Eva returned with something from the *farmacia*, she noticed the bag. I told her Nick had been through. She frowned and asked where Inge was. I'd introduced them the week before,

in the club, and they'd fallen into eager conversation, two
Scandinavian girls far from home. Inge had confided to Eva she
was four months pregnant by Nick. Now, when I told her Nick
had said she was still in Ibiza, Eva darkened; she'd taken an instant dislike to him. We stored Nick's bag on the floor of the armoire and thought no more of it.

That night the Club Jamboree and its upstairs annex—a
record bar called Birdland—were packed with Christmas Eve
revelers before midnight Mass. I sat at a table before the first set
with Memphis Slim and his young Chicago cohort Guitar
Murphy (later to gain modest fame in the Blues Brothers
movies), a scarf around my neck, sipping tea and sneezing. If
there'd been another decent drummer around I would have canceled that night. Slim, hearing my hacking cough, said, "Flying
low tonight, schoolboy." He'd caught me scribbling in my notebooks one day and I'd been "schoolboy" ever since. "Sounds like
you comin' down with somethin' evil."

I liked Slim, and I greatly admired the potent economy of
his lyrics. A tall, sophisticated man with an ebony baby face
and a stripe of white hair that swept back from his forehead,
he'd settled in Paris some years earlier, purveying his deft,
shouting blues of ominous irony to appreciative Europeans.
Drumming behind him was easy, his rumbling two-fisted piano
obviating much in the way of percussion help.

"You know, schoolboy," Slim said, sipping his Scotch, eyeing
me ruminatively, "you're a good drummer—don't get me
wrong—but lately you in it but you ain't of it." He drained his
drink and stood up.

Slim's perception smote me like a curse. He wasn't talking
race; great musicians seldom do (though "white drummer," a
cliché disguised as an oxymoron, would later dog me back in the

States). It's all about what you deliver on the stand. Slim's comment alluded to matters of heart: to play the music is to commit to live it. Some invisible force was leaching me away from the instinctive center to the watchful edges. I was detaching, not being there. Slim knew it, I knew it.

I was becoming thoughtful, earnest. My eyes were open when they should be closed—as in kissing, or sex. I was marking time, not making it; and drumming is nothing if not about time. Memphis Slim had unearthed a spy in our midst, a stranger on the very ground where we stood—and it was me.

The problem was that lurking inside the drummer was a second, larval character: the writer, watching the player, my creative abandon now coolly observed by a voyeur with an inexhaustible subject at hand—myself. When the physical and moral extremes of my life as a drummer threatened to annihilate me, the writer, rapt witness, would do nothing to save me. This parallel personage, locked in his own creative tumult, complemented and vied for my soul. (Eventually it would capture it, leading me to shed those skins, abandon a world of unpredictable conflagrations for one of small, carefully tended fires, put myself at a safe remove. But this would come later.)

Dispiritedly I mounted the bandstand, fever's heat flaring in my head. I settled on the cushioned swivel stool, gripped my sticks weakly, thumped the bass-drum pedal a couple of times.

On a good night, the cluttered, industrial paraphernalia of the modern drum kit—chrome, steel, springs, wood, skin, plastic—seemed to dissolve on a surging current of rhythm. Hands and feet worked independently but in perfect communion, the body near-weightless. A telepathic locus settled among the players in some fluid nonspace—elastic, panoramic, ranging—

each player both leading and following. The comparison with sex is too keen even to indulge. With someone like Tete, or Dexter Gordon, or Bud Powell when he was right, the music became a mysterious communion out along possibility's edges, the audience accomplices.

Not that night. That night each fevered limb was a log tumbling down some confused rapid, colliding haplessly with the others, trapping time in the claustrophobic corridor of the instant. Even Memphis Slim's rudimentary blues groove taxed my power to keep up. In my quavering hands, the snare drum made, instead of its usual sharp comments, only feeble, broken blurbs. The ride cymbal hissed as if air were being let out of it. The bass drum thumped doom. Below the bandstand, Christmas Eve celebrants milled maniacally, leering skulls. The Club Jamboree had become an infernal place.

After the set I stumbled to the bar in a sweat. Tete was sitting at his usual stool, dressed impeccably in suit and tie and cufflinks, smiling one of the strange smiles of the sightless. He brushed back his jacket sleeve, flicked open the glassed casing of his wristwatch, and felt the hands.

I'd never been around a blind person before Tete. His mastery of his condition amazed me. He handled nearly all his personal chores without assistance. In a taxi in traffic he always knew where he was. He stayed current with politics and culture through radio, television, and Braille, and by way of friends. We'd spent rich afternoons in his apartment with his Cuban wife, listening to Miles, Orff, Roderigo; we'd eaten to satiety in the quarter's restaurants (Tete's towel stuffed in his shirt collar, *caracol* and *langosta* juice running down his laughing fingers). Lately the issue of my drums, which still hadn't arrived from

Copenhagen, loomed uncomfortably between us—the house set was splintering, and I had no money to buy replacements—and I'd begun avoiding him off the stand. But Tete read people by their footsteps, even in the noisy club, and knew I was there.

"You are stoned tonight, Tony?"

Pot or hash, Tete claimed, tended to pinch my attention to a tiny point—a cymbal sound, a drum tap—whereas a drink or two loosened and socialized me. I swung harder, more freely, he'd say. I'd tested his theory and concluded he was right—further reason to distance myself from drugs at that point. The club's six-free-drinks-a-night policy (the one thing Carlos the boss was generous about) helped the process along.

I looked into Tete's black glasses, which reflected the club's lurid revolving lights. "No, Tete," I said. "Not stoned. Just sick."

Tete turned away, his fingers scurrying across the smooth bar for his whiskey.

Back in the hotel that night, Eva and I had a fight about Nick's bag. I lay awake until dawn, hallucinating, the clothes and bedsheets soaked in sweat. The next morning, Eva found a doctor who treated the whores of the quarter, and though it was Christmas convinced him to come to the hotel. Pneumonia, he confirmed, injecting me with penicillin.

That afternoon, I made a sickly, incoherent call to my parents in California that so alarmed them, they told me years later, that my father seriously considered getting on a plane and coming over to get me—a dread project, even in the retelling. They were losing their son to some invisible force they couldn't fathom and felt powerless to intercede. The college-capping "year abroad" they'd delusorily imagined for me before I settled down to some solid, paying profession had gone hopelessly awry. Now, further inflamed by Jacob's lurid intimations of my depraved European wanderings during his stay with them, they truly feared for my life.

That evening, swaddled in layers of clothing, I lurched across the Plaza Real to the Jamboree. We were scheduled to play a single set before dinner, then close up for Christmas night. Midway through Tete's tour-de-force, "Willow Weep for Me," I looked out to see the club swarming with police. The room had turned into a heaving, shouting sea of jostling bodies. Patrons crowded toward the exit. The clamor drowned out the music; we couldn't hear ourselves.

Tete stopped playing. He jerked his head around, side to side, like a rooster. *"¿Qué pasa? ¿Qué pasa?"*

I saw Luanne, a black American singer who sometimes sat in with us, being hustled out between two policemen, her teenage son running after them protesting. Luis, one of the bartenders, was being hauled off in handcuffs. Carlos, the club owner, stood in back, arms crossed, watching from behind his Ray-Bans, flanked by two of his goons and one of the *guardia civil.*

I guided Tete back to the safety of his barstool. There has been a murder, somebody said, and we were all to vacate the club.

We hurried upstairs. The Birdland was being emptied. An American known as Bad Jack who bartended the place was being led out roughly by police, a welt on his head. Carbine-wielding *guardia* milled along the west end of the Plaza Real. I hurried beneath the dark arches to the Hotel Roma.

Back in the room, I found Eva standing at the window, watching the confusion below.

"Somebody's been murdered," I said. "They're searching the buildings."

We found our little cellophane bag of Moroccan *kif* and

emptied it in the sink, forcing the last shavings down the drain with our thumbs. Then it occurred to me to check Nick's valise. I hurried to the armoire, hauled it out, and opened it.

Among Nick's expensive clothes I found two loaded hand pistols, a plastic bag full of sticky black opium, morphine spansules, needles, and ammunition cartridges.

I looked at Eva in horror. She was lifting clothes of Inge's out of the bag. "Why would Nick take this?" she said, holding up a Swedish passport.

"Maybe he keeps it for her, maybe they had a fight—I don't know. But we've got to get this bag out of here."

I rushed to the window. The *guardia* had advanced halfway around the plaza, several buildings away. Nick's arsenal would easily earn us life in Franco's prisons. How to get rid of the bag? Leaving through the hotel lobby was unthinkable, the plaza swarming with soldiers and police.

Eva remembered the rear exit, behind the reception desk at the bottom of the stairs, next to the empty coal bin. I grabbed Nick's bag and tottered down the stairway behind her, shaking with fever and fear.

The lobby was deserted, the unused exit door blocked by crates and chairs. We pushed open the breaker bar enough to slip through, and found ourselves in the darkened, empty street running behind the plaza.

Instinctively we turned away from the city center, toward the harbor. At a corner in the *barrio gótico* we stopped and tried to figure out where to go. *Guardia civil* patrolled the street corners. If we simply abandoned the bag, someone who might have already seen us pass, or even now watched from a window, could identify us.

"The train station," I said. "We'll check it into a locker."

It was a half-dozen blocks to the terminal by the harbor. We trudged through the icy night, feeling the city's eyes upon us. "I hate Nick," Eva said bitterly. Drenched in cold sweat, bearing the incriminating bag, I found my thoughts advancing to the homicidal: if I'd spotted Nick at the end of one of these dusky streets, I'd have been tempted to empty his Luger into him. At the same time my own self-disgust had reached flood level. I knew that, in my irresolute countenancing of Nick, I was as much the author of this moment as he was.

The Barcelona train station was near-deserted. Our footsteps echoed on the tiles as we crossed the cavernous foyer. The skeleton Christmas staff stared at us from behind counters. At the baggage check-in counter a grizzled, uniformed handler took Nick's leather bag, stacked it against the wall, and handed us a claim ticket.

"*Feliz navidad,*" he said, smiling.

"*Igualmente,*" we murmured back.

Back out on the street, we argued. Eva thought the ticket was as incriminating as the luggage and we should tear it up. "No," I said, "I want Nick to have to pick up that bag."

In a narrow street behind the *barrio*'s monumental, gloomy cathedral, we found a crack between two loose stones at its base and stuffed the claim ticket in.

Back at the hotel, we found the doors to our room wide open. Police had rummaged through cabinets and drawers, searched our luggage and clothing, torn up the bedding. Too weary and ill to check if they'd taken anything, I crawled into bed.

For the next five days I drifted in and out of consciousness, coughing and shaking, racked by anxious dreams of guilt and punishment. Each day I awoke long enough to take penicillin and hear news arriving by way of friends and the daily newspapers about the big bust in the Plaza Real. It was all Barcelona was talking about.

It seemed that an affluent businessman, returning home to his apartment in a good neighborhood of the city, had been accosted inside the entry by two armed men and a woman demanding money. He'd put up resistance, and in a panic the thieves had shot and killed him, then escaped to a waiting car with the money. Police had quickly concluded that the main perpetrator was Bad Jack, the American who tended bar at the Birdland, upstairs from the Jamboree, a hotbed of petty crime and rough trade. Bad Jack, whom I hardly knew, appeared to be a smooth blond wheeler-dealer who ran small scams around the club. His London girlfriend Macey had earlier been with a New York avante garde composer and musicologist I'd run in to in Tangier. The day after the Plaza Real raid, Macey had been arrested in Ibiza where she'd fled. Another suspect, a Spanish hustler I'd seen hovering along the walls of the Club Jamboree, was apprehended as well.

Apparently the plan had been hatched over time, and there were others allegedly in on it: Luis the bartender, Luanne the singer, some other locals I didn't know. The Spanish businessman had been carrying a lot of money home with him, the papers said, though the origin of the funds wasn't explained other than to say that the stolen money had been recaptured; nor was it ever made clear how Bad Jack would have known about him or what their connection was. The police had been ordered to round up all the musicians at the club as well the night of the raid; only boss Carlos's connections and Tete's status as Barcelona's favorite son had saved us from jail.

Each day brought new details and revelations. Crime or libertine behavior of any sort were always newsworthy under Franco's repressive watch, but a case involving foreigners was a bonanza for the xenophobic regime. From our room in the Hotel Roma, Eva and I tracked the unfolding drama with all the paranoid absorption of cabalists, scanning the papers, listening for rumors and reports. Then I'd tumble back into fretful sleep.

One afternoon I became aware of light in the room. I opened my eyes to find Guitar Murphy sitting by my bed.

"How you feelin', schoolboy?" he said, handing me a little Christmas gift, a gesture of true kindness: mittens to keep my drumming hands warm.

"What's happening at the club?" I murmured.

"A drummer from New York came through. He's covering."

"How is he?" I asked, thinking I'd been replaced, half wishing it to be true.

"He's okay. We want you back."

The following day Eva was scanning the newspaper when I heard her gasp, then break out sobbing. I took the paper from her and read the small item. A young woman's body had washed up on a beach on the island of Ibiza two days earlier, victim of a botched abortion. A doctor was being held. The Swedish Embassy had been contacted in an attempt to identify the body. An unidentified companion of the girl was being sought for questioning.

For the next several days we barely spoke. Sunk in sorrow and remorse, we mourned the beautiful Inge, whom we'd barely known. Nick was the unspeakable archfiend. Inge's death hung between us like a shroud. Eva and I knew without saying anything that our time together wouldn't survive it.

Still in the pneumonia, I lay there tossing, sick to my core. Each day the keening voice of the legless beggar of the Plaza Real rose through the window: *"Limosnas, por favor."* I have to get out of this life, I thought. I'm trapped in some toxic bacchanal with no exit. The club scene, the frayed relationship with Eva, the episode with Nick's cargo, and now Inge's death struck me with the force of judgment. The quota of human waste had exceeded the allowable. I wanted desperately to claw my way back to light, to feed life and be fed by it again.

Before I'd gotten sick I'd been reading Jung's *Memories, Dreams, Reflections*; and now, in a fever dream one night, I was an enlightened doctor-psychiatrist-writer—some saintly combination of Jung, Schweitzer, and Gandhi—ministering to an ill, unfortunate patient *who was also me.*

At last, one morning, I awoke to find sunlight pouring through the curtains. Children's cheery voices drifted up from the plaza. Water ran through the pipes again. My fever was gone.

I sat up in bed and said to Eva, "I'm going to become a doctor."

By New Year's I was back drumming at the Club Jamboree. Memphis Slim and Guitar Murphy left for Paris the following week, leaving us trading sets with the dismal house band again. The Tete Monteliu Trio continued playing smart, virtuosic jazz, but the magic was gone. My drums still hadn't arrived from Copenhagen and never would; It seemed Harold, the Montmartre's co-owner, was punishing me for not having made it to Mallorca to open up his club there. The winter chill had lifted, but not the frosty sentiments of Barcelonans toward foreigners since the murder; they shouted curses at us on the street.

Bad Jack, Macey, and the others were in jail indefinitely, since Spain had no *habeas corpus* law. We heard that Jack was certain to be executed by garotte and Macey was up for a long jail sentence, maybe life. Friends of Luanne the American singer paid her regular visits, bringing food and tidings, for there was a sense that she'd been unjustly swept up in this.

One night in late January a furtive Spaniard approached me at the bar and whispered that Nick was in town and wanted his bag. Wordlessly I walked the man to the spot in the alley behind the cathedral where Eva and I had stashed the claim ticket. I pointed to the cleft in the stones. The ticket was still there. The man took it and vanished into the night.

For the next few days I checked the papers, half hoping to read that Nick had been arrested picking up his luggage, but there was no mention of it.

In early February, I saw Eva off on the train back to Copenhagen. Through tears we vowed to reunite later in the spring, when the gig was over and the pressure off. Things would be better then, we told each other.

Tete was scheduled to leave for Berlin to play with Dexter Gordon, his first big gig outside of Spain. I wrote to UC Berkeley to apply for medical school in the fall. In March the French saxophonist Barney Wilen, who had recently recorded a cool, innovative soundtrack album with Miles Davis for a Louis Malle film, arrived at the Club Jamboree with his own rhythm section. Tete, Joachim the bass player, and I bade each other weary goodbyes.

I took a train to Rome, where Mick, my sculptor friend from

college, was living. Years later he'd speak of opening the door of his flat to greet the sunny youth he'd known in California and finding instead an ashen, hollow-eyed specter looking like death itself.

One night in 1975, after a concert in California, Dexter Gordon told me Eva had died two years before in Copenhagen of leukemia. She would have been twenty-nine.

I had seen Eva once more after Barcelona—which led to my seeing Nick again too. In mid-May of 1963, I left Italy and traveled by train back to Copenhagen to pick up my drums. From there I planned to take an SAS flight back to California and begin premed summer classes at Berkeley. Friends' letters had arrived, sounding the pedal tones of the emerging decade: Martin Luther King's nonviolent assault on Birmingham; friends drafted for duty in Vietnam; Harvard's firing of Richard Alpert for LSD experimentation. It was time to go home.

I hadn't planned to look Eva up. I'd thought it would be too painful, our vows in the Barcelona train station three months earlier surely no more than fumbling words of extrication. Besides, now I was with Anne, a girl I'd known in college who had tracked me down in Italy. As I was leaving the SAS office in Copenhagen with my ticket, I felt someone grab my shoulder from behind. I wheeled to find Eva glaring furiously at me. She'd seen me from a bus window, jumped off, and followed me.

Over coffee at a restaurant nearby, she flung her anger at me. She'd thought we'd meant it when we'd said we'd get back together and had been waiting all this time. Clearly I'd reverted to the jerk I truly was, going back to California with some girl from home. How disappointing, she said. How disgusting. How trite.

When eventually she'd calmed down—she knew as well as I did that it had been over in Barcelona—she said, "I saw Nick."

"Where?" I said, tightening.

"Here in Copenhagen."

Eva began to tell me the story. After having fetched his bags full of dope and guns and Inge's things from the Barcelona train station, Nick had wandered up through Europe, consuming the dope until it was gone. Finally he'd overdosed somewhere near Hamburg. While recovering, he'd gotten it in his mind that he was going to take Inge's clothes and passport to her parents in Sweden and, in some mad act of contrition, give them money. Now he was staying in Nyhaven, down by the wharves, Eva said, in a cheap seamen's hotel. Each day he got up and carried the leather bag with Inge's clothes and passport to the harbor. He'd stand there, ticket in hand, watching the ferries run all day to and from Malmö, in southern Sweden, unable to bring himself to get on board and complete his journey. Nor could he walk away. He'd creep back to his little room in Nyhaven, then the next morning get up and go back to the ferry landing.

"He's been there three months," Eva said. "Do you want to see him?"

Nick was the last person on earth I wanted to see again. But curiosity must have overruled aversion: in some awful way he represented a self I was bent upon casting aside. "From a distance," I said. "I don't want to talk to him."

On the way to the harbor, Eva reached into her purse and pulled out some snapshots. "I just got these developed," she said.

There we were, standing in the snow in the Plaza Real together in front of the Club Jamboree.

"Do you want one?" she asked.

I took it and slipped it into my jacket pocket. Our eyes locked. We hugged. I kissed her. She cried, squeezing my hand.

Down at the harbor, we hovered in the shadow of a building. I wouldn't have recognized Nick if Eva hadn't pointed him out. The taut, goateed gangster in the cool threads had dissolved into a slumped, dejected figure in a chopped bowl haircut, torn chinos, and sandals. A little potbelly pushed against a faded Greek boating shirt. His face had turned doughy, flaccid, as if the bones had simply crumpled away from the surface—leaving his eyes, those slits of deception, now round and basset-hound-like, rheumy with sadness. Hanging from his shoulder was the fancy tan leather bag Eva and I had stashed in the train station in Barcelona that night, now soiled and travel-worn.

I watched Nick gaze after the departing ferry until it disappeared, then turn and shuffle over to a piling, where he sat staring vacantly off into the gull-strewn sky over Sweden. All the rage I'd felt toward him faded into something tinged at least a little by pity. Nick had become ensnared in his own web of casual evil—first by love, then by Inge's needless death, and now by some dim awakening of remorse, bringing him to this impassable strait.

I see Nick frozen there, like the statue of the Little Mermaid in the harbor, eternally hung up between Copenhagen and Malmö. Did he finally get on the ferry? Did he turn away and drift back into Europe or the States, resume his old ways? Or did he simply wither and die in the seamen's hotel in Nyhaven? Or maybe he's still there at the wharf, waiting for the next ferry to go visit Inge's parents, who by now are probably dead.

===

Silvery rivers wound through dark wooded hills and slopes. Sparse towns interrupted flat yellow plains. The humpy cordillera of the Rockies feathered into brown wastes, sierras, and green coastlands. Hunkered against the vibrating hull of the SAS cabin, I pulled the blanket around my shoulders and pressed my forehead to the window as we flew into the setting sun. I was twenty-three years old, coming back to America after two years away.

The plane banked down over a vast, tilting sea of light. From above, L.A.'s gridded extent, so tawdry by day, looked like a jeweled carpet. The pilot cut the engines. Descent narrowed the spooling diorama to a tracking shot of streets, parks, houses. Down there—among the flats and canyons, the streaming freeways, the wide table of the ocean, the rickety pier—lay youth and memory. As the wheels hit the tarmac, dread gripped me.

I lurched off the plane, carrying a box of hardening Danish pastry I'd brought as a gift. Emerging from the terminal, I saw my father, his hair grayer, standing at the curb, waving.

Three

"... instead of drifting into sleep, I slid into my memories. Or rather the memories (so it seemed to me) rose higher and higher in some space outside myself, until, having reached a certain level, they overflowed from that space into me, like water into a weir. ..."

W. G. SEBALD,
VERTIGO

"*Philip, my nylons,*" Mom cried. . . .

Lately I've been looking through my father's photo albums for that fugitive image of our young family beside the Griffith Park Observatory, convinced now it wasn't a memory at all but a photo transmuted into memory. I can't find it anywhere. If the photo doesn't exist, then perhaps the moment never existed up there on the Hollywood mountain. Did Mom really tumble into those bushes? Was the bottle of gin on the car seat of the Buick Roadmaster? Was it her drinking or Dad's dereliction that incited the family's fall, eroding our Eden?

Maybe this primal scenario wasn't a memory or a photo at all but a dream, elaborated in imagination: a fictive construct I turn like a diorama, a kaleidoscope, a telescope (like the one in the planetarium scanning the stars), revealing changing patterns of meaning—a composed past I refigure and resurface as a jeweler works a stone, exposing a striation or fissure here, rounding a facet or edge there, burnishing and turning, positing and polishing. The moment on the hilltop, the luminous twilight, the iconic ballad playing from a car radio:

> *See the pyramids along the Nile*
> *See the sun set on a desert isle*

It is *their* innocence I want to recover, not mine. I want to lift my mother up from that ravine where she'd fallen, brush her off, set her upright and facing forward. I want to guide my father toward that shining new horizon, not back into the thickets of memory and defeat. The four-year-old boy looking up with wide trusting eyes, his little hands in theirs, wants to lead them away from the gathering storm and the encroaching night to that land of promise they'll never reach.

"Philip, my nylons..."

Early October 1999. Five months since my return to California to attend my dying dad. Summer brush fires abate along the ridges, smog diffuses into the ionosphere. Los Angeles eases into a faux-fall. Here in beachside Venice, gusty freshets strip the elephant palms of their crackly excess, purple bougainvillea blossoms scuttle through the unscreened cottage door. Blade-sharp light parses the stucco walls and weathered wood fences into planes, like paintings Diebenkorn once made here.

Twenty minutes away, a sense of calm, or abeyance, has settled over my father's house. Dad has all but vanished into his memory palace but appears no closer to death. I seem to be the one remaining person whose identity he doesn't confuse. Angela keeps him shaved, bathed, changed. Nell pays the bills, shops, keeps the household up and running. We use his funds to try to keep him out of the clutches of the American health-care system. I drive over a few times a week to pay checks, chat with Nell and Angela, and sit with Dad for a while, gazing glassily at the golf channel. The photo albums have migrated from living room to bedroom; but, subsumed by memory itself, Dad seldom looks at them.

A wordless, cautious intimacy has settled between us.

Nothing is resolved, yet attrition seems to have engineered what dialogue could never achieve. Dad has no fight left in him, which allows me in turn to drop my dukes. His son nearby, he is content for the time being.

What would California be like without him around? Unimaginable. Surely he was the incitement to the flights, the journeys, the escapes. Our conflicts, more than I ever acknowledged, shaped my existence—as peripatetic drummer, as literary voyager. In this paradoxical sense I am in his debt.

On the porch, Masako culls her long black hair by canal light, harvesting strands she will embroider into mysterious letters on silk. She'll exhibit the results at a gallery here in Los Angeles in January. Last month, her book on Mexican tiles near completion, she flew up to join me. We spent late-summer days walking the beach at dusk, seeing a few old friends, marking changes since we moved to Mexico fifteen years earlier.

Sometimes she comes with me to visit my father. He pretends to remember her but I think he's faking it. He'd always liked her, as far as I could tell. For years she'd politely endured the tiresome dinners, Dad's tape-loop litany of old show-biz glories, his calling her "sweetie" and pinching her cheek. This afternoon she'll fly up to San Francisco to deliver her book to her publisher and spend time with her family. I'd hoped to go too, my first trip out of L.A. since the vigil began; but Dad is so enfeebled, and Nell and Angela are struggling. No, it's better I stay.

At the end of the Santa Monica Pier, I hunker at the railing among the silent, smoking night fishermen with their bait, blankets, and buckets. Here, where the Japanese current slaps the barnacle-bearded pilings, where the sun of Western civilization daily sinks into the sea, where the last hubcap of the freeway clatters to rest, I gaze out at the bobbing buoys, awaiting the cooling night currents. At the horizon's dim edge, where the starlight stops, a freighter's lights bob in gathering mist.

Land's end, sea's end. It's all how you look at it, I suppose. In youth this beachfront served as a site of escape from family and place, time and sorrow. One summer I hitchhiked twelve miles from Coldwater Canyon every day just to be here at the rim of the continent, as far west as I could get without drowning. On a steaming July afternoon, in a motel room above a restaurant a block from here, I peeled off Sandra's wet bathing suit with near-unbearable excitement and beheld her for the first time. On the floor of a friend's flat in Ocean Park I watched Bobby Kennedy collapse backward over and over on a tiny television, gunned down at the Ambassador Hotel, a few miles east of here.

I turn and look down the pier, past the pinball arcade with the Skee-Balls in their troughs, Madame Doreena's crystal ball on velvet, the merry-go-round ponies frozen to their poles behind glass doors. In the sky above Santa Monica, a penumbra of lights wobbles in an aspic of shadow and mist. It's possible late at night to race across the city to Pasadena, a couple of climate zones and two freeway interchanges away, in as many minutes as miles: twenty. Three more days east will get you to New York, that city we left so long ago to begin a new life here.

A few hundred yards south along the boardwalk, an arc-lit crater in the ground marks a demolition site where a building had stood until a recent fire. A swank beachfront resort built by

Fairbanks and Pickford in the 1920s, the Hotel Monica had been reduced by the 1960s to a classic waterfront dive stocked with hookers, drunks, and renegade artists. There was a cavernous Isadora Duncan stage on the third floor, an Olympic-sized swimming pool in the basement, and a tacky bar called Jack's along the front. The red neon roof sign used to short out, so at night it read, from as far away as the freeway, HOT**MON-ICA. Jim Morrison used to hole up there, one of the guys from Steely Dan had a room upstairs, and Joan Baez had a unit along the front she kept until the recent fire. This was the hotel Drew had taken me to that high-school afternoon to visit the famous junkie bass player, refiguring my world. Later, on more than one occasion, I stayed there myself. At one point it became a fixed-rent HUD apartment development called the Sea Castle, the swimming pool a parking garage, Jack's Bar gone, and the high old arched rooms cut up into smaller units. The last time I stayed there, an earthquake in Santa Monica Bay literally threw me out of my bed. But it was the rats, and the water dripping through the ceiling from the rotting building's burst pipes, that drove me out.

I turn seaward again. My mind hurtles out across the ocean to sites of journeys taken and those yet to come: vaulting across Asia and the Middle East, North Africa and Europe, the Atlantic and the wide States, east to west. Then I'm here again, at the end of the pier, alone, staring at the back of my own head.

What *is* one's native state? Is it a place, a state of being? Is there such a thing in a shifting world? How far do apples fall from trees? Am I the gangly twelve-year-old frozen forever in my dad's ingratiating smile, or the guy who went out and made a life of his own? And what does it mean to be from a place that never stays still, where the earth continually shifts beneath your feet?

Night fog rolls in. The lights disappear, the mist becomes drizzle. The fishermen reel in their lines and begin the walk back to land. I join them.

On a still, cloudless June morning in 1963, I parked beside a high mesh fence topped with barbed wire encircling grassy, sloped grounds. A man in a pale-tan officer's uniform and cap greeted me at the guard gate of Oak Knoll Naval Neuropsychiatric Hospital in Oakland with a firm handshake, pushing his glasses up on his nose.

"I hope this proves to be an enlightening day for you," Chaplain Carter said as we strode briskly up a path toward a complex of barracks.

It had been six weeks since I'd arrived back from Europe. My return had occasioned great unease in the family. Dinners in the quiet home were filled with long, terrible silences, the dolorous chiming of the hall clock, the clinking of the family silver as Mom and Dad gazed stealthily at this gaunt, taciturn interloper who held his fork backward, stared fixedly into his mashed potatoes, and seemed to have lost all sweetness and civility. My parents seemed older, more subdued, and unable to hide their skepticism at my plans to become a doctor.

Europe still haunted me. I slept poorly, my dreams strewn with Tangier and Algeciras, Tete and Nick, Burroughs and Bud. Ringing phones made me jump. The suburban landscape was tinged, like a poor Technicolor print, with muted terror. Signs of deepening American entanglement in Southeast Asia flooded the news. At a golf course near my parents' house, I gazed out at duffers in plaid slacks lunging at errant TopFlites as if the world were still intact. I felt like the advance man for some awful beast come to devour the land, a blinking pterodactyl reborn in the middle of a backyard barbecue. Sometimes at night I entertained visions of Eva lying in my arms on the hotel bed in the Plaza Real, her thighs pale and downy in the bright Spanish light.

Accepted at the University of California's Langley Porter Medical School contingent upon my getting good marks in summer premed courses in chemistry, biology, and physics, I obtained Dad's lukewarm commitment to help with part of the expenses. The rest I planned to earn drumming and editing books. I imagined my seven-year path to Jungian psychiatry threaded between the twin poles of art and service, duty and inspiration.

I left L.A. in an old VW Karmann Ghia I'd bought for three hundred dollars. The last thing my mother said at the front door was, "If you need any mental help, we do know some psychiatrists."

In Berkeley I found lodgings in the basement of a decaying estate and onetime metaphysical institute, Clear Light College, on a hillside among a grove of trees, its grounds overrun with vines and broken masonry. Built in the 1920s by theosophist followers of Madame Blavatsky, now bobbing haplessly in the wake of the great agnostic citadel of learning nearby, Clear Light survived on cottage rentals and Wednesday-night lectures on such topics as "Auras: How to Read Them" and "A Cabalist Looks at Mu." My basement flat had a hatch-cover coffee table, a faded Persian rug, and a totemic wood statue left behind by the former occupant, an acid-popping sculptor who had fled to Mendocino convinced the second great San Francisco earthquake was imminent.

In the days that followed, I set up my drums, shipped home from Copenhagen, and began to practice. Nights, I jammed in Oakland blues clubs, in Berkeley lofts, at Bop City in San Francisco. Weekends, I played free-form jazz in a Berkeley club with saxophonist and pianist Ian Underwood (soon to become one of Frank Zappa's Mothers of Invention)—abstract investigations unmoored from melody, beat, or structure. Amazingly, people came to listen.

During the days, with little to do until summer school began, I'd wander alone among the ruins of the Clear Light campus or hike up in the hills among the pines, where the light was pale and sharp. Venturing into Berkeley, San Francisco, or Mill Valley to visit old friends, I'd hear talk of Dylan and electric folk music, the burgeoning Asian war, Zen, and psychedelics. Just as Galen in Tangier and his planetary conspirators had prophesied, drugs were breaking from the fringe into the middle class.

Some nights I'd spend with Anne, the girl from college I'd reconnected with in Europe, entwined in consoling passions and tossing discontents. Around us, war clouds gathered. One afternoon, her father, a navy chaplain and Presbyterian minister, took me on a tour of his warship, the USS *Ranger*, berthed at Alameda Harbor, readying for action in the Gulf of Tonkin. Walking me through the vast hold, he pointed proudly to the nuclear warheads hanging in the bays overhead. He didn't seem remotely aware of the rising tide of dissent ashore.

Driving me back to Berkeley afterward, he said, "How would you like to visit a neuropsychiatric hospital?"

I looked at him in alarm. "I feel fine."

"Oh, that's a good one!" he said. "No, I mean the naval hospital in Oakland. The doctors are doing good stuff over there.

My colleague Chaplain Carter will take you around. It may give you some ideas while you're waiting for your premed classes to start."

At the top of the bluff at Oak Knoll Hospital, I entered a freshly painted barracks labeled 49 MENTAL HYGIENE and followed Chaplain Carter down a hall past swabbing orderlies. We logged in at a reception table and received ID clips. In an adjacent office, a tall, chesty, granite-faced female colonel rose to greet us. Chaplain Carter introduced us, then left. The colonel shook my hand firmly and invited me to sit down.

"Understand you're headed for Langley Porter. Good. We need more doctors. What can I do for you, young man?"

"What sort of work do you do here?"

"Stress and motivation." She dug a Pall Mall out of her breast pocket and lit it. " 'S and M,' we call it." Her hair was short, her hands large. She leaned back in a wooden swivel chair and blew smoke out. "A joint army-navy project. We're dealing with the problem of the soldier who cannot shoot his gun or otherwise carry out his wartime duty. Needless to say, these men must be identified, treated, and made fit for all combat instances. In order to test such individuals, since until recently we've had no actual combat conditions in which to observe behavior, we *induce* fear by chemical means. So far we've had encouraging results. But now"—she leaned forward, her elbows on the desk—"we have a situation where we can test out our work."

"Southeast Asia," I said.

"Correct." She sat back. "Frankly, it's terrific for us."

When I asked to see the "S and M" facilities, she was evasive. Instead she walked me to another office and introduced me to a psychiatrist in a lab coat and officer's cap.

"This young fellow is interested in your racket," she said.

"Headshrinker?" The psychiatrist appraised me solemnly, puffing on a pipe. "Like to accompany me on inspection?"

We crossed the lawn to another barracks building. Hospital beds ran down either side of a long room. "Mental" patients stood at the foot of their bunks in myriad variations of at-ease. The doctor, his officer's uniform visible beneath his white coat, stopped to talk briefly and mechanically with each patient about his condition. "How's your appetite? Stool? Take your meds?" Chaplain Carter, also in full officer's cap and uniform, followed behind the doctor. "Read your Bible last night, fella? Did you pray?"

"Yessir" or "Nosir," mumbled each sheepish patient, saluting at the same time. I trailed this triple whammy of God, Navy, and Medicine down the line. Most men, not knowing what else to do, saluted me and said, "Sir."

"Vietnam. Vietnam. Vietnam," Chaplain Carter said over his shoulder, nodding at patient after patient.

I followed the doctor and the chaplain to the end of the inspection line and out of the barracks. A glassy-eyed man was scrambling up the wide, empty lawn in torn pajamas, shouting obscenities, spittle flying from his mouth. The doctor, backing away, called for orderlies. Two large black men in pale-green scrubs appeared and quickly subdued the man.

"Get him back to the Quiet Room," the psychiatrist snapped.

Watching the patient hauled off, I asked what the Quiet Room was.

"Violent cases," Chaplain Carter said, tilting his head in an attitude of pity.

"Thorazine. Straitjackets until they calm down," said the shrink.

"Time for therapy," Chaplain said, glancing at his watch as we entered the main building.

Twenty patients sat in a semicircle in a large room across from Chaplain Carter, two doctors, the pipe-smoking psychiatrist, and me. In an "Open Discussion," the patients were encouraged to talk about their treatment and their progress. Most sat stonily and said nothing. The several who did speak voiced complaints about the program, which the doctors seemed to regard as further evidence of mental disturbance. A poster was affixed to the wall depicting a ladder representing the road back to "mental health," the reward for reaching the top the privilege of going back on duty. A fawning, spiritless Latino who talked the party line was held up by the doctor-officers as a model patient, nearing the top of the ladder. The others regarded him with sullen scorn.

Afterward the doctors and Chaplain Carter held a discussion in a small private room, grousing about the patients in technical jargon. "Pure passive-aggressive," said one, waving a helpless hand. "More anal-aggressive, I'd say," murmured the shrink. The chaplain put in a pitch for more prayer.

"What about you, young man?" Eyes fell upon me.

"They seem confused by authority," I ventured. "It looks like they're trying to figure out how to act in order to get out of here with the least amount of damage. 'Well' seems to mean 'compliant.' "

I gazed helplessly into the supercilious silence. After papering over my remarks with finalizing comments of their own, the doctors adjourned.

"Well," said Chaplain Carter afterward at the door, "you do speak your mind."

"Sorry if I embarrassed you."

"No, no." He looked about the hall, which had emptied. "Listen. I know of a volunteer project you may be interested in." He gazed at me earnestly. "Down in the Tenderloin. Street work, with some very fine nuns. Idealistic. Meaningful." The chaplain patted me on the shoulder, then turned away. "See you after lunch."

Feeling bleak, I pushed through a set of double doors and entered a pavilion of gleaming steel bars and machines: the Prosthetics Lab. Sailors in various states of amputation and dysfunction exercised before mirrored walls, grunting over artificial limbs and devices under the eyes of therapists.

The limbs were brilliantly devised. Arms capable of lifting large weights, made light with new synthetic foams and nylons, worked from cables at the opposite shoulder. Hooks and spoon attachments performed intricate tasks. For the first time all day I felt I was seeing good work.

The shop foreman, a thick, ruddy man in a tee shirt, introduced himself. As he guided me among the patients and machinery, I noticed in a mirror a small, delicate man—a boy, rather—with thin, quivering red lips and terror in his eyes, sitting in shorts on the edge of a gurney. Two brand-new artificial legs, the chrome still shiny and unclouded, extended from his pelvis. An unwrapped gift sat on his lap. His soft, unshaven face was blank with fear.

The foreman was demonstrating the wonders of an artificial arm equipped with a spoon. "And here we have our Standard Navy Leg," he said, holding it up for me to feel. "Our leg tech is finally getting a workout, let me tell you. Gook land mines. You'll see the spoon attachment here on this arm, how it can rotate. . . ." The young man with his two brand-new Standard Navy Legs looked at me in the mirror with unfathomable grief, mouthing something inaudible.

"How about *this*? A leg for the ladies, with a *high heel* built right in," said the shop foreman.

"Ahhh!"

The image of the boy exploded in the mirror, arms flailing as he tumbled from his gurney. I rushed over, followed by the foreman. The young sailor, splayed on the linoleum floor, his robe askew, was crying as much in frustration, I thought, as in pain.

The foreman took one of his arms, I took the other, and we swung him and his new, useless legs back up on the gurney.

A bell rang.

"Twelve hundred hours," the foreman said. "Time for lunch."

Still stunned, I edged among the steel and chrome toward the exit, passing quadriplegics lifting themselves on crossbars, wheelchairs run by armless men using their mouths.

The cafeteria reeked of the soup of the day, boiled cabbage, and burnt coffee. I queued up among doctors, orderlies, and sailors. Clutching a soft drink and a dry sandwich wrapped in cellophane, I sat at a Formica table facing the door, wondering how patients were supposed to get well in a place like this. My own medical aspirations seemed impossibly distant. What had I thought that becoming a doctor would entail, lying in the Hotel

Roma in Barcelona in sweat-soaked sheets reading Jung? What mad course had I embarked upon?

I stood up and slid the remains of my lunch from the tray into a bin. Outside the cafeteria, the lady colonel reappeared and marched me to a lecture room where a heavy man with a sorrowful face was briefing the assembled upon the subject of "Disaster Plan—Revised," the title written out in large block letters on a green blackboard.

"Should disaster strike, there is the question of, uh, *priority*," he droned on. "Preference will be given not to those most critically wounded but to those who might be expected upon recovery to contribute most to further civil or national defense efforts."

I struggled to keep awake against the alternately disturbing and soporific litany; the night before, I'd drummed at the Berkeley club until one in the morning.

After the briefing had droned to a halt, the lady colonel said, "What would you like to see next? How about the Quiet Room?"

But I'd had enough.

At the top of the hill, outside 49 MENTAL HYGIENE, Chaplain Carter clapped me on the arm. "Keep it up, young man. We need more like you." He tapped his brow. "A big unexplored world in there."

Back at Clear Light that night, I lay awake until dawn, staring out through the dusty basement window snarled with creepers, watching the moonlight shift, feeling like a ticking bomb in destiny's mailbox.

"*...a ticking bomb in destiny's mailbox,*" I wrote feverishly and melodramatically in one of the journals begun the day I'd left L.A. two years earlier. They lay stacked beside my bed, seldom written in lately. California's familiarity made it hard to stay alert to things; shorn of travel's mystery and surprise, I wrote only when I was distraught. From time to time I'd try to read in them but found it painful, the entries self-pitying, pompous, often semi-incoherent behind the effects of hunger or misery, dope or drink, or simply derivative emulations of masters I'd been reading: sensuous Durrell, grave Camus, tormented Dostoevsky, florid Lawrence. I was casting about for some language of the self—a self obscure to me.

The night after my visit to the naval hospital, I sat disconsolately with Anne on the paisley-draped bed at Clear Light. My brush with institutional military psychiatry yoked to the service of the new war had left me shaken, unsure of my course.

"How can your father as a Christian justify what he's doing? Counseling men to kill?"

"He tries to console them, bring them to acceptance."

"And sleeps soundly at night."

"Those men were shaped by World War II, remember."

We leaned back against the wall, our hands finding each other. Miles Davis' *Kind of Blue* curled from a scratchy LP on the portable hi-fi on the hatch-cover table.

I'd first met Anne my senior year in college. A blonde, pretty sophomore studying literature, she'd fallen for me as editor of the campus newspaper, serving first as my cub reporter then as consort at weekend bacchanals at the house I shared with Richard Serra, a literature student with me before becoming a sculptor. Later when she'd showed up in Italy, where I'd gone after drumming in Barcelona, we'd rekindled our romance.

Soon after we moved to Berkeley, Anne had discovered she was pregnant. She was twenty, I was twenty-three, and we had no money. We didn't for a minute consider keeping it. A junkie trumpet player I knew with underground connections gave me the name of a Tijuana abortionist, code-named "Irene." Frightened and anxious, we drove down 101, crossed the border into Mexico, and followed a contact through the unpaved Tijuana outskirts to a shabby stucco house. I handed over the four hundred dollars I'd borrowed to "Irene," who turned out to be a furtive, balding man with a paunch. I waited in a tiny anteroom beneath an icon of a bleeding Jesus whose eyes followed me no matter where I stood, while "Irene" did his work behind a curtain. Sick with remorse, listening to Anne's cries of pain, I thought of Nick's girlfriend Inge, the botched abortion in Ibiza, her body washed up on the sand. When Anne finally hobbled out from behind the curtain alive, I felt wild relief. We drove straight back to Berkeley, Anne weeping and disconsolate, ice packs pressed between her legs.

Now, on the bed at Clear Light, the LP clicked off, the needle arm retracted into its armature. We slithered out of our remaining clothes and into the act that most seemed to affirm our connection. Afterward we sat on the bed smoking, sated but not happy. Anne and I seemed to love each other in some gentle, aesthetic manner—a sweetly melancholic sharing of vague griefs, leavened by fleeting patches of animal comfort.

"Oak Knoll freaked me out today," I said, stubbing out the cigarette. "I don't know if I'm going to make it."

"You'll feel better when summer classes start."

I picked up the paperback book that had fallen between us in our grapplings. Left behind by the flat's previous occupant, its thumbed pages had become sacrosanct to me in recent weeks. An ex–Anglican minister's gloss on Buddhism and Japanese meditation practice, it contained mellifluous descriptions of states of being that I'd intuited but never encountered as religious philosophy or practice. It had wreaked an inordinate effect upon me, a few mere lines setting off chains of luminous realization—especially after a couple of hits of pot. I'd wander the leafy derelict grounds of Clear Light, peculiarly alert, disengaged from frustration, rage, and the oppressions of the moment. Alan Watts's *The Way of Zen*, with its smooth rhetoric of clever paradox, contained a literary seduction; but behind that lay gleanings of another order of consciousness, an essential wordless reality—intimations of cessation, silence, breath; illumination; and the cleansing void of understanding.

By the end of my travels, I'd come to see Europe as a museum of exhausted human possibilities, the territory of Sartre's *No Exit*, Beckett's *Endgame*. Any suspicions I might have had that communism was a road out were quelled by my visit to East Berlin. Modernism, Europe's great revolt, was enervated, reduced to mere gesture; Europeans hungered instead for the American music I played, the new American literature of release and revolt I read and aspired to write.

In Rome I'd taken a couple of LSD trips with a lapsed scientist and psychedelic messiah sent my way by a California friend—vaulting mental journeys deconstructing mathematical theorems and bead games, Bach, and snowflakes. In Paris I'd undertaken a nocturnal peyote voyage in which the room had dissolved into sensuous, malleable organic stuff, a gluey lava lamp of color, sound, and sensation. Hallucinatory Morocco had opened other windows onto the unnamable, confirming earlier pantheistic realizations that had come through poetry, music, and ecstatic dawn beach walks. Now, as the American war machine geared up and social disturbance swept the land, the inner landscape seemed to hold more promise.

Summer session began at last. I found myself among students far younger and infinitely more innocent, though only a couple of years separated us. I felt corrupted by experience, ravaged by travel, lost forever to the world I'd grown up in. My fellow aspiring doctors, most of them the very types I'd avoided while growing up, already talked about how much money they'd make, the Wednesdays off, the private planes. Terrible anatomical banter circulated: A gynecologist meets a proctologist at a convention. "We're neighbors," goes the punch line. Chemistry, biology, and physics lectures and labs were deadening. I had trouble with homework, taking tests, things I'd always done with ease. I soldiered on toward midterms, trusting to a sign from somewhere, a glimpse of a road out, a renewal of faith and facility.

Meanwhile, characters from street days in Europe and North Africa—backpackers, drug dealers, itinerant bards and musicians—passed through Berkeley expecting a place to crash and drugs on offer ("I'm a friend of Petrus from Copenhagen . . . Jacob from London . . . Galen from Tangier"). Musicians invited me to play at clubs and all-night sessions. Student-activist friends demanded I come demonstrate with Mario Savio at Sproul Plaza and rage against punch-card tyranny and the spreading war.

A UC biophysicist I'd met invited me to a party at his home one weekend. He was earnestly engaged in experiments giving patients LSD and tagging them with tracer molecules to see where they went in the body, an attempt to map consciousness. Two anthropologists, just back from the upper Amazon, were there, passing out the hallucinogenic *yage*, enthusing about its visionary high. Another drug scholar had brought magic mushrooms, psylocybin, from the *bruja* Doña Maria in the Sierra Masateca mountains of Oaxaca. I performed on an African slit drum with the Nubian oud-player Hamza el Din and a pale, willowy junkie guitarist, Sandy Bull, who had a couple of albums out on Folkways. The Beat poet Michael McClure read his "beast" poems, consisting of mere animal noises.

A few weekends later, this same troupe caravaned across Richmond Bridge to a party on Alan Watts's Sausalito houseboat. Our host—stoned, I assumed, but in fact quite drunk, I was told later—held forth fatuously in a kimono, his arm around his Japanese secretary. Watts's sloppy, garrulous persona seemed to betray the luminous dance of awareness he described in his texts. Observing him, I wondered: could we hold an author accountable for his behavior? Paul Bowles in person had seemed entirely consonant with his work. Was Watts merely a Zen publicist? Could one write convincingly about states of understanding without having achieved them? Language bore the possibility of con, deception. Burroughs, I thought, understood this perfectly, and had indeed made it his enterprise to unmask language.

Against this undertow of distraction, I slogged on through premed classes. Only my nightly readings in Buddhism offered sense and solace. Freud's relentless, solipsistic examination of the overstuffed furnishings of private biography now seemed suspect; a century of psychoanalysis hadn't proved that it worked. At least Jung had moved on to shared archetypes and myths, patterns of thought—searching, I'd begun to think, for what Siddhartha Gautama had gleaned twenty-five hundred years earlier. If each individual's mind is built the same way, then becoming aware of the mental shapes and forms common to all thought might release the ill effects of unconscious behavior. Zen's logic-cracking koans intimated a way out. Of course, I hadn't yet spent a single minute meditating. Still, these insinuations of a path all seemed to point in one direction: Asia. Moving past fallen idol Watts, I next embraced the more stringent, technical D. T. Suzuki; a translation of the Diamond Sutra; Arthur Waley's little volume of Lao Tzu. I heard of a temple in San Francisco where a Japanese Zen master taught meditation, and I thought of going there.

My midterm-exam grades came back: B's and C's. I was distressed but not surprised. This meant I'd need to get nearly all A's from then on to secure my entry into medical school in the fall.

Over the summer I'd written a few long letters to my parents, confiding impressions and doubts, debating human purpose with quotes from *The Brothers Karamazov,* the psychoanalyst Frantz Fanon's radical *The Wretched of the Earth,* and Suzuki. A week after midterm exams, in August, I received a letter from my father. I walked out onto the grounds of Clear Light College and opened it. Reading it, I felt the oxygen drain from the air. He said he'd been thinking about it and had decided he couldn't help me with medical school after all. He didn't believe I was really serious about this, he said, and maybe it was time for me to go out in the world and find a real job.

I walked Telegraph Avenue for hours that night, crushed. I couldn't believe he'd do this to me, and in this manner. It was less the withdrawal of the money than the moral support. Dad had always been reticent about his finances (he remained so until a few years ago, when his enfeeblement finally forced him to disclose things to me, since there was nobody else); and yes, I knew the big bucks from the old Durante radio days were gone. Still, he was a provident man who had always saved, and he had the job with the advertising agency. I was sure he could have managed it. I could only understand his refusal as another attempt to undermine and cripple me.

Trudging the dark streets, I tried to figure out how I might negotiate medical school on my own. Get a day job? Play in clubs or bars at night? There were no loans available; I'd already checked. It seemed impossible.

The next morning, I elbowed through a free-speech demonstration at Sproul Plaza to the UC Berkeley admissions office and withdrew from my premed classes. I drove back to Clear Light, threw myself on the bed, and wept.

I sit beside my father as he sleeps. His chest barely rises and falls. I remove the remote from his hand, dim the sound on the cartoon channel where Popeye, his neck twisted into a corkscrew by his massive bearded nemesis, reaches for a can of spinach to revivify.

No spinach for Dad: too late. How can I hold old grievances against this attenuated figure, a faint stream of breath whistling through his sunken lips? His defeats and disappointments were already embedded in him by the time I took my stab at becoming a Jungian shrink. We do the best we can: a father myself, I know this now. Dad, a Depression child, a fallen show-biz figure, hemmed in by fear and loss, didn't realize how much slack there was in the social fabric then—that the young, white, and educated could test boundaries on the cheap; that his assets would appreciate for the rest of his life. No, I wouldn't have busted his piggy bank. Fearing that the forces that had abridged his path would hobble his son's, he wanted to rein in my hubris. Having lost control of his destiny in the outer landscape, where men take their measure, he compulsively tried to control those close at hand: my mother, my sister, me. My request for help had put him in an impossible position, reawakening his own losses. His message was: "Don't ask. I bear a wound of my own too great to permit it. Don't you see?"

No, I didn't.

Whether I'd have made it into medical school, let alone through it, had he not withdrawn support, was moot; probably not, though I'll never know. But I read it as another gesture of abandonment at a key moment, invoking for me Dad's earlier abdication of the family and Mom's subsequent ruinous drinking. When, years later, my mother died and my father began looking to me for support and sustenance, surely that old wound colored my reactions.

For over thirty years, we never spoke of this incident. Then, one day over lunch—he was in his late eighties by then—he alluded to that time he hadn't backed me for medical school and hoped I didn't hold it against him. I was so taken aback I couldn't begin to form a response. I shrugged and said, "That was long ago, Dad."

Driving home that day, I tried to decode his statement. Why mention it now? Was this true remorse? Was he, late in life, trying to clear accounts? Or was he being ingratiating as a prelude to demands for further devotions and services?

I gaze at my sleeping father, his mouth wide open now. Hairs sprout from his nose, his ears. This snoring man, who precedes me down the genetic chain, composes his death mask.

Reaching to turn off the television, I think: if Dad's final vision of this world is a Popeye cartoon, it could be worse—a halfway-decent sendoff into the next: that journey through the realms of *bardos*, Buddhist stages of the afterlife, which the Tibetan Book of the Dead details so precisely.

Leaving the bedroom, I avert my eyes from the photo albums, wary of their toxic allure.

23. Rage

Broke and without direction, cast out into the Bay Area's political and social tumult of 1963, I tried to survive by drumming—at all-night sessions in downtown Oakland lofts with sullen jazzists in dashikis; with a cool, vacuous white piano trio at a Sausalito restaurant affording a view of the glittering city across the bay; behind a topless sensation in a North Beach strip joint one weekend, summoning the old rim shots and "Night Train" licks from Duke's Supper Club days; with scruffy young art students in Mission District storefronts, playing rock-blues-jazz fusion soon to congeal into the San Francisco rock movement. I drove to gigs and sessions, unloaded my drums, engaged the night's prevailing idiom, then packed up and drove back to my basement flat at Clear Light.

These outings provided little joy or passion. The bop virtuosi I'd worked with in Europe, still young men but already beyond competition, were elaborating their innovations nightly before benign, reverent audiences. The American musical landscape I returned to teemed with anxious cultural battles, the air littered with dissonant clusters of sound, Coltrane understood as an emissary not of transcendence but of black rage. Noisy, pained, and bitter, "jazz" was eating its own flesh. The rousing din of Western percussion that had once lured a boy out of the hushed L.A. suburbs into color and sense now sounded crude and strident to me—an expression of American military aggression, even.

Meanwhile, I was finding another music in silence.

Bell chime... Smell of joss... Shoeless legs gathered beneath me on zabuton pillow... Eyes cast downward, unfocused... Attention centered in the hara, *the pit of the stomach... I am not the thoughts that form but just a little behind my own head, watching them....*

At the Zen Center in San Francisco's Japantown, I'd sit among gong chimes and the rustle of bodies, listening to the shaven-headed abbot give a commentary on the Diamond Sutra. Back out on Post Street, the lights and traffic rush seemed an assembly of sense illusions, mere manifestations of mind. I'd climb back into the Karmann Ghia, becalmed. *Turn of key, whoosh of engine...*

Unable to subsist on drumming, I took a job packing books at the University of California Press warehouse—a refuge for old Bay Area lefties, Wobblies, and unionists, who, when I'd load a box too quickly, would say, "Hey, man, where's the fire? You're making us look bad." It was among them that, on a small black-and-white television, I saw JFK wave to the Dealey Plaza crowd from the back of the open limousine, then fall backward, again and again; and watched Oswald take it repeatedly in the gut from Jack Ruby. The ceaseless replays, embedding public trauma into private dreamscape, seemed perfect metaphors for the endless repetition of human folly. Only the individual mind, Buddhism counsels, can free itself from the futile wheel of recurrence.

Anne and I began to talk of going to Japan as soon as we'd saved enough money. She'd spent high school years there—her father had been stationed at the navy base in Yokosuka—and loved the idea of returning. Friends at the Zen Center said there was teaching work to be had in Kyoto, the old capital undamaged by war. As new protests swept Berkeley, Lyndon Johnson authorized more troops to be sent to Vietnam, and racial ferment in the American South spread through the rest of the country, I packed books by day, played music at night, and dreamed of Kyoto.

That Christmas, in Los Angeles, I sat benumbed at the family table. I now saw my father as bent upon cutting me off at every turn, a censorious element I had to ignore if I was ever to find my way. This was something I, at twenty-four, was deeply worried about: my progress in the world. My future appeared stunningly modest. A washout as a doctor, losing momentum as a drummer, having nothing to show as a writer, an academic career now unimaginable, I was in fact employed at a menial job, packing books. Surely, had I possessed enough of that mysterious "talent" Dad so adulated, it would have shown by now. I felt humiliated, weakened in front of my parents, a deep disappointment. The thought of going abroad again offered, among other allures, flight from the specter of my own failure.

My father was then fifty-eight, my mother fifty-one. Still employed part-time at the ad agency as an "entertainment consultant," he played golf with old cronies and puttered around the house, his den blossoming into a repository of memorabilia from the glory years: clippings and photos of himself with Uncle Jimmy, Uncle Paul, the other radio greats. A resurgence of his show-business fortunes no longer a remote hope, Dad was digging in—taking, in effect, early retirement. Rooted in postwar complacencies—a McCarthy-muted landscape of nuclear families and few questions asked—he saw the country, reeling from JFK's assassination, descending into new chaos. The slightest allusion to events in the world beyond—worse if they came from Berkeley, hotbed of civic unrest—invoked bristling rejection. My mother watched our inflammatory dinner-table scrimmages in silent anguish, torn between the two men in her life— her affinities with me, her loyalties with him.

During this trip home I noticed for the first time the serious erosion of her health and spirit. Asthmatic, sipping black coffee and smoking cigarettes all day, she seemed increasingly isolated in the house, the fierce intellect that had always driven her to study and read sapped—a woman embalmed in a city, a marriage, a life she'd wished other than it had turned out to be.

The Christmas visit at an end, I headed back up Highway 101 into an uncertain new year, knowing I'd have to shape my life now without reference to my father. If this had been his intent in withdrawing support for medical school, it had worked.

In the passport photo shot soon after, I wear a thick knit tie, a white shirt, a navy pea coat. My hair, neat and shorn though not short, appears combed back off my forehead as if for the photo. The faint beginnings of a mustache graze my lips. Along the picture's edge, in embossed letters, are the words: PHOTOGRAPH ATTACHED. DEPARTMENT OF STATE. SAN FRANCISCO. I'd just turned twenty-four. Hovering about my eyes is an expression I tend to read, here in the Venice cottage, as wounded, worried, questioning. Struggling to disentomb some message or revelation encoded in a visage I can barely read as myself, I am blocked by the mystery of time, the impenetrability of the past, the inscrutability of snapshots. How little one's face in a picture tells us: both a mirror-gaze into a labyrinth and a flat surface rejecting interpretation.

I want to read, behind that high, pale forehead, my mother's suppressed rage, internalizing in me and fusing with my own rage at the path my country was taking, with its dark, corrosive American war games and social perturbation; rage at my father;

rage at my own cloudy fate and failure: rage that will run forward in time until delivering me, fitfully and finally, into writing.

In Berkeley that January, a senior editor at the UC Press heard that a literary man was working in the warehouse. He summoned me to the main office. I was interviewed for an editor's job, hired provisionally, and given a small desk and a stack of scholarly monographs to edit. On my last Friday in the warehouse, my Wobbly friends teased me: "Joining the bourgeoisie. Bunch of phonies. You'll regret it."

In a way, I did miss the irreverent sociability of the warehouse, my days spent now in airless rooms beneath fluorescent light among hunched, humorless men in tweed jackets and bifocals. Some of the press's books were interesting: titles on European New Wave cinema; Rudolf Arnheim's brilliant *Art and Visual Perception*; Theodora Kroeber's landmark study of the lone survivor of a California Indian tribe, *Ishi in Two Worlds*. Lashed to my cubicle, I redacted lesser works—monographs parsing radiation theory, Inuit dialects, nature imagery in Thoreau and Emerson—and stared at the white partition enclosing me, imagining escape.

One evening in a Berkeley Laundromat, waiting for my clothes to dry, I looked over and saw Sandra, my girlfriend from high school. The last I'd heard from her was a letter she'd written me to Paris, a final plea either to come home and claim her or to let her go. I'd written her a withering reply, full of bitterness and despair, rejecting her and all I considered she stood for: home, hearth, church, and the dull American middle class of constancy, jobs, simple love.

I'd felt ashamed afterward, but if Sandra still bore any hurt she didn't show it. She was getting a doctorate in biochemistry at Berkeley, she said, and was engaged to be married. I offered my congratulations, happy for her and relieved that she'd moved on in love. As we parted, she gave me her telephone number and told me to call her.

For the next few days and nights I couldn't get her out of my mind. I knew she wanted me to call, or part of her did; and I knew that if I called we'd most likely have sex. I'd felt it in the Laundromat as we parted, or thought I had. This could be ruinous to her engagement, her new life. How much more ill behavior could I inflict upon this sweet and good first love?

All through college our heated investigations had continued, the tender, gradated, precoital intimacies we'd first explored together in high school never abating in ardor. When I was at Stanford and she was at a college for women in Oakland, I'd drive across Dumbarton Bridge every Friday night and pick her up at the reception desk, where matrons looked you over, then had you sign in, declare where you were taking the young lady, and promise to bring her back by eleven. We'd drive straight to a motel, climb out of our clothes, and spend our four allowable hours in bed, not pausing for so much as a pizza. I'd head back across Dumbarton Bridge, wobbly-legged, starving, and barely awake, to my dorm at Stanford. On vacation trips home during college, we'd drive to our old sites in the hills, convene in available bedrooms.

I didn't tell Anne about the encounter in the Laundromat. The impulse to call Sandra lingered. Our erotic past throbbed relentlessly in my mind and body. I began to think about love, its kinds and qualities. Was I capable of love? Did I truly love

Anne, or were we together by default, lacking the will to break off? I wondered if making a commitment to her would strengthen what seemed to be flagging between us.

I never did call Sandra; but for a long time I'd think about what might have happened if I had. I'd imagine a single, explosive sexual encounter late at night in a car in the Berkeley hills, releasing us both at last. I'd imagine us remaining perfect, secret lovers down through the years, each holding the erotic key to the other, even as she went ahead and married the unknowing biophysicist and had a family with him. Surely first encounters model our later sexual lives: if Honey Bare, the stripper at Duke's Supper Club, initiated me into sensual abandon for its own sake, it was the innocent, tender, inexpert romance with Sandra that retains in memory the inexhaustible erotic charge.

Soon after I began my editing job at UC Press, I was hired to drum nights in a San Francisco theater for a British comedy revue, a spinoff of London's witty, satiric *Beyond the Fringe*, providing musical transitions between sketches from behind a semi-opaque scrim, visible as silhouettes to the audience. Each night I drove back across the Bay Bridge after midnight. My waking hours were balanced between books and drumming, language and music—kindred arts yet different, twin passions that seemed to hold something of what I was about. A core of identity? I found little else by which to define myself. Yet the manuscripts I edited by day were not mine any more than the music I played by night. After Europe with Bud and Dex and Tete, playing in a pit band for a comedy revue was mere shadow play; and correcting dull monographs was far from the Parnassian heights I dreamed of scaling with my own writing. Exhausted from working two jobs, performing neither well, I consoled myself with the thought that soon I'd have enough money saved for Japan.

I stand on the stairs of a wedding chapel in a suit, my arm around Anne. She wears a white silk dress and holds a bouquet of flowers. A sunny day, it would appear, in June 1964. In the commemorative portrait, we smile, though we both look stiff and unhappy.

Two months earlier, after a weekend of deliberation, I'd given notice at the UC Press, quit my gig with the comedy revue, and given up my flat at Clear Light College. Then I'd called Anne and broken off with her. The life I'd been living wasn't adding up, I'd said, and a clean break was the only way. Even going to Japan had become so intertwined with her that I'd given that idea up as well. Instead I was moving to New York to try and survive by writing and playing music.

It was time once again to escape into a new scenario.

A week later, beset by regret and confusion, I'd called her back and said I'd been thinking about it and maybe we should get back together and go to Japan after all. That being the case, we should probably get married, since her parents would have fits if we didn't.

Anne received this backhanded marriage offer by saying she'd think about it. A few days later, she agreed. I began researching cheap freighters to Yokohama or Kobe, imagining a brief civil ceremony to legitimize us, then a hasty departure for Japan; but it turned out Anne's mother had different ideas. A full-blown wedding grew up around us, her father pulling strings to fly all the way back from the USS *Ranger* in the Gulf of Tonkin to preside. So it was into his kindly, tear-filled eyes that I gazed as he united us at the Monterey Peninsula Naval Languages Institute. A reception afterward at their house in nearby Pebble Beach brought together our families and a few stray friends from along the California coast. After a few nights' honeymoon down the coast in Big Sur, we drove to San Francisco's Pier 15, on the Embarcadero, and boarded a freighter for Yokohama.

Friends and family came to see us off that night. Then the ship backed slowly out of its berth, turned, and glided in dark silence between Alcatraz and the Embarcadero. As we passed beneath the Golden Gate, I thought how close it looked, almost as if I could reach up and touch it. Then we were through and out into the black Pacific. Shivering, I turned aft to see the bridge lights and land's end, dipping, dimming, then disappearing.

"Your father has stopped eating," Nell says on the phone.

"Since when?"

"Three or four days ago. He won't chew or swallow. Angela can get a little soup down him, that's it. He's wasting away."

Driving to Dad's place, I feel alarm and some perplexity. I'd never credited him with having the resolution to end his own life. An older sister of his in an East Coast nursing home had stopped eating as a protest against going on, burdening her children further. A tough bird, that aunt. But Dad isn't made of the same stuff. What's going on?

A cool early-November morning along the ocean road. Snowy gulls cluster on empty sand among bleached driftwood and kelp. Satchel-mouthed pelicans cruise just above the glassy surface, then jackknife and dive, piercing their reflections. Yesterday, on the stretch where I run, I passed a whale carcass ravaged by birds and crabs and sand fleas, an offshore breeze bearing the salty stench hundreds of yards.

As I approach the canyon turnoff to my father's house, every bone in my body wants to keep going up this coast road, ribbon of flight in youth—anywhere but to that site of upbringing and strife, now a temple to dying without surcease. At moments like this, I feel imprisoned in some cruel, interminable jest, in which my invincible father will in the end outlive me. I will remain in purgatorial service to false rumors of his imminent demise, then, like my mother before me, beat him to the grave.

I pull up to the house. Opening the front door, I inhale the odor of ammonia, iodine, and stale tobacco mixed with the elusive aroma of human failing. Angela cleans regularly but nothing stanches it. I traverse the carpeted corridor to Dad's room and find him in the rented hospital bed, only his head visible on a fluffed pillow. Sound asleep, he looks tiny, emaciated, barely alive. As I approach the bed, his eyes pop open. He looks sweetly up at me like a becalmed child.

"Tony boy," he murmurs. "My son."

He raises a gnarled hand, more skeleton than flesh, to the one person he still recognizes. I take it without aversion and squeeze it. A lump rises in my throat. Tears form at the corner of my eyes. Helplessly ambushed by compassion toward the one man for whom I could never summon much of it, I look away.

How small would I have to make myself to hold anything against this ash-cheeked specter, reduced to such an infantile state? How small, indeed, have I made myself all these decades, knotted and hobbled by a son's resentments? Today I only feel tenderness. The tears are for myself as much as for him. Why did release have to come this way, and this late?

"Dad, what's going on? Why aren't you eating?"

"Tony boy," he mumbles again.

"Aren't you hungry?"

He nods.

"Do you hurt somewhere?"

He opens his mouth and closes it a couple of times, like an expiring fish. He casts his eyes downward along his nose.

"Open your mouth, Dad."

I lean over and peer in. His lower denture hangs from its metal implant, broken away. The gum is inflamed, blood pooling the cavities.

"Does it hurt?"

He nods.

I call Angela and Nell in, show them the reason Dad can't eat. A grave, speedy discussion ensues. I telephone his dentist, who gives us the name of a colleague who makes house calls. He agrees to come that afternoon.

On visits home, a few hours always seemed an eternity, restlessness quickly driving me out on one excuse or another. Now, with Dad's permanent retraction to his bedroom, it's become a little easier. Still, waiting in the living room for the dentist to arrive, among objects, smells, and sounds that always represented stasis to me, I feel the panicky urge to run away, to somewhere, anywhere.

I thumb the daily paper, but it doesn't occupy me for long. Until even a few months ago, Dad would stare at a page of the *Los Angeles Times* for hours, as if decoding a Mayan epigraph, while Nell and I would watch him and wonder what he was experiencing. Little, I expect; but holding the newspaper to his eyes represented the comfort of repetition, and connection to the daily events of a vanishing world. For forty years, wherever I might be, I had only to glance at a headline or the nightly television news to know what my father was thinking about and what his opinion of it would be. This uncritical absorption had caused his politics to list to the right without his noticing, driving my mother, an astute mind and a lifelong liberal, to distraction. He'd become an unmitigated recipient of the American consensual view of events, devoid of leavening influences from elsewhere. Too bad, I always thought; for this was something his son could have provided—a window to the outside. But those virulent arguments of years ago had taught me that new perspectives upset him grievously, threatening the bulwarks of narcissism and memory he'd erected around himself.

In the silence, among dust motes stirred by shafts of sunlight through cracks in the curtains, I scan the bookshelf, whose only additions in the last thirty years seem to be either those I'd written, grouped in a section of their own, or books I'd given them as gifts, which often remained unread. When I was a boy, their books (and maps, photos, and records) modeled the world, my only stable set of references as we lurched from home to home, coast to coast (ten different houses or apartments, I counted once, and thirteen different schools).

The remaining volumes tended toward old Book-of-the-Month-Club selections from the 1940s, sequential tomes such as Churchill's memoirs or André Malraux's *Man's Fate*, their faded cloth spines echoing the dimmed currency of the words within. Mom's burgeoning interest in mysticism and the mind surfaces in Richard Wilhelm's translation of Jung's *Secret of the Golden Flower*, shouldered between a Christmas Humphries book on Buddhism and Karen Horney on psychoanalysis.

A small section of Japanalia tracks my Asian peregrinations: a big book on imperial Japanese gardens that interested Dad for some years, a Charles Tuttle edition of Lady Murasaki's diaries I'd bought Mom when they visited Anne and me, a Yukio Mishima novel I'm sure they never read. (A Zen scroll bought for five dollars at a Kyoto flea market in 1965 now hangs in my Venice studio, one of the only remaining Japanese artifacts of my years there; the rest Anne kept.)

As I take down the Murasaki and open the flyleaf, a parchment-thin blue aerogramme flutters out onto the beige carpet.

I bend down and pick it up. It bears a Japanese stamp. Written in blue ballpoint pen, dated May 14, 1965, it begins with an attempted haiku:

White morning
Mount Hiei floats upside down in the pond
A crow calls from a pine tree

We'd been in Kyoto just over a year by then. Four seasons in a land ruled by seasons, where on designated days in spring and fall the entire nation changes the colors it wears, and the shedding of cherry blossoms is a nationally televised event. My letter home bears a voice I don't quite recognize: quiet, formal, poetic. No trace of the hallucinatory scribbler of Tangier, the drug peddler of Paris, the bop drummer of Barcelona. I was twenty-five years old.

We lived in a tiny teahouse on the grounds of a small villa owned by a silk merchant's daughter. Summer among water bugs and tatami and typhoons, silk dye shimmering in river canals like iridescent carp. Monk's lunches of tofu and green tea in the compounds of Nanzen-ji, Noh plays by candlelight at Heian Shrine. Gardens and inns, pachinko arcades, salary men reading S&M comic books on the trains. A civilized culture, to be sure, but one far stranger than Morocco.

Soon after we'd debarked in Yokohama Harbor, I'd found myself rather too tall and pale and ill-put-together, an excess of limbs and motion, moving among a compact, impassive, purposeful mass of people in dark suits. Fumbling with chopsticks over food I didn't know, my wallet accumulating business cards I couldn't read proffered by curious, polite strangers, I couldn't figure out where I was, what I seemed to represent to these people, or why I'd come here. Once we'd stepped off the bullet train, we'd made our way to our first house, in the northern part of Kyoto, only a few blocks from Daitoku-ji, the Zen temple where I'd planned to slay the dragons of the mind.

Bamboo shadows brush the stairs
But no dust is stirred . . .

Several mornings after we got settled, I walked to Daitoku-ji, intent upon taking up the Way. A few blocks beyond the last noisy eastern boulevard, a stone lane turned into an earthen path, a wooded pine forest pressed in. The footpath ended at a tall, unvarnished wood *torii* gateway, behind which lay ancient Daizen-ji, the subtemple I sought. On the grounds, stillness ruled. I found the central monastery, a large wooden building nestled among the pines. I passed shaven-headed monks in brown robes, raking pebbled gardens. I listened to the rustle of *tabi* slippers along the burnished wood corridors, the splash of a bucket emptying, the hiss of a broom sweeping a floor as the monks went about their chores. In a reception room facing onto a simple sand garden, I saw the abbot, the *roshi,* observing the tea ceremony with two men in business suits.

I turned around and left. I knew in that instant I wasn't going to become an adept, a lay monk. Some deep identification with Buddhism had already impressed itself upon me and would never leave; but somewhere en route to Daitoku-ji, the kaleidoscopic reality of Japanese daily life had altered my direction. I never went back.

By the end of our first year in Kyoto, we'd taken our place among a small community of foreign scholars, potters, priests, and Zen students, among them the poets Gary Snyder and

Philip Whalen. I taught English to students and businessmen, lectured on American culture to Japanese Fulbright scholars, wrote essays on aspects of teaching for obscure Japanese magazines. In letters home I sound like that young instructor—opaque, intellectual, disclosing little. In fact, I was happy to be far away again, crafting an expatriate life away from America and my parents. Buzzing through the back streets and lanes and geisha quarters on a little 50cc Suzuki motor scooter, my teacher's jacket and tie flapping, I came to know the old capital's contours and moods. Though I'd left my drums behind in California—the clatter of Western percussion had no place in a Zen world—my students took me to odd little coffee bars and tearooms, introducing me to the intense, weird Japanese jazz scene. With a *nisei* friend from California I studied *gagaku*, Japanese court music, stately and slow, coming to understand rhythm not only as human heartbeat, step, or dance, as in Africa or Europe, but as interruptions in silence: the irregular sounds of nature: water, wind: the duration of time itself.

The Kyoto YMCA occupied a cramped downtown building, teaching haven to a dozen or so foreigners from the far reaches of empire—scholars, writers, drifters, Buddhists, artists—delivering serviceable English instruction for tiny wages, using oral methods not dependent upon knowing much Japanese (I'd cobbled together the rudiments of teaching English as a foreign language from a manual I'd read on shipboard). Soon other classes fell my way: teaching executives at the Daimaru and Takashimaya department stores, instructing private students at home. Gradually I penetrated the universities—Doshisha, Kansai Gakuin, Kyoto University. The inordinate respect accorded the role of *sensei*, teacher, in Japanese society invested me with a curious status, venerated for my purported skills yet strangely quarantined from ordinary life. Never in the nearly two years I was there was I invited beyond the *genkan*, the entry, of a Japanese home; the only interiors I ever saw were on television soap operas.

Twice a week I traveled to the nearby port cities of Osaka and Kobe to teach. One of my employers, a Europhile who wore a beret and constantly interjected French words into our conversation, dealt in *shunga*, Japanese erotic scrolls. His lifelong dream was to publish a book of his collection with English text. Each week, in a Kobe waterfront pub, he'd unscroll his treasures—a horizontal tumult of disrobings, leering faces, and exaggerated genitalia—then I'd go back to Kyoto and try to make something of his transliterated Japanese texts (my first, but not last, venture into erotic writing).

When I wasn't teaching, I wrote. I began a novel based upon my Europe experiences that bore an uncanny resemblance in structure and language to *Naked Lunch.* Hunched in tiny downtown coffee shops and tearooms between classes, I recorded the Japan around me in notebooks. On trains or trams to my classes, I filled them with verbal portraits of people snoozing, or reading, or staring out windows, imagining their lives, investing them with narratives. I spent hours at the Kyoto Zoo sketching animals in language—the dour pacings of a tattered gorilla, the loll of a hippopotamus, the strut of a purple-wattled cassowary. Sometimes, standing at the back of a crowd writing, I'd notice people had turned and were gaping at me, the true ape uncaged: the foreigner, the *gaijin.* Kyoto was still a provincial inland city, spared the war's ravages and postwar GI invasion; there were only three hundred *gaijin* in residence, most of them missionaries. People took my classes, I sometimes thought, less to learn English than to observe the antics of a Westerner, to watch my exasperation grow when I couldn't manage to get my students to pronounce *"sit"* as anything other than *"shit."* Insular and self-referential, Japanese tended to be as poor at learning languages as Americans.

If I was something of a freak, it was worse for shapely, blonde Anne, ogled and sometimes groped on the streets by schoolchildren and men. Trying out our young marriage in a place where nobody looked like us and everybody looked at us, glaringly visible yet isolated, simultaneously esteemed *sensei*s and "hairy barbarians" (the implication of the term *gaijin*), both insulated us and engendered strain. We lost weight; we suffered constant colds from the extreme changes in climate— icy winters around a *kotatsu* heater, simmering summers with an inadequate fan. A diet of rice and vegetables harvested from depleted postwar soil, and little meat, further sapped us. Still, we lived in a deeply aesthetic world, where, along the eastern Higashiyama hills beyond our teahouse, the tips of the pines hovered like ghost heads, gongs pealed in the mist, and in the fall russet *momiji* leaves lit the land in flame.

By our second year in Japan, sunk into a chill winter, we were making a living but saving little. Anne contracted berberi; soon afterward, I lost six weeks to hepatitis. By then it was clear we'd never be accepted in Japan as anything more than exotic professionals, channeled into places and roles reserved for foreigners in a closed society. I began to identify with the plight of Lafcadio Hearn, Japan's foremost explicator to the West in the preceding century. An esteemed Tokyo university professor and honored figure in Japan, he made the mistake of taking Japanese citizenship. Abruptly his salary was slashed, his honors were stripped, his quarters were reduced. He'd become a mere abject citizen of no pedigree, neither fish nor fowl, a man who didn't know his place, hence an object of scorn. We began to talk of leaving Japan when we'd saved a little more, taking a Messageries Maritimes freighter around the world to Europe, then working our way back to the States at some vague future point.

Friends passed through that winter with dire reports of escalating developments in Vietnam. In early 1966, students surged through the streets of Japan in bloody antiwar street demonstrations; one of my best students was killed. News from California suggested a radicalizing new American moment: Black Panthers, Pop Art, rock and roll, mass psychedelia. Letters from my mother intimated her health had worsened. We decided it was time to return home and try again to put some sort of American life together.

On departure day, dozens of students came to Kobe to see us off on our ship. Paper streamers joined us to our well-wishers on the pier, who tirelessly waved and cried. Tears streamed down our faces too as the ship pulled away, rending the streamers.

The *Brazil Maru* was a huge passenger vessel bearing dejected Japanese emigrants to a new life in São Paulo. The bar was crammed at all hours with melancholy drinkers. I saw a man lose his entire stake in a running twenty-four-hour mahjongg game and jump overboard. Nightly slide shows in Japanese illustrated the promise of the new land. In the tiny, bilious cabin where Anne and I bunked, I lay wrapped in my own fragile hopes and deeper dreads, the future uncertain once again. How would Anne and I survive together in clamorous, discordant, pressurized America after our time in delicate, refined Kyoto? Normal American adult function remained mysterious to me. Music seemed lost to me as a path; now I only wanted to write. But what sort of reception could I expect for my first attempts at fiction?

Was I addicted to exoticism? Had I drifted into displacement as a steady state, fated to wander endlessly? I knew there were plenty of other Americans like me along the airways, the steamer lines, the donkey trails. I'd run into them brandishing their little stamp-filled blue passports before dour border officials, catching last planes out as some countries closed off while others opened. I'd see them out there, circling earth, their papers in order, attuned to travel advisories, terrorist alerts, and border skirmishes, pockets full of undigested currencies, punched stubs, names of cheap tasty restaurants in exotic capitals scribbled in matchbooks. I'd notice them in hotel lounges, plazas, and cafés where foreigners deposit themselves to drink or wait, or in remote village bars, watching some American football game or election on television. I'd watch them staring blearily at Samsonites, garment bags, and backpacks tumbling onto shiny aluminum conveyors, seldom speaking, eyes flicking, never steadying on anything for very long. Artists, intelligence men, traders, drifters, addicts. Never stopping, never adhering, taking brief comfort in the purchased hospitality of peoples whose smiles of welcome hid fathomless scorn. To them, earth was a single city, its countries neighborhoods of a vast polyglot metropolis.

Though I studied them, peopled my notebooks with them, I was no different, really. If their axioms and evasions were becoming known to me, it was because they were mine.

On a flat, cloudless May day, the *Brazil Maru* pulled into L.A.'s San Pedro Harbor. We'd been away almost two years.

From the deck I looked down and saw a tiny figure at dockside: my father, having come, uninvited, to meet us.

Standing above his bed, I gaze up at a pair of framed Utamaro woodblock prints of geishas on the far wall. Anne and I had bought them, I remember, on Shinmonzen-dori in Kyoto one afternoon right before we left.

The visiting dentist, a bony man in a loud striped sweater, stands across from me, brandishing a metal implement. Nell and Angela hover anxiously behind us near the bedroom door.

"Now, if you could, just hold your dad's mouth open, please," the dentist says.

I reach down and pry open his jaw. Dad's mournful, trusting eyes fix upon mine. The dentist reaches in to do his work. From time to time I give Dad the high sign with my free hand.

"Here's the problem. See?"

I peer into his mouth where the dentist is shining his light. One of the pins holding an implant has come loose. Dad hasn't been eating because his lower denture won't hold, which prevents him from chewing.

"Looks like we'll need to put in a new implant," the dentist says.

"Will you have to anesthetize him?"

"Afraid so."

I wonder if Dad's body can take this. I remind the dentist he's ninety-four years old, and frail.

"We'll need to get his doctor's opinion," the dentist says.

"What would be the alternative?"

"No more solid food. Just liquids, intravenous feeding."

Until his imminent end, is the unspoken implication. *Out of his misery.*

My father seems to understand. He looks miserable. I glance back and see Nell's and Angela's frightened expressions, looking to me for an answer.

"Hold his mouth open again, please," the dentist says.

As he digs in Dad's gums again, our heads come close together. I can smell the dentist's minty breath.

"Hey, we're in luck," he says. "The implant is unscrewed, that's all. Just needs tightening."

He reaches for another tool, ratchets the implant tight, then hooks Dad's lower denture back into place.

"Piece of cake," he says.

"You mean that's it?" I say.

"Yup."

Dad will be able to eat again! He'll live longer! I feel an odd happiness at this little victory, this reprieve. We can't go on; we'll go on.

"Is that better?" the dentist asks my father amiably, packing his tools in his bag. Dad, his jaw trembling, is unable to reply. Angela rushes off to prepare him some food.

I write the dentist a check and see him off at the door. I turn around to find Nell standing there, a beatific smile on her face.

"You know," she says, "you're all your father cares about now."

How strange, I think, getting into my car a few minutes later, that things would turn out this way.

25. The Palm Reader

I sat disconsolately on the edge of a bed in a Holiday Inn motel in Ames, Iowa, my head in my hands, my stomach rumbling with hunger. I needed to use the bathroom and thought of going on ahead to the lobby but felt I shouldn't. My roommate, the North Indian drummer Kumar, would expect to find me here when he finished his interminable morning ablutions. Splashing, chants, snapping towels: I couldn't imagine what he did in there, why it took him a good hour each morning.

I looked at Kumar's little framed image of the fire god Kali on the dressing table. Soon he'd emerge from the bathroom in fresh-pressed white shirt and dhoti, patchouli flooding the air. A small dark man with thick, straight oil-slicked black hair and pocked cheeks, he'd stand before his icon, palms together in prayer. Then there'd be the careful attaching of the silver wristwatch band, the zipping of the leather handbag, the slipping into the thonged sandals. We'd knock on Chatterjee's door, he'd appear equally abluted, reeking of strawberry attar, and off we'd go to another tasteless motel breakfast among gawking Midwestern folk.

We'd been on tour over two months, crisscrossing the country by car and plane. By day I took drumming instruction from Kumar, then shepherded him and Pankaj Chatterjee, maestro of the ancient, multi-stringed sitar, across the American heartland to our next concert. Each night I appeared onstage as musical explicator and tamboura player, sitting crosslegged on the rug-covered dais behind the two virtuosi, plucking the drone instrument that establishes the key and scale of the music with my right hand, keeping the *tala*, the beat, with my left, while these master musicians from Calcutta spun sublime ragas to enthralled, if mystified, audiences.

It was early December 1967, and ever since George Harrison had taken up the sitar with Ravi Shankar and the Beatles had embraced Maharishi Mahesh Yogi, an infatuation with Indian music gripped the country. The hippie era was in full swing, and we were part of it somehow. Dressed in white Indian garb, my hair down to my shoulders, I'd step to a microphone and deliver a brief explanation of Indian classical music. Then I'd settle onto the dais in a cloud of sandalwood incense, strum the tamboura in my lap, and contemplate the hippie girls in the front row clutching flowers and gazing reverently up at us.

Our three-month tour was to culminate at New York's Town Hall in a week, part of an Indian Music Festival also featuring Ravi Shankar and the peerless sarod artist Ali Akbar Khan. On mornings like this, I wondered if I'd make it. Countless nights in Holiday Inns, flagging conversation with my two wards during day-long drives across barren landscapes, and dismal meals of coleslaw, unfrozen peas, and mashed potatoes in Howard Johnsons had rendered me terminally roadsick. I desperately missed Anne and our new baby daughter, Maya, alone back in San Francisco. A few weeks shy of my twenty-eighth birthday, I was tangled in yet another exotic artistic odyssey with no clear outcome. Only the divine music each night redeemed me.

I parted the motel curtain and peered outside. Patches of snow lay on the parking lot, the empty field beyond. A lone truck moved slowly across an access road. The day before, we'd arrived by plane from Kansas City and been met at the airport by Amiya, a graduate student at the university where we were to play that night, assigned to us as host. He'd delivered us to a suburban house and into the worshipful arms of the local Indian community, amid rich aromas of incense and curries, deep bows, clasped-hand greetings of *"namaste."* Parathas and biryanis prepared by sari-clad women erased our weariness, making us feel loved, if only for a moment. More often we arrived in featureless mid-American college towns, checked in at motels or hotels, received brusque written instructions telling us where and when to appear, played before an audience dim beyond the footlights, and were left to our own devices afterward. How strange this must have seemed to Kumar and Chatterjee, coming from a teeming, fecund, music-obsessed land where adoring crowds thronged train stations to greet them with flowers, food, and gifts. Two dark men in dhotis, they were met by silence and suspicion in small-town America, and as the tour wore on, I could hear melancholy creeping into the music.

In the overlit pink-and-orange hotel coffee shop, Kumar took the top off the pepper shaker and emptied a third of it on his eggs, a move always guaranteed to turn the local diners' heads. Chatterjee, still awaiting a packet of spices from India ("the one thing I forgot to bring," he'd say, shaking his head and clucking *"acha"*), addressed a lumpen stack of pancakes. Later that morning Amiya was to deliver us to our flight to Chicago and a concert at Northwestern University that night. Then on to Ohio for engagements at Oberlin College and the Cleveland Museum, a recital in Buffalo, and finally Manhattan for the climactic Town Hall Concert. While Kumar and Chatterjee talked in Bengali over coffee, I finished a letter home to Anne.

It had been a year and a half since we'd returned from

Japan. Serene, ascetic Kyoto had quickly receded into a Lilliputian time-warp in the face of the American cultural tumult that greeted us upon re-entry. Passionate prophecies poured from babbling tongues, artists disappeared into local sanitariums, friends essayed ecstatic leaps from buildings. Poets broke bread with Hells Angels, Black Panthers wrote literary apologias, warships bore body bags across San Francisco Bay.

Seeking some peace, Anne and I migrated down the coast. We rented a cabin in the woods south of Carmel, along the Big Sur road, that had been occupied by the novelist and folk musician Richard Fariña and his wife, Mimi, whose sister Joan Baez lived nearby. Fariña, a few weeks after I'd met him, had been thrown from a motorcycle following a publication party nearby celebrating his first novel, and died. It was in that cliffside cabin that we learned Anne was pregnant.

Build a house, write a poem, have a child. So had Robinson Jeffers, craggy bard of the Carmel coast, once counseled. While the greater culture beyond splintered, Anne and I would pursue just such a handmade, authentic existence. I worked on a construction crew, laying up house frames in the fog in jeans and gum boots. I edited books for would-be local authors. At night I wrote at an old wooden table overlooking the thundering Pacific. Pregnant Anne and I walked among the tidepools and sea-lion enclaves of Point Lobos; explored Henry Miller's old Big Sur haunts; hiked Bixby Creek, where Kerouac had spewed his amphetamine-fueled *On the Road* in Lawrence Ferlinghetti's cabin.

One weekend I drummed with a pickup band at the Monterey Fairgrounds; Janis Joplin sat in for a couple of tunes. But after jazz and Zen, rock-and-roll drumming felt clamorous, mindless, repetitive. My life as a working musician to all appearances behind me, I set out instead to finish the novel begun in Japan. At night I lay listening to the child kicking inside of Anne while U.S. battleships on maneuvers fired rounds of artillery offshore.

Maya arrived at a hospital in the pines, perfect and beautiful, a reason for hope. We bore her tiny swaddled radiance home to our cabin overlooking the sea. At dusk we wandered the coastal strand, a new little family, our Irish setter racing ahead to fetch driftwood we tossed. A sweet life, without ambition—a rustic bohemia that should have sufficed.

Then, one Sunday afternoon at Big Sur Hot Springs, I heard the North Indian sarod master Ali Akbar Khan perform a raga with a young Calcutta drummer. In these passionate, deep melodies, I thought I heard a way out of the prison of Western musical forms. Sublime polyrhythms on the pitched pair of Indian hand drums, the tabla—a fount of metrics from the Indus, wending back to Sanskrit and the Vedas—seemed to weld music and speech, braiding the twin strands of my life together. When I learned that Ali Akbar Khan and his drummer would be teaching classes in Berkeley that summer, I knew I had to be there.

The pastoral idyll was over. In May 1967 the three of us, plus dog, moved to San Francisco and a flat in North Beach. I continued editing books for money, and I began my tabla studies.

Ali Akbar Khan's music school, funded by a wealthy newspaper heir and his wife who had a passion for Indian dance, drew a quirky band of disenchanted Western musicians to study at the feet of this genuine master. Working with the drummer I'd heard in Big Sur, I progressed relatively quickly—up to the level perhaps of an eight-year-old Indian student. I'd sit before the two drums, the smaller of wood, the larger of metal, each with a hide skin on top, producing an astonishing variety of sounds with fingers, hands, and the palms of the hand—though nothing compared with the range, speed, variety, and emotional inflections the best drummers wrung out of them. I began performing around the Bay Area in small concerts with Ali Akbar Khan's best sarod student.

In our San Francisco flat, Anne's behavior was taking odd, distressing turns. She often seemed inconsolably sad, dispirited. Her father, the navy chaplain, an eager disciple of *Games People Play* shrink Eric Berne, whom he called "the next Freud," arranged for group-therapy sessions with Berne. Before long she wanted me to join her. I attended a couple of sessions and couldn't wait to get out of there. Berne, a hook-nosed, pipe-smoking man in mustache and tweed jacket, presided over a half-dozen poor souls confessing impotence, fears, and insecurities as if he had answers, which it was clear to me he didn't. Whatever my human failings, this miserable convocation hardly seemed the way to unburden them.

We struggled on in North Beach with our baby daughter, our marriage fragile, money scarce, while around us in the streets mania deepened. It was the Summer of Love, in the press's coinage, and the world's media had descended upon the Bay Area like an occupying force, turning daily life into spectacle. We pushed baby Maya in a stroller through the Haight-Ashbury; the Panhandle, where the Diggers were giving away free food; Golden Gate Park during the Human Be-In. I filmed with an 8mm camera the march through the city to Kezar Stadium, listened to Eldridge Cleaver, Jerry Rubin, and Timothy Leary make portentous speeches. It was hard to make plans or address personal life when the world as we'd known it seemed on the verge of coming apart.

Late that summer, the owners of the Indian music school announced the arrival of India's new young lion of the sitar, the "next Ravi Shankar," thirty-two-year-old Pankaj Chatterjee, for a three-month concert tour of the U.S. They needed a tour manager and tamboura player. Seeing a chance to study one-on-one with a great drummer, make a little money, and escape my difficulties with Anne, I applied for the job and got it.

So, on that snowy morning after breakfast in Ames, Iowa, I sat on the motel floor across from Kumar, my feet folded beneath me, my hand drums, silver tuning hammer, and Johnson's baby powder to dry the hands before me. Kumar recited patterns of sound aloud—*"Dha deri kita taka. Kita taka deri deri"*—each syllable corresponding to a distinctive hand stroke on one of the two drums, all within the ornate rules of Indian metrics. I repeated them vocally; then we played the results in unison. If there was a drumming beyond jazz, beyond Africa even, this was it.

At eleven, Amiya knocked on the door. Outside, snowflakes whirled. I grabbed my drums and luggage. We headed out into another day of travel.

Amiya drove us down flat, icy roads past stands of barren trees, Kumar in front next to him, Chatterjee in back with me, his sitar in Indian cloth-and-foam padding stretched across our laps.

Chatterjee was an educated, lively man deeply versed in

both Indian and Western culture. A true musical prodigy, he'd made his concert debut at the age of six. Along the unfolding American highways, we'd spoken of the Bengali writer and composer Rabindranath Tagore, the differences between Western and Eastern music, James Bond, the caste system, *atman*, and the nature of the soul. I'd tried to introduce him to my musical enthusiasms, but he found most contemporary Western music cold, anxious, ugly. Yet this improvisatory genius whose *ragas* reached the loftiest realms would fiddle with the radio dial while I drove, lingering on the "easy-listening" stations, enchanted by the idea that twenty-five strings could play in unison. "In my country," he'd say, waggling his head, "you can't get two or three musicians to play together. This is the general problem of modern India, you see. Too much individualism. Everybody at cross-purposes." At gas stations, while Chatterjee and Kumar went to the men's room, I'd switch the radio to other music on the airwaves that year: Stevie Wonder's "Signed, Sealed and Delivered," Eddie Floyd's "Knock on Wood," Aretha's "Chain of Fools."

At the Ames airport, we were told our flight to Chicago was delayed because of snow conditions. We waited in the small coffee shop, Amiya stirring cardamom and other spices into our Lipton's tea in Styrofoam cups to make Indian *chai*.

The three Indians chatted and giggled in Bengali. Then Chatterjee turned to me and said, "Amiya comes from an old Calcutta family of fortune-tellers. Not the usual chaps on the street. These are Brahmins, trained priests. Good families consult them on every important matter—births, weddings, business matters."

"I trained in palm reading for seven years," Amiya said.

"Longer than for my doctorate in metallurgical engineering. When I go back to India I'll practice both."

Outside, snow flurries danced in the air. The few planes on the tarmac were grounded, and none were landing. Amiya said something in Bengali. Chatterjee turned to me. "Amiya has offered to read our palms."

Amiya, stirring his tea, smiled softly. Tall and lean, with limpid eyes and dark, sensitive features, he was dressed neatly, like an American student, in khakis and button-down shirt and loafers. "Only if you wish to, of course," he said.

"You can start with me," Chatterjee said jovially.

Amiya moved his chair across from Chatterjee's and cradled the sitarist's left palm in his hand. He studied it, tracing various lines with his forefinger.

"You see here," Amiya said. "The lifeline is very strong. No breaks. You'll live long. And here, it looks as if your wife—you're married, yes?—will bear you a second child. Late next year. A son, it would appear."

Chatterjee beamed with pleasure. "Yes, we've hoped for a son."

"Really, this is an exceptional palm. The lines are clear, and correspond to each other properly. You will have a long life, great success in your career, many grandchildren."

Chatterjee lowered his head modestly, thanked Amiya in Bengali.

But, then, this was hardly a surprise. Chatterjee seemed to have everything going for him. From a high Brahmin family, his path had been smooth from childhood. At thirty-two, five years older than I, he already had fame, money, a lovely wife, and two children, and was nearing the peak of his art, the heir apparent to Ravi Shankar. Living within an art sanctified by centuries of culture and tradition, he was spared the vain, individualized Western search for identity. He seemed to have little neurosis about him, only humility, calm, and stunning command on his instrument. I envied but didn't begrudge him his good fortune. That it would last throughout his life made sense to me.

Kumar's palm was a mixture of good and ill fortune. He'd been sent to study music as a boy and had quickly risen through the ranks of India's young tabla players. A fiery drummer, he'd performed on a famous recording with Ravi Shankar when he was still quite young, and now, in his late thirties, was a highly regarded player. Amiya's reading suggested he'd have a reasonably long life with a few setbacks and injuries, including an upcoming illness in the family. His musical trajectory wouldn't take him much higher than this. Kumar seem unsurprised at the reading, and reasonably content. His fortune, too, seemed to add up.

The readings were deep, and we were growing serious around the table.

Amiya pulled his chair across from me, took my pale upturned left palm in his, and smoothed it out as if it were a piece of parchment. He studied it for a long time, his dark forefinger gently tracing the indentations. Then he spoke softly—reluctantly, it seemed: "Your present work will not last, and you will abandon it."

I wondered what work he was referring to. Tour manager? Tabla player? Sometime editor, unemployed musician, underground filmmaker, unpublished novelist? What in fact was my work at this point?

Then Amiya said, "I'm sorry to tell you, but your marriage will not last much longer."

I looked dully at the floor. How to respond to this, even to think about it? I'd been missing Anne and my little girl terribly lately and couldn't wait to get back to them; yet in some uncanny way Amiya's prediction didn't come as a surprise.

Amiya said something in Bengali. Chatterjee said, "He wants to know if it's all right to tell you the rest."

"Of course."

Amiya said, "You are greatly torn between spirit and matter. You will achieve some fame." He traced a line running up the center of my palm. "And see here? This is the lifeline. It is broken."

"What does that mean?"

Amiya looked carefully up at me. "You will die in middle age, violently, while traveling."

I looked down where Amiya's finger lingered on the deep fissure curving up the middle of my palm. Clearly it was sundered midway, breaking jaggedly off from its root, then crossed by another line. The fatal rupture lay before my eyes.

"I am very sorry," Amiya said, his large brown eyes regarding me with helpless compassion.

I felt numb, as if the snow and ice and gray sky outside the airport waiting room had entered through the glass into me. The sounds of the airport dimmed, the fluorescent lights seemed to flicker weakly. Kumar and Chatterjee looked off into the air, anywhere but at me.

On the plane to Chicago I sat next to Chatterjee. His long, beautiful wood sitar with its seventeen metal sympathetic strings and ornate inlaid ivory rested in the seat next to him.

Your present work will not last. True, as my twenty-seventh year came to a close, I had no idea what I wanted to do with my life. This was a thorny matter Amiya had unearthed in my palm. Did I imagine I'd become an Indian master drummer at this late date? I had a wife and child to support, and no money but what this tour put in my pocket for Anne and Maya. My wanderings, my murky struggles with art and identity, had added up to little. A hopeless eclectic, a perennial student (a term thrown at me by my father), a financial flop, I saw friends and family giving up on me. Lately I could read it in their eyes. A botched life, foretold in my palm, a text etched into my very skin.

Your marriage will not last much longer. Anne and I had been having difficulties since the beginning. Sometimes I wondered if marriage, Japan, the pregnancy weren't just stratagems to raise the stakes with new commitments. Anne's unfathomable sadness only seemed to worsen. Was it my fault?

You will die in middle age, violently, while traveling. The verdict tolled like a judgment. So it was all worthless anyway, the remaining years a mere hollow, abortive exercise. Where would my end come, and when? And when did middle age commence?

Chatterjee, seeing me glumly sunk down in myself, said in his chirpy Indian English, "These boys are correct. It is a science. But you must remember"—he reached over and tapped my knee—"there is always the element of *will.* You can change your fate by your own intention. I have seen the lines of the palm change on a man. So don't be so downcast, my friend."

I looked at him miserably.

"No destiny is absolute," he said. "By your own efforts you can improve your karma." He giggled slightly. "Besides, when you think about it, isn't this what we're all doing, whatever our state? All we can do is our best during our allotted time."

As the plane dropped through snowy cloud cover onto the O'Hare tarmac, Chatterjee's words, tendered as consolation, served only to distance his perfect fate further from my hopeless one. I stood and left the plane, a walking ghost, trapped inside the cracked shell of a futile, abbreviated life.

Four nights later, on the road from Cleveland to Buffalo, our rented car hit an ice slick and fishtailed on a narrow bridge in the dark, barely missing a plunge into the freezing river below. We came to a halt pointed in the other direction, uninjured but shaken. The instruments were intact, fortunately. I got the car turned around and drove my frightened Brahmins to Buffalo. I could feel their alarm: the person entrusted with their lives was starting to self-destruct.

"At least I'm not middle-aged yet," I tried to joke as we pulled up to the downtown hotel that night.

"Chatterjee's good fortune will protect us both," Kumar said.

"Let's hope so," said Chatterjee, sounding a little less than certain.

A few nights later, all of trendy New York turned out at Town Hall, it seemed—rock idols and ballet stars, film celebrities and critics, musicians of every stripe and idiom. The Indian community in its best finery mingled with newly minted hippies. Chatterjee's rich, meditative morning raga, transporting in beauty and depth, made his name in the city. After intermission, an evening raga built to an exhilarating call-and-response, a flurry of counterrhythms and wit, bringing the crowd to its feet. Sitting behind Kumar and Chatterjee with my tamboura, as in the photo that appeared in the newspapers, I was proud for my maestros, the travails of the tour—and a troubled year in the world—eased by this triumph. We took three encores.

A few days later, I was back in North Beach with Anne and baby daughter Maya, exhausted and emptied. My final tour check arrived, enough to last us through Christmas and beyond. Anne seemed even more distant, unreachable. We'd sit on the bed at night trying to talk about it, but I couldn't get through to her. I had missed her and Maya so terribly much; now, home at last, I felt like a stranger. Was it the therapy? Was there some-one else?

Ten days after my return, heartbroken and dazed, I left our apartment in North Beach, Amiya's dire predictions echoing in my ears. Our split had played out with the mute inevitability of a dream. I hitched my way south down Route 1, through Big Sur, hoping to find work in L.A., another life, some path of es-cape from the message of doom engraved in my palm.

26. The Loved One

November 1999. Six months in California indentured to my father's decline. Masako has returned to our house in Mexico, since there's no reason for her to live through any more of this. Neighbors and acquaintances have fallen away, leaving only Nell, Angela, me, and occasionally my sister or the grandkids.

Yet a paradoxical cheer gathers around Dad's house. Swathed in dream and forgetfulness, he has become trusting, pliant, grateful for the slightest attentions. When I visit him he looks up at me innocently, sweetly, reminding me of my daughter in her crib long ago. Thin and weak, he mostly sleeps now. His few remaining words are mumbled words of gratitude. Seeing him fills me with improbable affection.

In a way, the less of him there is, the easier it is to like him. Nothing intercedes between us any longer; only tenderness prevails. Forgiveness has come almost without my noticing, on a level deeper than personality. Not one of the things that separated us all those decades has been resolved, yet we're peaceful. No more axes to grind, riddles to tease out of family or fate. What passes between my father and myself now might qualify, I suppose, as one of love's humbler forms. The irradiated pages of the family photo albums drawn shut, I carry them back to the living room and replace them on the shelf.

In a leatherette booth of a Mexican restaurant in Santa Monica, my sister, Meg, and I slosh margaritas, talk about what we'll do when he goes. We agree we have to do something. Our mother had insisted there be no ceremony when she died; then, one day, she was gone—erasure, void. The grandchildren in particular have since confessed to feeling confused, bereft of the chance to grieve or say goodbye. All attention in the weeks and months following had gone to my father, to the exclusion of anyone else. I tell Meg I can't recall having had a moment to reflect upon my mother's death, Dad's needs had so dominated things. Typically, he hadn't seemed to notice.

I stare at the laminated menu, an illustrated montage of tostada salads, fajitas, nachos, burritos—items seldom found in Mexico proper and certainly not in the region where I live. The gringo menu makes me aware of my exile here in L.A., land of the teriyaki burger—a vast, mutating food court. I settle upon a "fiesta combination plate," fearing the worst.

Dad sometimes spoke of his older sister, who, when she passed, had her ashes scattered about her rose garden. Other times he talked about our burying his at Meg and her husband's ranch. The subject of death has generally confused him, as have most matters of substance, and by now it's far too late for him to express his wishes. Meg and I concur that there's never been the slightest whisper of anything religious, which would have confounded us. At this point we couldn't summon much of a gathering even if we wanted to, since he's outlived all but a few friends and colleagues. We incline toward something at her ranch with immediate family—a relief, as I'd dreaded the thought of being called upon to deliver some sort of encomium, for fear of what I might say.

If Meg and I, four years apart growing up, had become distant as our adult lives diverged, we've rediscovered each other during the seventeen years since my mother's death in surprising, pleasurable ways—stealing moments at family holidays or on the phone, reviewing Dad's rise and fall and peculiar stultifying egoism, decoding Mom's drinking, speculating about what had really happened behind closed doors when we were kids. Breaking the seal on family secrets, we've excavated buried cities of youth, held up shards to the light. Like surgeons, we've examined lesions that burned, scarred, cauterized. Growing up a continent away from other family members, in a nuclear quartet isolated by alcoholism, career rupture, and uncertain social status, our secrets never named or spoken of, Meg and I have had to plumb the mysteries and trade revelations for ourselves.

Tonight we talk for the first time about what might happen when Dad dies. Usually we banter about his longevity. Even now, into our second margaritas, we speculate darkly as to how many more years he might endure in this vegetative state, a hoary icon, a monument to the body's obstinacy, as the family funds dwindle to nothing.

"But when—if—he does go," Meg says, "what about the bequests?"

I burst out laughing. Several years ago, Dad, in his dotage and with nothing left to do, began fiddling with gifts of money he planned to leave to others. The bequests existed as codicils, written addenda to his will. This became an obsession, a sort of Dickensian accounting based upon who was naughty or nice. Each time I saw him he'd tweaked the list yet again, raising or dropping people as they called or failed to, sent holiday greetings cards or didn't. My repeated urgings to leave the bequests alone fell on deaf ears. I queried his lawyer, who pointed out

that if bequests are changed too often the estate could be contested later on the basis that the old person was not of sound
mind. Most of them were in amounts far too small to warrant
such scrutiny—a few thousand to a nephew, a lesser gift to an
old crony—but he was changing them so often that I finally
suggested he just let me jot them down informally on pieces of
paper, offering my blood assurance they'd be honored.

Over his long life, Dad had managed to store away some assets, mostly in the form of stocks, bonds, and cash from the sale
of the avocado ranch he'd bought in the 1960s. It was the ranch
proceeds that enabled him to stay in his home. Still, if he lives
on another few years, we'll run out of money and have to take
out a mortgage. Even now there isn't enough left to pay death
taxes and bequests without selling the house.

"It can't be worth much," I say to Meg. "A tear-down, don't
you think?"

"You might be surprised. The market's coming back. And
believe it or not, those postwar ranch-style houses are cool these
days."

Impossible to imagine anyone lusting after that low-slung,
one-story lath-and-plaster place whose featureless rooms bleed
into one another.

The arrival of food rescues us from further discussion of bequests, which would soon have touched upon Kitty, the ex-show-
girl, still a sore spot among the women of the family—though
things have cooled off since Kitty's bequest collapsed from ten
thousand to zero on Dad's final go-round.

When it came to money, my father had always played his
cards close to his vest; I never knew what he had or didn't have.
Ever since he refused to help me with medical school, I didn't
want to hear about it. I always suspected he was worth more

than he let on. Finally, one day when he was nearing ninety, he said, ceremoniously, "Son, I think it's time you knew a few things about the family affairs."

Joking about this with Meg over enchiladas, I recall a time a few years back when she was in temporary difficult straits and asked Dad for an advance of ten thousand dollars against her inheritance. He didn't respond. I interceded for her, begged, pleaded. Still he wouldn't cough it up. Finally Meg drove down from Santa Barbara and literally thrust a pen and checkbook in front of him. The magnanimous charmer, the popular and kindly show-biz great, a hero once to his adoring daughter, had ended up in her eyes a suspicious, frightened geezer hoarding his *gelt*. No, longevity hasn't served him well.

"I loved living in that house when I was a kid," Meg says—words she'd never hear from me. "But these days it's such an effort to come visit."

How ironic that I've arrived at a tentative peace with the idea of him, while Meg, who had idealized him, is left with resentment and frustration. But, then, her fall from innocence came much later than mine.

Meg says, sounding suddenly pragmatic: "If he goes soon, it's winter. Christmas season. Bad time to put the house on the market. Spring would be better."

A mariachi band belabors a table in the next room with "Las Mañanitas," the Mexican birthday song, my cue to call for the check.

"How many times," Meg says, "I've wished Mom could see the way things have turned out for you."

"You too. Believe me."

"No, I mean that you really got somewhere with your writing. Your life."

I reach for my wallet. "I didn't give either of them much reason for hope."

Yesterday, as I was leaving my father's house, Nell said something similar, about how pleased my mother would be at what I'd become. Then she added, "And how good you are with your father."

I winced inwardly. Still, she couldn't have said anything kinder.

"I guess, when all this is over," Meg said, "you're outta here."

"I expect so."

"You earned it," she said. "But I'll miss you."

I awaken before dawn, agitated and restless. For some minutes I don't know where I am. A mist hangs over the canals, so thick I can barely see the water a few yards away. I slip into my clothes and make coffee among traces of dreams of remote places. At first light I get into my car and begin driving aimlessly into the city, taking the surface streets, avoiding the freeways.

From wide, near-deserted Venice Boulevard, I angle north across the flats toward the Hollywood foothills. Wending up fabled, tawdry Vine Street, I feel myself entering my father's territory, a landscape that later became mine *en passant*: Dick Monahan's Drum Shop, Gold Star Recording Studios, the Capitol Building like a stack of records. Turning west down Sunset Boulevard, I realize I am unthinkingly tracing a route I once wrote into a novel. It's all too much, a hall of mirrors.

Driving slowly along cheerless Sunset Strip—past Schwab's Drugstore, the Château Marmont, the Player's Restaurant,

Tower Records, the Whiskey, the Rainbow Grill—I realize I might never drive these streets again. The journey begins to take the shape of a valedictory tour.

In California, private and public memory merge in recollection. Mom is Susan Hayward drying out after an onscreen bender. Dad is *Father Knows Best*, Willy Loman, Mister Magoo. Schwab's is less a drugstore than the soda fountain where Veronica Lake was discovered sipping a milkshake, the Château Marmont less a hotel than a stage set for dramas of fatal excess. My childhood recollections of L.A.'s Chinatown were permanently refigured by Polanski. Does it matter what is real, what simulacrum? Ed Ruscha's *Sunset Strip* series models this drive, the Eagles' fast-lane mini-epics etch its subtext. Proust's madeleine, to a kid growing up here, is whatever hit single was playing when you were fourteen.

Sheared hillsides, garbage piled on the street beneath outsized airbrushed billboard heads. Such extravagant desolation. The Strip in early glare exposes last night's revels, a janitor sweeping tissues and condoms into the gutter at the corner of King's Road. Hollywood's permanent morning-after. It was here, in this monument to transience, that I, my family, my society were projected into a 1950s dream future that would never arrive. At Union Station, where elegant Cary Grants and Loretta Youngs once swept off trains and into each other's celluloid arms, tattered winos and immigrants huddle beneath the soaring carved beams, curl up asleep in the grand Deco leather chairs. Enough to break your heart.

Turning left, I drop down the first steep block of La Cienega Boulevard, with its broad vista across the basin past the airport. Drifting with scant traffic, I pass low buildings that figured in my life after I arrived back here in 1968: the Tropicana Motel, the old Doors office, Elektra Records. I pass the block where Warhol had his first Pop Art show at the Ferus Gallery, and where earlier the old émigré painter Warshawsky rendered that canvas that still hangs in Dad's dusky hallway: Mom as Madonna of the Lakes.

Which of these telephone poles, I wonder, had Mom wrapped her car around that night long ago, climaxing the epic spree that occasioned the overnighter in the Hollywood jail and her first long sanitarium sabbatical? I slow and pull the car to the curb. Switching off the engine, I lean my forehead against the steering wheel.

My mother would sometimes assume a tone of hauteur, of moral superiority—a censoriousness, directed mostly toward me. Upset at some failing of mine, she'd flash the heat of her anger. It seemed she held some abstract, unannounced standard of behavior I couldn't see, and it was crushing to feel that I hadn't managed to meet it. I just knew I was selfish and small and hadn't behaved properly or performed up to expectations. Normally sensitive and compassionate, she became unkind and mean in those moments, in the name of some corrective principle. It wasn't something she controlled well. Maybe it was the stern moral training, that harsh Puritan legacy inflicted upon her by her mother's family. Of course she'd been crushed by her own fall, her sobriety never ameliorating her sense of guilt and failure but instead encumbering her with an endless penance. Since it was difficult to gain her praise, I just tried to avoid her blame. I respected her values and her attempts to live up to them, even impose them on me; but being at the end of her moral censure was withering. It was hard to measure up.

Her anger became embedded in me. I enacted it unconsciously upon those around me in love or work. Like her, I harbored an unseen, undisclosed measure of performance. If I imagined slowness or laziness or selfishness or ineffectuality in those close to me, it stirred me to rage in that same way as it had her. I felt undermined by the perpetrator and suspected this was intended somehow. It took me years to untangle that rage.

My mother, I see now, had pinned her hopes on me to redeem us both—indeed, the entire family. She was pouring her thwarted expectations for herself into me, a burden I neither understood nor could bear. How disappointed she must have been.

Morning traffic streams past. I get out of the car and enter a little coffee shop. As I sit down at the counter I hear a radio playing:

And the days dwindle down to a precious few
September ... November ...

It's too neat. Schnozzola, rasping the signature song of his late years. Uncle Jimmy, who brought us all out here to this coast so Dad could produce and direct his radio shows. Years later Dad would make the pilgrimage to the house in Beverly Hills and sit next to the great aging comic in his wheelchair and blanket, as if visiting a living saint. "September Song." Brecht and Kurt Weill had done their time in L.A. too. Sipping hot, tasteless American brew, I feel a sadness as deep and dark as the antediluvian La Brea Tar Pits nearby.

And these few precious days
I'll spend with you. ...

"Those people out there," Morrison said, gesturing beyond the walls at the streets below, "don't know they're going to die."

We were sitting in the Doors' office at the corner of Santa Monica Boulevard and La Cienega. Morrison had a Nagra portable tape recorder in his lap that he was itching to use. The band had finished recording what would stand as their penultimate album together, *Morrison Hotel*, at the Elektra Records studios across the street. During a recent Florida concert, Jim had allegedly exposed himself to the audience and in the wake of his desperate theatrics, concert promoters had blacklisted the band. Grounded while awaiting his court trial in Miami, he had time on his hands. He suggested we alleviate the desultory afternoon by taking the Nagra out on the street and querying passersby as to their awareness of their own mortality.

A few doors down La Cienega, in a two-story stucco edifice called the Clear Thoughts Building, Morrison was overseeing the cutting of *Feast of Friends*, a film he was making with Frank Lisciandro, a fellow UCLA film-school grad and the mutual friend who had introduced us. The Kem moviola spooled interminable takes of Jim in leather pants walking down a deserted highway outside of Palm Springs in wavery heat: the Lizard King *in situ*.

Morrison and I had become casual friends that year. Our educations and experiences were not dissimilar, and we shared certain literary and cultural interests—Blake and Rimbaud, European art films, jazz and essential blues. I found him good company when sober, more interesting artistically and intellectually than his detractors suspect—he read continually and deeply—if less than his rock adulators imagine. I'd try to catch up with him during the days, when things were calmer, saner, before afternoons inevitably slid into blowsy, incoherent nights at a strip club half a block away called the Topless Extension, Morrison's de-facto clubhouse and watering hole. There the conversation grew fatuous, the circle of acolytes around the leatherette booths wider and drearier, and eventually I'd become bored and slip away. Still, I was in Jim's debt that summer of 1969, for he'd done me a true favor.

A year and a half had passed since I'd left Anne and Maya in North Beach. Arriving alone and broke in a city I'd never known as an adult, I hadn't the slightest idea how to gain a foothold in the material world, something I'd scarcely bothered with in my twenties. Travel and experiment, inspiration and ecstasy, protest and rebellion—the era and all it had floated—had panned out enigmatically at best. Ships of possibility, personal and social, spiritual and political, had foundered on the shoals of chaos and sickly excess: assassinations, war, riots, madness. Johnson had ceded stewardship of the American ship of state to the ghastly Nixon; worldwide student protests were met with billy clubs and machine guns. A week before leaving San Francisco, I'd gone with some Bay Area friends to a *Whole Earth* magazine conclave in the Marin woods with Stuart Brand and other utopian disciples of Buckminster Fuller, and thought: No, this fuzzy tech romanticism is no road out either. An unemployed writer and musician with a broken marriage and a daughter to support, haunted by an Indian fortune-teller's prophecy of failure to be followed by violent death, I needed a purgative and a purgatory. It was time for pain, realism, the friction of materiality: L.A. or New York.

Not long before she died, my mother said to me, with surprising breath and vehemence, "I hated the sixties. I wish they hadn't happened." Taken aback, I wanted to ask her more, but she was in no shape to elaborate. By then it was 1981 and the sixties had already been framed and labeled by those who curate such things with the lapidary care of botanists (each decade bearing its own associative media-driven iconography: wartime black-and-white forties, doo-wop peroxide fifties, me-decade disco seventies), none of it remotely describing what it felt like to be there.

From a suburbanized distance, my parents had witnessed television's version of the age, the first time the tube truly defined American reality. Places and events I was living through came to them as sound bites, slogans, and rhetoric. Ominous nightly footage from campuses and draft boards, war zones and rebel headquarters brought intimations of anarchy, chaos, and revolt into their living room. Tim Leary, Huey Newton, and Bob Dylan were brand names to them without their having the slightest idea of who these figures were or what realities were attached to them. My parents were frightened for themselves, their country, their son. The *artiste-manqué* offspring who showed up in L.A., a refugee from the Dionysian sixties, must have appeared no longer quite human to them but a disturbing exemplar of these awful developments going on outside. My friendship with Morrison, self-declared "erotic politician," whose fuck-the-mother-kill-the-father slogan was now scandalous public coin, hardly helped.

In fact, my days of rebellion and excess were essentially over by the time I married Anne and left for Japan in 1964. To me the interesting developments had occurred earlier: the tilted landscapes of Bowles and Burroughs; the visionary films of Jordan Belson, Bruce Connor, Stan Brakhage; the rapturous explorations of Miles and Coltrane; the shattering social critiques of Camus and Fanon. Now it was the time of mass spectacle.

I suspect what my mother most meant when she said she hated "the sixties" was the toll it took on our family. Perhaps it was easier to blame the breakdown between father and son upon a "generation gap"; whereas I saw (and still see) it in more classical, deep-rooted terms. She would have taken offense on purely aesthetic grounds too: long hair, slovenliness, bell-bottoms, and tie-dye an affront to Paris couture, Bonwit Teller, and Mainbocher. Free love, outspokenness, the lack of discretion or civility—and her son "abandoning" a young wife and child—would have grieved her, the breakup with Anne anathema to both our sets of enduringly married parents (to Anne's I became an instant pariah).

I desperately needed money but didn't dare ask my father for help, fearing the repetition of the medical-school humiliation. Clearly he was uncomfortable presenting me to his work colleagues or contacts. So I began a series of sideways, crablike, scuttling moves—a frenzy of intense, eclectic, mostly misdirected activity, using the only two skills I had at my disposal—music and writing—in an attempt to commercialize myself.

The record business was flush with new rock-and-roll coin, suggesting a youth market to be mined. Writers, photographers, artists, and illustrators were flooding into L.A. to service the new phenomenon. Odd or unusual minds were for hire, the odder the better if they seemed to breathe the Zeitgeist. A playwright who worked at a record company threw me a few assignments writing publicity releases for rock acts; an aspiring movie producer offered me five hundred dollars to write a film treatment from an idea I'd thought up in the car driving to meet him. I fetched my trap drums from my parents' house and dusted them off, hoping to get session work in the recording studios. I finished *White City*, the novel I'd been working on since Japan, in hopes of selling it.

Coincident with this flurry of enterprise, I began to write songs. It was, after all, the era of the singer-songwriter. Like my father, I played a little piano, and I'd sung on occasion when I was a drummer. At a friend's house, while he was at work, I composed, over the course of a few months, some fifty songs, many shamelessly indebted to Van Morrison's early, brilliant albums *Astral Weeks* and *Moondance*. I sang them into a tape recorder, then sent copies around to music-publishing houses, producers, and record companies.

I seldom called or visited my parents, sensing they were just as relieved not to hear from me. Penniless, I stayed ("crashed") with people I barely knew, some of them women whose beds I shared. It was stimulating to be released from marriage back out in the world of desire and attraction; since I'd last been single, social relations had eased to the point where there seemed no good reason not to sleep with someone you might be interested in.

The sitar virtuoso Ravi Shankar, following Ali Akbar Khan's example, had opened up a small school in a run-down two-story office building in a nondescript neighborhood south of Hollywood. He'd even flown in his personal guru, Babaji, to bless the place, an incense-drenched rite lasting an entire day, and including among the guests George Harrison. The presence of Taranath Rao, a master tabla teacher from Calcutta, was an irresistible lure; and as often as I could I'd come to sit across from this chunky, bespectacled fount of knowledge, inhaling ornate spoken syllables, then disgorging them as drum strokes. Immersion in this divine percussion study kept the confusing world outside at bay for a few hours, but hardly fed Anne and baby Maya in the apartment up in North Beach.

Among the sitar students was the guitarist and composer Lowell George, later to found the band Little Feat (and die a few years afterward of a variety of excesses). We began composing songs together and rehearsing with a bass player, envisioning a Cream-like power-rock/jazz trio. One afternoon Lowell took me to a party in the Hollywood Hills at the sprawling house of one of the Monkees, the Beatle clones who had hit it big on television. Naked, stoned rock stars fondled starlets on the lawns, groped in the sauna. I was unable to shake my awareness that in an adjacent canyon Aldous Huxley had written *The Doors of Perception*, his elegant, influential examination of psychedelic experience, which had shaped the ethos of the era—and lent Jim Morrison the name for his band. This, I thought, is where Blake's Road of Excess had led to: the Monkees. How deeply wrong things were. How had I ended up here? I felt terribly lost and alone among the cheap hedonism. I missed my daughter, and Anne, and my own real life, whatever that might be. The fateful palm reading in the Iowa airport hovered over me like a scythe.

One of my demo tapes reached the head of April Blackwood, a large music-publishing company. He took me into a studio with a team of L.A.'s best musicians and over the course of several days recorded me singing a dozen of my songs. My filmmaker friend Frank brought the tape to Morrison, who arranged a songwriting grant for me through a foundation he'd endowed as a tax maneuver. I drove to his lawyer's office in Beverly Hills and was handed a check for three thousand dollars, a lifesaving amount at the time—money for Anne and Maya, and enough left over for me to rent a small apartment with a piano.

Through another writer friend of Morrison's, I found a literary agent willing to shop my novel. Meanwhile, I took any paying work I could find—designing ad campaigns for movies and record albums, composing and recording music for a couple of small films, collaborating on a screenplay from a story of mine that the actor Robert Ryan optioned with the promise of a sale. The Doors' label, Elektra, also with an eye toward signing me as a singer-songwriter, financed a demo session in their studios, recorded live one night with only piano and bass before a gallery of wine-swilling friends.

With Christmas 1968 approaching, Anne and I decided to give it another try. She and Maya came down to L.A. to join me. I rented a roomier place in Westwood, and to pay for it took a holiday job in a bookstore near the UCLA campus run by a local underground weekly. Another aspiring writer who clerked there told me a local editor was commissioning good authors to write classy erotic books along the lines of Paris's Olympia Press, which had of course published Nabokov, Beckett, Henry Miller, and Burroughs.

I drove to the San Fernando Valley and entered a long, one-story building. Once inside, I realized it was an adult-movie-

and-book factory. A bearded man named Larry ushered me into a small office and explained he'd been given a budget by the owners to develop a line of "literary" erotic novels. A list of disconcertingly good and well-known authors were writing for him under pseudonyms. I'd sent him my lone novel ahead of our meeting, and on the basis of that he hired me to write a novel for fifteen hundred dollars. I invented a pseudonym, and in six weeks delivered a comic satire in which the title character, a purveyor of various imaginary substances to the rich and famous, was privy to a vast erotic canvas that included couplings among virtually all the famous figures of the day—a Boschian *Garden of Earthly Delights.* I thought of it, written in a mood of dark relish and self-disgust, as in the spirit of Swift, my envoi to the broken decade. In spite of its tonnage of sex, I feared Larry would find it less arousing than funny; but he hired me to write a sequel.

I continued my Indian-music studies, appearing on a television show playing tabla while Ravi Shankar explained what I was doing. I'd become my drum teacher Taranath's prized student and confidant, even as my other activities and practical needs were distancing me from this passionate pursuit. The guru-student relationship in Indian culture is intense, absolute, sacrosanct, and claustrophobic. I kept recalling Amiya's prediction that I'd give up the drumming.

Word came that Grove Press wanted to publish my novel *White City.* The advance wouldn't be much, but that was hardly the point. Grove was then publishing the hippest, most interesting American and international authors. Rescued and redeemed! A writer in the world at last! The same week I received a call that Robert Ryan had raised enough money to take my script into production. Meanwhile, Elektra Records had heard my demo tape and was reportedly preparing a contract. Things were starting to happen.

In Westwood, Anne and I were trying to make go of it, and it was a joy being with my daughter again. Yet, for all my prospects, there was little money on the table. We migrated up the coast to Santa Barbara where rents were cheaper, and found a tiny cottage near the beach. I spent weekdays in L.A., chasing money, sleeping on friends' couches, coaxing my projects along. Everything seemed on the verge of breaking, yet nothing was quite in hand. I was certain, like every fool before me, that my ship would come in any minute. In our tiny cottage in Santa Barbara, Anne and I argued. Pressures grew. Finally I moved out.

At a friend's wedding one weekend I met Lauren, the sister of the bride, who had flown out from New York for the event. Twenty-five, smart, beautiful, and heiress to a movie fortune, Lauren lived in the Dakota Apartments in Manhattan. She told me she was directing, financing, and starring in a feature film. When I asked her what it was about, she said, "Me." Fore-warned, but fatally enamored, I drove with her to L.A. after the wedding. We spent the night at the Tropicana Motel, a hallowed Hollywood tryst-and-overdose site on Santa Monica Boulevard, across from the Doors' office. The next morning, before she flew back to New York, Lauren said she'd decided I should write original songs for her movie.

Broke, smitten, and oblivious to Anne and Maya, I borrowed enough money to fly to New York. I arrived to find her apart-ment at the Dakota a virtual film set, swimming with kliegs and cameras. Each morning, when the crew arrived, I'd disappear into the city and write songs. Nights, Lauren and I would go to

Max's Kansas City downtown, or carry on in her bed. After some days, I began additional recording in an East Village studio, sessions paid for by Bob Dylan's manager, Albert Grossman, who'd taken an interest in my music and wanted to present me to Columbia Records.

I'd yet to see a frame of Lauren's expensive, consuming film; but she was so smart and alluring, and putting so much into it, I had to believe it was something good. Finally, one night, she took me to an editing room off Times Square. Gravely she told me, as we rode up in the elevator, that I was the first person to see footage except for her editor. We sat on stools before a Keller rig, watching takes of Lauren drifting through her rooms at the Dakota, hair flowing; Lauren with her little shih tzu; Lauren staring into a mirror at her own visage. Operatically self-indulgent beyond my worst imaginings, it was something only a supremely narcissistic, wealthy young woman could dream of doing. I was dismayed, because I was in love with her.

Afterward, in a Chinese restaurant nearby, she asked me what I thought. I tried to choose my words carefully, but it was no good: she knew. Devastated, Lauren rushed to the restaurant bathroom and vomited.

The next day I took a room at the Chelsea Hotel. Lauren and I did keep seeing each other, and I finished recording the songs for her film, but that night in the editing room had dealt our romance a fatal blow. Lauren's self-involvement was such that you were either with her or against her. I already knew from my father what a narcissist needs from the people close by, and I knew I wasn't willing to provide it.

In debt, dejected, and sick with remorse at my abandonment of Anne and Maya, I flew back to L.A. As if in sympathetic response to my failed marriage and foolish affair, news of my various projects arrived in succession like a series of hammer blows. A feminists' strike had crippled Grove Press, my editor had left, and though I could keep the partial pittance of the advance I'd been paid, they would not be publishing *White City*. Robert Ryan's backers had evacuated to Europe to chase another film project, leaving my script in limbo. A few of my songs were being recorded by others (for which I'd receive some advance money, and various small royalties, for decades), but the publishing deal with April Blackwood was off. Ditto the recording contracts with Elektra and Columbia. Lowell George had joined Frank Zappa's band, ending our collaboration. Even the press that had published my erotic novel folded, leaving me with a completed sequel and no payment.

Lauren finished her feature, engendering much publicity by virtue of her family and means, but it incited only modest interest. In response she—in an act of amazing *brio*—made a second film, again all about herself, also greeted with faint praise at best.

Soon after my return to L.A., I visited my tabla teacher Taranath at his small apartment in East Hollywood. He cooked us an Indian vegetable meal in dhoti and tee shirt, regaling me with marvelous drumming anecdotes from Indian lore, then handed me his shoes and asked me to go get them shined. I walked to a nearby shop, got them polished, left them at his door, and never came back.

A few days later, I played on a Columbia Records session with the guitarist Ry Cooder and some other good musicians, backing a folk duo of the day—a passionless, boring gig. I simply couldn't share the general enthusiasm for such trivial music. Afterward I packed my drums in my car—the drums I'd hauled from gig to gig, city to city, country to country for almost twenty years—drove to the Hollywood Drum Shop on Vine Street, and took what they offered me for the whole kit.

Why shed those skins? Why renounce an activity, act, art soldered to my identity since the age of eleven? Drumming, which had raised me up out of childhood, had dismissed me. The beat had fallen silent. The writer had devoured the drummer, subsumed and supplanted him.

Still, for years afterward, I'd remain haunted by the sense that I'd left something of myself behind, entangled among the snares and cymbals, tom-toms and sticks. At times it seemed, to the writer I'd become, that the words on the page were mere detritus of the drummer's sloughed life, faint tracings of realms the music had traversed on a good night.

That summer of 1969, I moved to a tiny beachfront room above Jack's Bar at the Hotel Monica, a few floors below the room I'd visited with Drew that afternoon in high school and met the famous junkie bass player. My marriage over, my hopes shattered, I wandered the oceanfront each day, stood alone at the end of the pier watching the sun die. Nights I lay awake in the dark listening to the bar jukebox below pound B. B. King's "The Thrill Is Gone." Drummer, writer, wanderer, Zen adept— all seemed lost identities now, mere relics of spent adventures. None of it had taught me how to live, or how to love.

It was on one of those smoggy summer afternoons that I ended up at the Doors' office with Morrison. After we'd exhausted the idea of asking people on Santa Monica Boulevard if they knew they were going to die, we adjourned to the Topless

Extension, where before long we were joined by some of the regulars.

In retrospect, the evening takes on the aspect of a wake. Tom Baker, a handsome actor who'd achieved marginal notice in Andy Warhol's film *I, A Man*, playing an inarticulate sex object—on the basis of which he'd come to Hollywood hoping for a career in film—was there that night. A few days earlier, Morrison had arranged a screening on Tom's behalf for the production heads at Universal, the most conservative studio in Hollywood at the time. I'd sat with Jim and Tom that day in the darkened screening room watching executives in suits twitch nervously at the onscreen underground erotica, until one by one they'd departed, leaving nobody but a hooting Morrison and his entourage. (Baker, to his credit, did some good theater work in L.A. before dying, I was told, of a heroin overdose.) Also there that night was Tim McIntyre, a vastly talented actor and musician who'd fallen so deeply under Jim's sway and example that, after Morrison's death, he set out to imitate his idol and succeeded—dying early of cocaine-and-alcohol excess. Journalist Jerry Hopkins, who had introduced me to the literary agent who sold my novel to Grove, was there too. Jerry would make better coin of his experience with Morrison, co-writing a best-selling book about the Doors, *No One Here Gets Out Alive*, before opting for the sensual life in Bangkok. Nico, the blonde German Warhol beauty and occasional singer, sat with us that night, silent and adoring, tangled in a futile obsession with Morrison that surely trailed her to her death in a motorcycle accident on Ibiza.

After a while I left Jim and the crew and drove back to the Hotel Monica. It was the last time I'd see Morrison. In November of that year, he'd be convicted in Florida of "vulgar and indecent exposure." There'd be a last Doors album, Paris, death in a bathtub, and *poète-maudit* immortality.

Despairing and defeated before self, family, and world, I made plans to leave California again, for good this time, to someplace far away. I wondered how I could do this without seeing my father. I couldn't bear the thought of his judgment and—I was certain—satisfaction at his son's perfect, utter failure.

When does middle age commence? Thirty-five? Thirty-eight? I'd often wonder in the years following the palm reading in the Ames airport.

I traded aerogrammes with Kumar and Chatterjee for a year or so after the 1967 tour, then they dried up. In 1970, I was in London and saw a poster announcing Chatterjee's concert appearance at a large auditorium the next night. From the balcony I heard him play, accompanied by an exciting young tabla player from Delhi. Chatterjee was brilliant. Afterward, in the dressing room, he greeted me with a broad smile and an embrace. We talked for a while. He looked hale and content, not a day older. His wife had indeed borne him a son, as Amiya the palm reader had predicted. He was becoming known internationally, and had recently been awarded India's highest musical honor. Yes, things were going well, he admitted modestly. When I asked him about Kumar, he told me the drummer's mother had grown suddenly ill and died the year before—a shock, because they had been close—but he was working around India and doing well nevertheless. Chatterjee asked me how my tabla studies were coming; I had to tell him I'd abandoned them. When he inquired about my wife and daughter, I said we were no longer together. We didn't speak of Amiya's prophecies, but didn't have to; they hung heavily in the air between us.

In the years to follow—well into middle age, however one chooses to define that term—I moved through the world stalked by a shadow. At the outset of every voyage—and there were scores of them, almost as if I was compelled to test my fate— with each lifting of a plane off a tarmac, each lurching forward of a train or bus or car, a knot gathered in my stomach, a sense of involuntary surrender, and a tension as familiar as my own breath. *Maybe this one is it.* I was a man waiting to die.

I never confided Amiya's prediction to anyone but my wife, Masako, and even then half in jest. But it tainted my life, and in many ways configured it. I awaited my foreordained violent end with the dull certainty of a man on Death Row. I worked furiously, fighting against time, trying to accomplish as much as I could before my inescapable early end. I learned to make money and survive. I remarried, happily. A rich relationship grew with my daughter. I wrote and published books, lyrics, articles, essays, reviews, work in many media. In many respects I flourished; yet I was ruled by a dark star. It was almost as if I'd set myself upon a course of redemption—by effort of that "will" Chatterjee had spoken of on the plane to Chicago that wintry day.

Sometimes, recalling his words about how the force of one's own intention can alter one's karma, I'd wonder if, through all this activity, I'd altered mine in the intervening years. But I had only to look down at my palm to see the ruptured lifeline intact, unchanged by a millimeter.

One evening in 1987, at a dinner at a friend's house in the Hollywood Hills, I found myself sitting next to a woman I'd known in Berkeley years ago, at Ali Akbar Khan's Indian-music school. A pretty woman, more now perhaps than in her youth, her graying hair tied back in a bun, she was one of those who, like me, had found breathing space in cultures not her own. Unlike me, she'd kept in touch with the Indian musicians—I recalled she'd had a romance with one—and she was dressed in a sari that evening, with the *puja*, the red dot, on her forehead. We began to talk about those days twenty years ago. When I mentioned my tour with Chatterjee, a frown crossed her face.

"It's so awful what happened," she said, "and to such a great artist."

"I've been out of touch," I said. "Tell me."

"Well, I saw him in concert two years ago. He looked terrible even then from the heart condition. By his recital here a year ago he'd wasted away to nothing. Such a wonderful man. And of course the great sitarist of his generation. Now he can barely walk. He only performs occasionally, and then one raga at most."

It was devastating news. Chatterjee, of all men. How undeserving of such a fate! I thought. Then, commingling with the shock and sorrow, came the other dawning realization.

I excused myself and stood up. I walked quickly through the living room and stepped out onto a balcony, fighting for air.

I looked out at the city lights below, a tangle of thoughts whirling through my head. Amiya had been wrong! If Chatterjee's perfect future was false, then so was my doomed one! Amiya knew nothing! It isn't an exact science at all!

But what of the split with Anne? The abandonment of my musical path? Hadn't Amiya foreseen all that? No, of course not. He'd predicted a few things by mere chance, and I'd yoked his random prophecies to my own grim ends.

Then I thought: what if Chatterjee had, for some unfathomable reason, changed his palm for the *worse* by the force of that very same will? But, recollecting the months spent with that cheery man, and the message in his music, I found this impossible to imagine.

Gazing out across the lit expanse, I felt a wave of sadness rise and engulf me. Then I began to laugh, darkly and bitterly. Tears streamed down my face, my stomach hurt. All those years enslaved to a bogus divination! If I were to die while traveling—a reasonable prospect, considering how much I did of it—it certainly wouldn't be because it had been foretold by a palm reader in the Ames, Iowa, airport.

The city lights below seemed brighter, as if a current of extra voltage surged through them. The view was strangely familiar—a perfect *déjà-vu*, in fact.

I turned and looked back over the rooftops up the hillside. The dome of Griffith Park Observatory loomed directly above. I was only a few hundred yards below that spot on the hill where I'd first stood—in memory, photo, or dream—a boy with my family, new to California, full of shining hope.

November 29, 1999. Nell calls just before 8 a.m., weeping softly. "He's gone," she says. "Angela found him this morning. He went peacefully."

Perfect, I think, climbing into my clothes.

I arrive at my father's house to find a police car and a coroner's black limousine outside. The front door is open. Two policemen are standing by the door, two more in the living room. I don't remember cops when my mother died, or my grandfather before that. Is something wrong? Routine, they say. A Neptune Society attendant proffers forms to sign, asks me questions about the disposition of remains.

I call my sister to tell her our father has returned to his native state. Then I go in and look at Dad for the last time.

He lies on his back, pajamas slightly twisted, his right arm across his chest, his left hand by his side. His mouth is slightly open, his visage composed and emptied. The room is perfectly quiet. Shafts of morning sunlight hit the carpet. A bird twitters in the bougainvillea outside the window. A car starts up in the distance.

I turn and leave the room.

Epilogue

"Whatsoever of it has flown away is past.
Whatsoever remains is future."

AUGUSTINE,
CONFESSIONS XI

On a warm spring day, the first of the new millennium, we gathered as a family at my sister's ranch near Santa Barbara. Each of us brought something to commemorate my father. With a shovel I hacked at the sealed black box the Neptune Society had returned his ashes in, but I couldn't break it open. So we simply laid the box into the hole we'd dug, covered it in flowers, shoveled earth in, and said our farewells. We sat around a picnic table and ate, wanting to talk about my father but not finding much to say.

I've spent the several weeks since then wading through a paper world of accountants, lawyers, Social Security people, tax forms. In Dad's den I crated up the old radio tapes and transcriptions, swing-band 78's, and family memorabilia. A "For Sale" sign is stabbed into the lawn out front. Meg had thought we should probably paint the place and update it; but the realty agent, effusing about "classic midcentury modern," advises showing it as is, and expects a quick sale.

I've distributed most of the photo albums and art among the family. Rummaging through the last of his things, I admit I do keep looking for an old black-and-white of the family standing beside the planetarium—Dad the show-biz maestro in hat and suit, Mom the beauty in gloves and veil, me standing proudly between them, looking out into the shimmering twilight. I haven't found it, and I doubt I will.

But in the end it isn't about photos, it's about experience lodged as memory in the vitrines of the heart.

Along this coastline strewn with half-realized dreams, I've seen them all off now: grandfather, mother, father. I always figured when Dad went I'd clear out for good. But what entangles one in a place? Recently I've had odd thoughts of keeping the little place in Venice, planting a fresh flag in native soil. As Eliot's lines go:

And the end of all our exploring
Will be to arrive where we started
And know the place for the first time. . . .

But this urge may pass. Meanwhile, tomorrow, I board a plane for distant parts.

From among my father's memorabilia I did rescue a framed picture of Dad at nineteen in the University of Pennsylvania Inter-Fraternity Jazz Band in 1924, his C-melody saxophone in his lap. I set it on the piano top in my writing room in Venice, opposite the one of me at fifteen drumming on the television show *Spotlight on Youth.* Sometimes when I'm at the piano the photos seem to blend and merge, and all I see is a couple of young guys in love with music. The rest seems to melt away.

Acknowledgments

I hasten to thank my immediate family—my sister, my daughter, my wife—who endure the discomforts of having a Monster in the House with astonishing generosity, tireless support, and unconditional love. Among countless books that have informed my thoughts about Los Angeles and my native state, of special value were William Alexander McClung's illuminating *Landscapes of Desire* and Mike Davis' peerless *City of Quartz* and *Ecology of Fear.* I'm especially indebted to my editor at Broadway Books, Charles Conrad, who believed in this book from the beginning; and to my literary agent, Bonnie Nadell.

A Note About the Author

Tony Cohan's books include the novels *Canary*, a *New York Times Book Review* Notable Book of the Year, and *Opium*, a Literary Guild selection. His last book, *On Mexican Time*, a memoir of his life in Mexico, was a national bestseller.